Landmark Visitors Guide

Yorkshire Dales

Ron Scholes

Ron Scholes is an author, landscape photographer and travel lecturer. He has been a regular contributor to countryside programmes for BBC local radio, and to the *Yorkshire Journal* and *Outdoor Pursuits* magazines. His latest books have included, *The Ravenber, a Coast to Coast Walk*, *Towns and Villages of Britain – Cheshire, Arran, Bute and the Cumbraes*, *Walking in Eden* and *The Dales – A Poem*.

Ron is a retired Headteacher, and a former long-serving leader for Youth Hostels Association Walking Tours at home and abroad. He has completed many of the long distance walks in the UK, including routes from Cape Wrath to Lands End and the Isle of Wight to Anglesey.

Ron Scholes
Master of Education: Diploma of Advanced Study in Education; Fellow of the Royal Geographical Society (FRGS); Chartered Geographer (C. Geog); Member: Outdoor Writers and Photographers Guild.
Ron Scholes email: ron.scholes@btinternet.com

Brd

301

D1396419

Top: Cautley Crags and
Cautley Spout, Howgills

Above: Golden
Pheasants in a Yorkshire
wood

Left: Refreshment stop
in Arkengarthdale

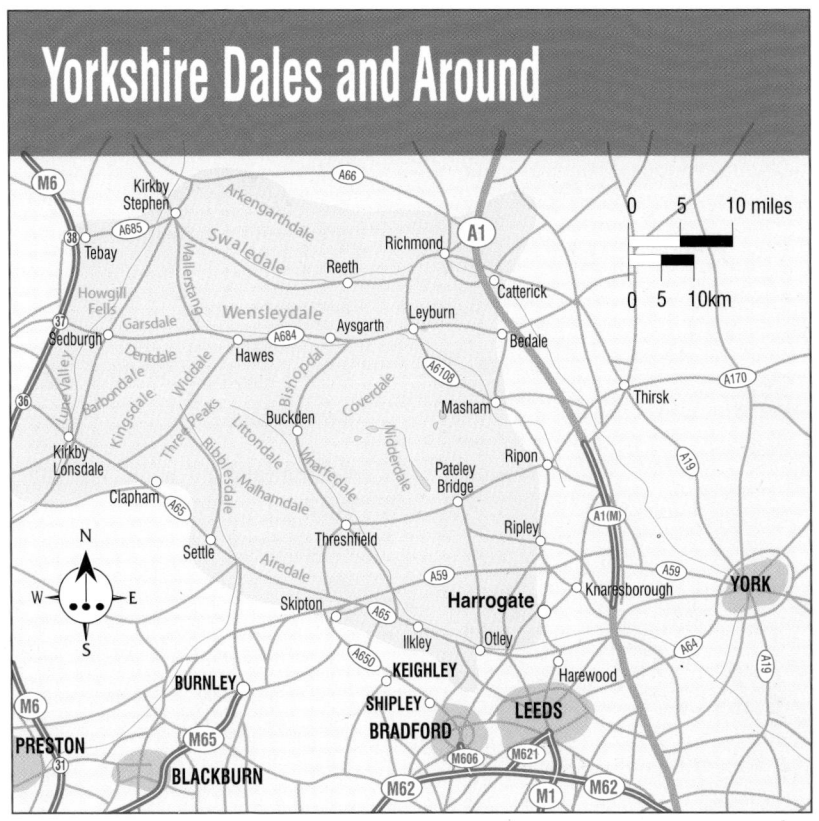

Yorkshire Dales and Around

Notes on the Maps

The maps drawn for each chapter, whilst comprehensive, are not intended to be used as route maps, but rather to locate the main towns, villages and points of interest. For exploration, visitors are recommended to use the 1:50,000 (approximately 1¼ inch to the mile) Ordnance Survey 'Landranger' maps. For walking, visitors are recommended to use the 1:25, 000 (2½ inches to 1 mile) Ordnance Survey 'Explorer' and Outdoor Leisure maps.

Dedication

Landmark Publishing thanks Michael Bell of Bells Bookshop, Halifax, Yorks (01422 365468) for supplying the material upon which the maps are based.

Contents

Welcome to
The Yorkshire Dales

The Yorkshire Dales is a place of outstanding natural beauty, gentle and pastoral areas contrasting with wild, open spaces. Within this attractive canvas are farms, hamlets, villages and the occasional market town, each settlement alive with flourishing community activities. In 1954, the Yorkshire Dales were designated as a National Park though not all the dales were included. Sadly Nidderdale and the northern half of the Howgills Fells were omitted.

There are special places to see in every dale, both natural and man-made: waterfalls like Aysgarth Falls and Hardraw Force in Wensleydale or those at Ingleton; the limestone caves such as Ingleborough Cavern and White Scar; Malham Cove and Tarn and Gordale Scar in Malham-dale; Bolton Abbey and The Strid in Wharfedale; Fountains Abbey in Skelldale; How Stean Gorge and Brimham Rocks in Nidderdale; and the hay meadows and stone barns in Swaledale.

As well as natural attractions, there are castles, historic houses, abbeys, museums, gardens, art galleries, mills, factories including a rope-maker, open farms and even breweries to visit. There are numerous information centres, both for the National Park and for general tourist enquiries. Alongside all this, Art and Craft Exhibitions and Music Festivals are held annually in the major dales, as well as drama productions, talks and children's concerts. Agricultural shows are also a vital part of the community life in the area, giving the farming

Top Tips

Sedbergh & the Howgill Fells
A book town surrounded by rolling hills and beautiful dales

Fountains Abbey & Studley Royal
Finest example of a 12th century Cistercian Abbey and one of the best examples of a Georgian Water Garden

Ingleton Waterfalls Walk
4 ½ mile ramble, lovely glens with vigorous waterfalls

Settle-Carlisle Railway
Famous route, wild terrain and over spectacular viaducts

Bolten Castle
Imposing type of 14th century military architecture

Descent of Gaping Gill
364ft pothole, an annual winch meet by two potholing clubs

Brimham Rocks
Fantastically shaped outcrops of gritstone, sculptured by wind, rain and frost

Upper Swaledale
Fine moorland scenery, waterfalls, famous stone barns and attractive villages

Interesting Masham
Its two famous breweries and visitor centres

Bolton Abbey
Priory ruins, nature trails and exciting Strid

community the opportunity to meet and enjoy a day out while competing in the many classes on offer.

The nature of the underlying rocks exerts a strong influence on the scenery of the Yorkshire Dales. The earth movements and climatic changes of prehistoric times gave the area its basic shape. Superimposed on this are the changes to the landscape brought about by the activities of man over the centuries.

Geology

In the Ordovician Period there was a general subsidence of the very early Pre-Cambrian continent and part of Yorkshire was submerged. The shallow sea received tremendous quantities of muds and sands that were deposited layer on layer and are therefore known as sedimentary rocks. These deposits eventually formed the dark sandstones and siltstones of the Crummack Dale Grits and the Horton Flags.

Later came the slates, grits and siltstones of the Silurian system that underlie all the Dales area: they compose the Howgill Fells the Rawthey Valley and the western parts of Garsdale and Dentdale. An area of Silurian slates forms the impervious bed of Malham Tarn, an interesting feature in a countryside of spectacular limestone scenery.

At the end of the Silurian system the Caledonian earth movements squeezed deposits of shales, silt-stones and sandstones into a complex of folds, with the resulting surface being continually eroded throughout the following period, the Devonian. This surface was then submerged beneath the sea of the Carboniferous Period. Deposits and sediments settled in the deep northern

troughs, eventually forming the pure limestones of the Craven area of Yorkshire. These accumulated sediments, of great thickness, are known as the Great Scar Limestone. The limestones and the shales were formed in moderately deep water and were composed largely of the shells and skeletons of microscopic marine life.

The strata above the Great Scar Limestone is called the Yoredale series, so well exposed in Wensleydale, the valley of the Ure or Yore. These limestones were formed in shallower water conditions, together with layers of shales and sandstones. This resulted in an alternating succession of limestone, shale and sandstone, with the same rock layers featuring again and again. Each band of limestone weathers out into a scar and with the shales eroding away easily this has formed the stepped valley sides as in Wensleydale. The local streams tumble over these giant steps with spectacular effect, creating splendid waterfalls such as Hardraw Force and Mill Gill Force.

Later, in the Upper Carboniferous division, particles of rock, soft muds and sands were carried by rivers and deposited in deltas and on the sea floor. Gritstones developed from the coarser sediments and shales from the finer material.

In the course of time, the deltas and estuaries of rivers silted up and became luxuriant swamps of dense tropical vegetation. The sea level periodically changed and further layers of sand and silt were deposited. The newer sediments separated the layers of plant remains that were compressed into coal seams. Then a succession of earth movements pushed up the rocks into a fold that we now know as the Pennines.

Ice Age

A very important event affecting the scenery was the Ice Age; although there were at least three periods when northern England was covered by great ice sheets. During each glacial interval glaciers filled the dales and subsequently moved slowly along scouring and smoothing the sides and bottoms of the valleys. Great thicknesses of boulder clay were deposited on the dale floor. The glaciers were able to transport huge blocks of stone, such as the Silurian boulders now perched on the limestone at Norber near Austwick. The passage of a glacier created a typical U-shaped valley such as Wharfedale.

Many lakes and tarns on the fells are the work of glacial ice. Semer Water in Raydale was created by the impounding of valley streams by a dam of morainic material. The outflowing and short-lived River Bain has forced its course through the deposited glacial debris.

Man's influence

Stone Age

The major Ice Ages were separated by periods of differing climatic conditions. Early man came across the land bridge of Europe and existed by following wild animals, such as mammoth, woolly bison and deer. To survive against the bitter cold they lived in caves. They knew how to make fire and how to prepare animal skins for clothing. Remains of animal bones and primitive implements have been found in the Langcliffe Scar caves near Settle.

After the retreat of the last great ice sheet the temperature rose and the covering of mosses, rushes and sedges gave way to large areas of grassland, and in time, trees. Possibly around 6500 BC, the sea level rose due to the vast quantities of melting ice and the land bridge was submerged from the mainland of Europe.

The Neolithic peoples brought with them skills in the working of flint for implements and weapons. They also carried out the practice of burying their dead in long earthen mounds or barrows. It is believed that they also constructed henge monuments consisting of circular banks and ditches in an area between the valleys of the Ure and the Swale.

Bronze and Iron Ages

New immigrants arrived from northern Europe with a knowledge of metal working; it was a combination of copper and tin known as bronze. The

Lynchets

During more peaceful times the people began to cultivate the lower slopes of the Dales. In the Grassington area of Wharfedale there are many examples of irregular fields and hut circles. The use of a simple plough only scratched the surface of the ground and even on gentle gradients the soil would creep down the slopes to form terraces called Lynchets. This evidence of ancient farming patterns may be seen through-out the Dales.

Bronze Age people erected stone circles and standing stones and many examples may be located in the upland areas of Britain such as on Ilkley Moor, where there is the Twelve Apostles Circle. The whole area of Rombalds Moor, overlooking Wharfedale, contains a number of decorated stones in the form of 'cup and ring marks' also attributed to Bronze Age peoples.

The introduction of iron working gave new colonists a great superiority in the production of tools and weapons. Unrest was destined to become the normal pattern of life throughout the area. The hillfort idea developed from the principle of a refuge easily defended by an earthen rampart with a deep external ditch.

The Romans

The Romans built a legionary fortress at York (Eboracum) in 71AD. The site grew in importance over the succeeding years and the fortifications were considerably enlarged. Gnaeus Julius Agricola conquered the whole of this northern area of Britain and a series of auxiliary forts were constructed to guard routes across the Pennines; at Bainbridge, Elslack and Ilkley. Gradually, the Roman road system was extended in order to exploit the region's natural resources and lead mines were opened up in Wharfedale, Nidderdale and Swaledale.

York's defences were further strengthened along the river frontage of the military base. By 400 AD, the Roman garrisons in the north were under attack from invaders and local tribes and in 410 AD Emperor Honorius advised the towns to organise their own defences. The Roman forces left Britain and withdrew to the continent.

Saxon and Norse invaders

Saxons invaders made the sea crossing to the east coast of Yorkshire and settled

Place names

The interpretation of place-names has played an important role in the understanding of landscape history. The first Saxon settlers who made clearings in the dense forests used the suffix element 'leah' for their settlements; it could also mean a glade or open space, or it could denote a meadow or pasture land. These settlements can be recognised in the modern day form of 'ley', as in Pateley Bridge – Paeth leah, a leah by a path.

Other settlers preferred more open ground above the flood levels of the valley and their enclosed homesteads had the suffix element 'tun'. Kellington was the tun of Cylla's people and Horton(-in-Ribblesdale) – Horh – tun, the tun on muddy ground. Another form surfaces in the place-name elements, that of 'ham or hamm'; this can refer to homestead, village or land. Addingham – the ham of Adda's people and Stittenham – a place with a steep slope are two examples of this element.

on the Yorkshire Wolds. They then spread westwards to the valley of the River Ouse and on into the valleys of the Ure, Nidd, Wharfe and Aire. Small bands passed through the Aire Gap to the Craven area and into Ribblesdale.

At the beginning of the tenth century a new Scandinavian invasion began with Norsemen landing from Ireland. In the summer months, they grazed their flocks of sheep and herds of cattle on the higher hill slopes. This rational use of pasture is emphasised by the word *saeter* 'saetr', a pasture, which now appears as sett, seat, satter and side as in Swaledale – Gunnar's saeter; Gunnerside.

The landscape as we know it, of hamlets, villages, farms and fields, began to take shape some time before the arrival of the Normans. After the Conquest, the existing Saxon boundaries and parishes continued to expand.

Normans

After the Norman Conquest the dales came under the influence of the monasteries, who in turn were supported by the great feudal landowners. Huge stretches of countryside were given to the religious houses, namely, Fountains, Bolton and Jervaulx. Farms were established to attend to the rearing of sheep and cattle and the boundaries of these granges spread across moor and hillside.

The villagers, cottars and bordars, were tied to the land and laboured in the fields for the benefit of the lord of the manor. Many dales settlements gained a stone-built church in the twelfth century, whilst the peasants existed in rough thatched shelters of wattle and daub.

In the northern Pennines the Conqueror designated vast areas of upland as Royal Forest and Chase. In upper Wharfedale the village of Buckden was the home of the guardians of Langstrothdale Chase. Here the Norman lords hunted the deer that gave Buckden its name. The Forest of Knaresborough covered an area of country around the castle of Knaresborough and Haverah Park was an enclosure within this Royal Forest.

Settled times

Many of the stone-built cottages in the Dales date back to the seventeenth century. Supplies of good local building stone were readily available, such as sandstone, gritstone and limestone. Notable features include mullioned windows, door lintels often bearing an inscribed date, and roofs made from split sandstone slates. It is interesting to note that many of these can still be seen on buildings, large and small, while exploring the Dales today.

Many of the farmsteads in the Dales built in the seventeenth century have stone-mullioned windows, low-pitched roofs and were constructed in the traditional Norse long house style. Here the living quarters, barn and byre lie under the same roof.

In the Calder Valley, the cloth trade combined with farming produced a dual economy, which was controlled by a thriving class of yeomen clothiers. They left us a heritage of splendid stone houses like Greenwood Lee at Heptonstall, a former merchant clothier's house dated 1712 and Clay House, Greetland, dated 1650.

Stone field barns

A traditional farming system is the common structure behind the dry-stone walls and the field barns that form such an integral part of the Dales landscape. The walls enclosed the grazing land and the stone barns provided storage space for hay and winter housing for a small number of cattle. The earliest barns were probably built in the seventeenth century and Swaledale is well endowed with many types of these familiar structures.

Other man-made features

Due to the physical nature of the landscape, fewer ancient routes in this country are better preserved than those in the limestone and gritstone areas of the Pennines. The search for lead and other minerals and the transportation of wool and woollen goods, meant the construction of paths, tracks and green roads. Many of these ancient routes that criss-cross the northern Pennines represent a priceless national heritage. There is no better monument to man's involvement with the landscape than these ancient ways that wander across the beautiful dales countryside.

Dry-stone walls vary in age and some tumbled remnants may date back beyond medieval times. A good example is provided by the village of Conistone in Wharfedale. Starting from the centre of the village, there are irregular enclosures around the old dwellings, then there is a pattern of larger rectangular fields bordered by walls, dating from the seventeenth to eighteenth centuries. Further away higher up the fellside are huge areas that were enclosed at the time of the Enclosure Acts in the late eighteenth and early nineteenth centuries.

A typical dry-stone wall has two tapering sides bound together by throughstones. The cavity in the middle is packed with small stones and the top of the wall is capped by coping stones. These unique boundaries stretch from the dale bottoms, up the fellside slopes and across the highest moorland.

Lead mining had a great effect on the landscape. After the Romans, lead mining in the Dales was a fitful process of individual workings until the seventeenth century. Occasionally, small groups of miners formed partnerships exploiting outcrops and shallow surface deposits, using primitive methods of ore dressing and smelting. Gradually, new techniques came and as the mines went deeper into the earth; water was the miners greatest enemy. In the eighteenth and nineteenth centuries all the mechanical processes were greatly improved with the help of water and steam power. Workings, such as old tips, crumbled buildings, adits and hushes may be discovered on many lonely moor tops and valley sides.

Natural history

Along the valley floors (Swaledale is a prime example) are extensive hay meadows where many wild flowers flourish such as wood cranesbill, buttercup, meadow vetch, globe flower, pignut, sweet cicely and red clover.

This is encouraged by the creation of Environmentally Sensitive Areas (ESA's), where the grassland may not be ploughed and the livestock must not be allowed to graze in the weeks before the grass is cut. Also, the grass is not cut until the wild flower seeds have ripened.

On the upper limestone slopes, the grassland, which is close-cropped by rabbits as well as sheep, contains a variety of lime-loving plants and herbs such as bird's-foot trefoil, yellow rock rose, harebell, eyebright, mountain pansy and purple wild thyme. On the limestone pavements, the clints and especially the moist and shady grikes, provide sheltered homes for hart's tongue ferns, spleenworts, wood anemone and wild garlic. Look carefully and note how the limestone surfaces are covered with lichens.

The impressive limestone scars and outcrops provide homes for the peregrine falcon, ravens, jackdaws and house martins. The cliff ledges support a rich flora including the colourful purple saxifrage and rock rose.

The extensive areas of gritstone moorland are covered with a surface of peat, blanket bog and mosses and such plants as cotton grass, liverworts and lichens. Drier patches of moorland support the growth of heather, that adds colour in late summer, and there are little corners where specialist moorland plants can survive, such as starry saxifrage, bird's eye primrose, tormentil, grass of Parnassus, cloudberry, cowberry and bilberry. The moors are carefully managed to retain the grouse population and are also home for curlew, lapwing, snipe, merlin and golden plover.

This book explores the Dales area by area, starting in the north-west and finishing in Nidderdale. Each chapter includes a suggested car drive and walks for that area. Some of the walks are given in detail, others are in outline only. It is important that all are followed using the appropriate Ordnance Survey map as changes may occur after the writing of the text. An additional chapter is included which gives brief details of places around the area which visitors may be interested to see.

Details of places of interest are included with opening times and telephone numbers. These will vary from time to time and it is always wise to check before visiting. Many places are now opening all year round and the Yorkshire Dales may be enjoyed in all seasons. Those visiting away from the busy summer months will find many compensations such as quieter roads, clearer views and less crowded shops and tearooms. Go in winter, prepared for all weathers, and the reward may well be snow-covered hills, waterfalls at their very best and as always in the Dales, a very warm welcome.

Water fowl

The two large stretches of water found in the Dales, namely, Malham Tarn and Semer Water, are wildlife havens for birds. Summer visitors include the mallard, coot, great crested grebe and little grebe, moorhen and Canada goose. Winter residents include teal, whooper swan, golden-eye and tufted duck.

1. North-Western Dales

The Moorcock Inn lies at the junction of the A684 and the B6259. This is a windswept area of high ground between Wensleydale to the east and Garsdale to the west. From this point the north-facing dale of the Mallerstang is border country between the counties of Cumbria and North Yorkshire; so we shall trespass into Cumbria to visit the Mallerstang, Grisedale, Garsdale and Dentdale.

Before 1974, the Mallerstang lay in Westmorland and Grisedale, Rawtheydale, Garsdale and Dentdale were part of Yorkshire (West Riding). The short strip of land between the Moorcock Inn and Aisgill was in Yorkshire (North Riding). The northern boundary of the Yorkshire Dales National Park descends from Swarth Fell, crosses the watershed at Aisgill and follows the long escarpment of the Mallerstang Edges. Unaccountably, Wild Boar Fell and the northern section of the Howgill Fells are excluded from the National Park.

Mallerstang

In the past, the first record of Mallerstang Forest was in 1284 when Roger de Leyburn died possessed of Mallerstang Castle and Forest. The dale before that time would have been considerably wooded, but now only small patches survive such as at Jenny Wood and in some of the gills.

The dale stretches for 5 miles (8km) between high hills that rise to over 2,000ft (600m) on either side of the narrow valley. The upper heights are capped with millstone grit, with the magnificent head of Wild Boar Fell thrusting its shattered crags above a

Memorials

Mallerstang Edge commemorates two famous owners of the Manor of Mallerstang. Hugh de Morville, in Hugh Seat, 2,260ft (689m) was one of the knights involved in the murder of Thomas à Becket, the Archbishop of Canterbury. The other famous owner was the redoubtable Lady Anne Clifford, Countess of Dorset and Pembroke. Just beyond the summit of Hugh Seat, on the border between Cumbria (Westmorland) and North Yorkshire, stands a stone pillar. On its western face is inscribed 'AP 1664 – this is Lady's Pillar, Anne Clifford's boundary stone'.

limestone plateau. This majestic hill, a landmark for miles around, dominates the dale; it has stood changeless from age to age, whether cloaked in snow, bathed in sunshine or part-hidden in mist like a Chinese watercolour painting. On the opposite side of the dale, the stony escarpment of the Mallerstang Edge forms a continuous barrier of high ground which is seamed by watercourses and cliffs – a perfect complement to Wild Boar Fell.

Hell Gill Beck flows rapidly from the high fells south of Mallerstang Edge and enters a deep limestone chasm. At this point, a bridge crosses it carrying an ancient road known as the High Way. This old fell route was used by Lady Anne Clifford on her journeys down the dale, and as legend has it, also by the Highwayman, Dick Turpin, and his trusty old nag, Black Bess. Before becoming the River Eden, the beck tumbles 60ft (18m) over a limestone cliff, to form the spectacular waterfall known as **Hell Gill Force**.

A sculpture collection to celebrate the River Eden was commissioned to mark the new millennium by East Cumbria Countryside Project and local communities along the river. One such work is:

> **Sculpture:** 'Water Cut' by Mary Bourne
>
> **Location:** Lady Anne Clifford's Way, Mallerstang
>
> **Map Reference:** SD 786 985 OS OL 19; Landranger 98

The tiny chapel at **Lunds** on the banks of the infant Ure stands 1,066ft (325m) above sea level and was closed many years ago. An old corpse road leads by

---

Jew Stone

On the village green at Outhgill stands the Jew Stone. This new limestone pillar was reinstated on 21 September 1989. In 1850, William Mounsey of Rockcliffe near Carlisle, traced the course of the Eden from its mouth to its source. He erected a slate pillar inscribed on one side in Latin and on the other in Greek on the northern rim of Red Gill, the source of the Eden. Unfortunately, navvies from the railway construction camps found the stone and smashed it into pieces.

High Dyke to the High Way and access from the B6259 is along a rough track through a narrow belt of conifers.

Higher up the hillside, the building called Shaws, once a much-loved youth hostel, was formerly the home of Robert Andrew Scott Macfie, a Liverpool businessman and a former editor of the *Gipsy Lore Journal*. He is remembered in the dale as the man who paid for the services of lecturers to visit this isolated farming community. The speakers arrived by train in winter time and talked to the local farmers on methods of improving their rough pasture land. R A Scott Macfie died in 1935 and is buried in Lunds churchyard.

Travelling northwards the B6259 reaches **Outhgill**. This small community contains Mallerstang's church, a Wesleyan chapel, built in 1878, and a few scattered farms and dwellings. St Mary's Church has a foundation of 1131 but the present building is mostly of 1663 when it was largely repaired by Lady Anne Clifford. An inscribed panel over the south door records that she did it, 'after it had layne ruinous and decayed some 50 or 60 years'.

Three-quarters of a mile (1.2km) further along the road stand the ruins of **Pendragon Castle**, raised on a knoll close to the banks of the Eden. Traditionally it was the stronghold of Uther Pendragon, father of King Arthur. Originally a late Norman tower built without extensions it was attacked and burnt by the Scots in 1341; then restored by Roger de Clifford between 1360 and 1370. The castle was ruined again in 1541 by the Scots, prior to their defeat at the Battle of Solway Moss in 1542.

It remained in a tumbled condition until 1660 when Lady Anne Clifford restored the stronghold. She had finally inherited the Clifford estates after a lengthy and bitter lawsuit; then set about re-roofing the keep, building an enclosing wall, outbuildings and gates and also constructing Castle Bridge over the Eden. The castle is private property but free admission is granted by permission of the owner.

Between Pendragon Castle and the village of Nateby, on the west bank of the Eden, are the ruins of **Lammerside Castle**. Reputed to be the home of the Whartons, the building was originally a fourteenth century pele tower. It is possible to note the remains of two floors and part of the tower. The site can be visited by means of a footpath that runs across the pastures above the river.

A short distance northwards the same right of way reaches **Wharton Hall**. This ancient building, now a farm, is one of the area's best surviving examples of a late medieval manor house. Later,

Thomas Lord Wharton erected a new Great Hall and kitchen. But it is the Gatehouse that remains an impressive feature; it was originally three floors high. Today, although roofless and without floors, it still bears the Wharton coat-of-arms and the date 1540. The Great Hall is no longer standing, although the back wall remains together with the spacious kitchen and its very large fireplace. To the west, note the fine lynchets on the slopes leading up to the railway.

At **Dalefoot** there is a flat grassy area between the road and the river. This is a pleasant spot to pull off the road for a picnic or a rest. Moving on, Nateby with its Black Bull Inn is a convenient point for walks along the River Eden and also the key to the Swaledale back door, where the B6270 climbs over the shoulder of the Mallerstang by way of Lamps Moss. A car can be parked at the top of the pass and walks undertaken to High Pike and High Seat and to Nine Standards Rigg.

At **Stenkrith Bridge**, the Eden's pleasant journey is interrupted when the river enters a wooded limestone gorge. Throughout the ages the turbulent waters have transported stones and pebbles that have gouged and scoured pits, hollows and channels in the limestone bedrock. The noise created by the rushing waters has earned this spot the romantic name of 'The Devil's Mustard Mill'. Access to this location is by means of a convenient path opposite the road junction beyond Stenkrith Bridge.

Kirkby Stephen

Kirkby Stephen is a busy market town lying where the valley of the River

St Stephen's Church, Kirkby Stephen

The parish church of St Stephen with a fine perpendicular tower dominates the northern approach to the town. The Norman stage of 1170 was built on to a Saxon foundation with a further replacement of 1240. This structure has been altered and enlarged to its present form. Its interior monuments consist of tomb chests of two famous local families, the Musgraves and the Whartons. Other interesting monuments include: a Scandinavian hog-back tomb stone and fragments of an Anglo-Danish cross shaft; there is also a splendid pulpit of polished red and green marble dated 1892.

Eden broadens out after its journey through the narrow confines of the Mallerstang. It is situated on one of the main cross-country routes from the north east to the Lake District and the Lancashire holiday resorts. The surrounding attractive moorland and valley scenery has meant a welcome increase in tourist traffic; the town is a convenient stopping-off point on Wainwright's Coast to Coast walking route. There are numerous accommodation facilities, including a popular youth hostel. There are also a number of interesting shops in the town; the modern Tourist Information Centre offers a wide range of literature and information.

The wide main street has a number of narrow ways leading from the thoroughfare culminating in the Market Place. This area of the town bustles with activity during the typical Monday market, where one side faces the entrance to the church. The impressive pillared cloisters were built on the direction of the will of John Walker, a purser in His Majesty's Navy and a native of this town. There are eight columns supporting a triangular gable

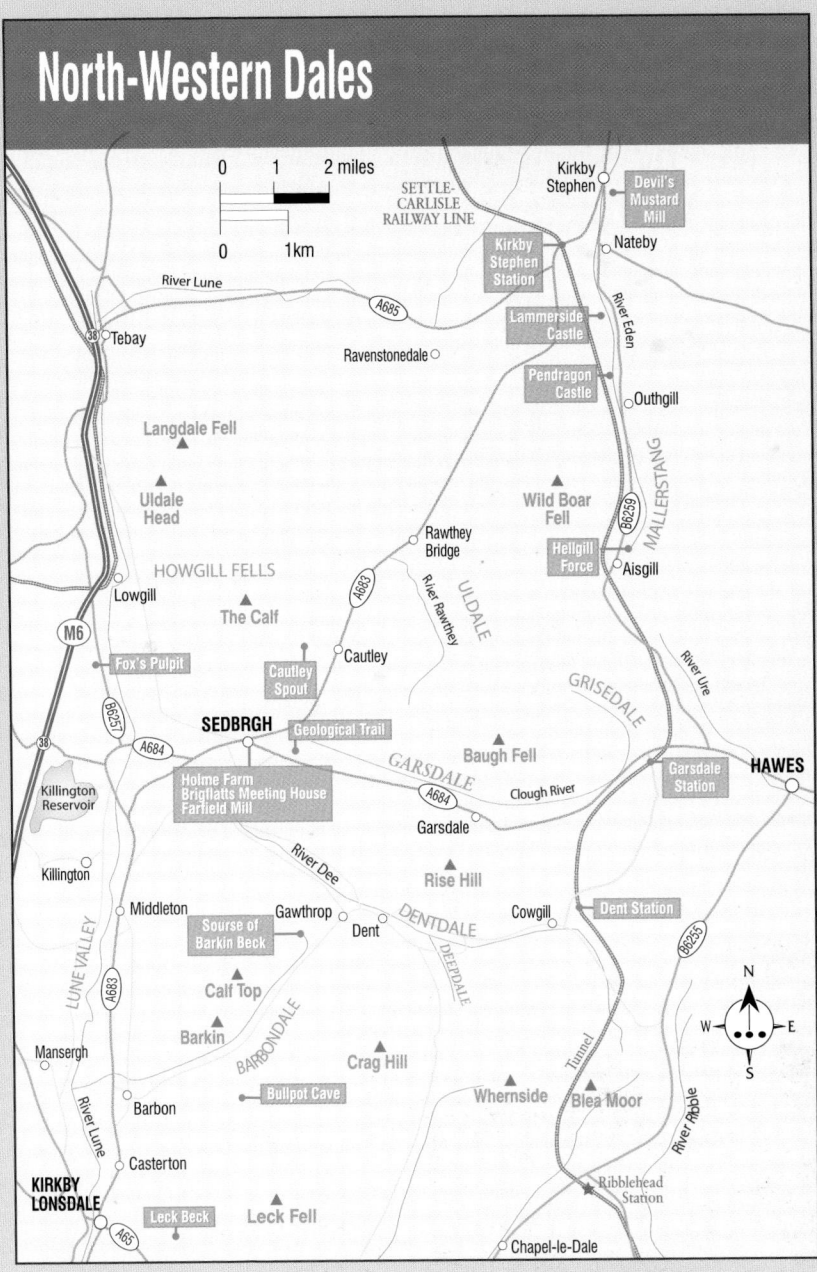

North-Western Dales

0   1   2 miles

0   1km

SETTLE-
CARLISLE
RAILWAY LINE

Kirkby Stephen
Devil's Mustard Mill
Nateby
Kirkby Stephen Station
River Eden
Lammerside Castle
Pendragon Castle
Outhgill
River Lune
A685
Tebay
Ravenstonedale
Langdale Fell
Uldale Head
Wild Boar Fell
MALLERSTANG
B6259
Hellgill Force
Aisgill
Rawthey Bridge
HOWGILL FELLS
Lowgill
The Calf
River Rawthey
ULDALE
Fox's Pulpit
Cautley
River Ure
Cautley Spout
GRISEDALE
Geological Trail
SEDBRGH
GARSDALE
Baugh Fell
Garsdale Station
HAWES
Holme Farm
Brigflatts Meeting House
Farfield Mill
A684
Garsdale
Clough River
Killington Reservoir
River Dee
Killington
Rise Hill
Cowgill
Dent Station
Middleton
Gawthrop
Dent
DENTDALE
B6255
Sourse of Barkin Beck
LUNE VALLEY
A683
Calf Top
DEEPDALE
Barkin
BARBONDALE
Crag Hill
Mansergh
Tunnel
River Ribble
Barbon
Bullpot Cave
Whernside
Blea Moor
River Lune
Casterton
Ribblehead Station
KIRKBY LONSDALE
A65
Leck Beck
Leck Fell
Chapel-le-Dale

N
W   E
S

M6
B6257
A684
A683
A65

Opposite: Looking across the Rawthey Valley to Cautley Spout and Yarlside

and bellcote. On the inner wall is a notice announcing the terms of the Market Charter.

Kirkby Stephen to Uldale

The A685 climbs gradually beyond Kirkby Stephen to pass beneath the Settle-Carlisle railway and the site of the town's station. Further on, take the A683 road to Sedbergh. The view embraces a landscape whitened by a capping of limestone and an emerging valley pointing to the velvet smooth rounded hills of the Howgill Fells. Soon you cross the Dent Fault that raised the Carboniferous Limestone high above the Ordovician and Silurian rocks. A lane leaves the main road for the hamlet of **Stennerskeugh**, where a footpath heads for the grassy ridge of Little Fell and an exhilarating climb to The Nab on Wild Boar Fell.

A little further on down the main road, a quiet lane called 'The Street' affords access to the Stennerskeugh Clouds. From this lovely area of shake holes, limestone outcrops and pavements, or from the nearby Fell End Clouds, there's a pleasant walk to Wild Boar Fell by way of lonely Sand Tarn. Here, the millstone grit becomes evident.

At **Rawthey Bridge**, the River Rawthey appears having travelled in a south-easterly direction along the sprawling flanks of Baugh Fell. Here, for part of the way, the river forms the boundary of the Yorkshire Dales National Park. From the main road below Cross Keys, a walking route climbs the hillside and traverses left along Bluecast-

er Side. It turns east and makes a gradual descent across the moorland slopes of the narrow valley of **Uldale**, to arrive at a footbridge across the Rawthey.

Here, as the river flows vigorously beneath a bankside canopy of trees, it tumbles over a number of rock steps in this lovely sylvan setting. A footpath continues straight ahead along the steepening sides of the right-hand bank with the noise of falling water in one's ears. Eventually, the main waterfalls are reached, as the Rawthey cascades over impressive limestone ledges.

The right of way to Grisedale is taken by crossing the footbridge over the Rawthey and climbing up the track through a copse of mixed woodland. To the left, there is a view of attractive Needle House surrounded by fine specimens of beech, birch and pine. The track continues to Uldale House, a fine robust dwelling of considerable interest. During the surveying operations of a route for the Settle-Carlisle railway, there was a possibility of the line coming through Grisedale and Uldale. As there would be a road as well, the house was built as a speculative venture for the purpose of operating as an inn. Above the door is a panel inscribed: 'I.S. HULL 1828'

Beyond Uldale House and the crossing of Whin Stone Gill, the line of the footpath heads across the moorland slopes above the river to Rawthey Foot and continues over the watershed into Grisedale.

Grisedale

The lovely green valley of **Grisedale** (the valley of the pigs) was the subject of a television documentary *The Dale*

That Died. From Garsdale Head a narrow strip of tarmac leaves the A684 and travels across the moorland before descending to Grisedale Beck. A short distance farther on the hard surface terminates at East House.

Farming in the hills has always been a difficult business and, sadly, lack of a steady income forced many of the families out of the dale. Now there are only a small number of inhabited farms and others lie abandoned, ruinous and empty. However, all is not lost as some life has returned to the valley with former dwellings converted into

The Howgill Fells

The **Howgill Fells** occupy a triangular area of high land between the Lune and Rawthey valleys. In appearance, they are quite unlike the rugged Lakeland mountains or the western dales of North Yorkshire. Their appearance is particularly distinctive: velvet smooth, gently domed, grassy ridged, yet steep sided and not inter-rupted by walls or fences above the lower meadows. Access is unrestricted for the walker with a remarkable concentration of summits, making it a hill-walking area par excellence. Conditions are good underfoot and there are the rewards of extensive views to Lakeland, Mallerstang, Wild Boar Fell and Swarth Fell and from Morecambe Bay to the Pennines.

holiday homes. Afforestation has crept into Grisedale and there is a sizeable plantation on the slopes of **Baugh Fell**. It would be more beneficial to the landscape generally, not just for commercial purposes, if stands of broad-leafed trees could be planted in sheltered spots; they would provide a visual contrast as well as being of benefit to birds and wild life.

Lonely Grisedale is a quiet and unsung place; but for many people it is a favourite dale for moorland walking. There are the sprawling slopes of Baugh Fell on the western side and the more inviting flanks of White Birks Common and Swarth Fell on the other. Baugh Fell is a vast upland triangle of moorland drained by many streams; its extensive featureless plateau is dotted with a number of tarns, overlooked by the summits of Knoutberry Haw 2,218ft (676m) and Tarn Rigg Hill 2,224ft (678m). From Grisedale Common there is a pleasant grassy ascent to the gritstone summits of Swarth Fell and Wild Boar Fell overlooking the Mallerstang.

This splendid range of hills is suitable for all grades of circular and linear walks only limited by the prevailing weather conditions. It should be borne in mind that the central mass of high ground could be confusing in mist and that one should be proficient in map and compass skills.

In the neighbourhood of Cautley, there is a small parking space on the roadside by the Cross Keys. From here a footbridge crosses the river and a path follows the glen towards the foot of Cautley Crags. Ahead, the spectacular long-stepped waterfall of **Cautley**

Selected Car Drives

1. Howgill circuit

Distance: 28 miles (44.8km)

Leave Sedbergh on the byroad north in the centre of the town opposite the church. This lane runs along the western slopes of the Howgill Fells in the Lune Valley. At Low Borrowbridge it passes the site of the Roman fort, and joins the A685 to Tebay.

Continue through the village and bear right at the roundabout along the A685 towards Newbiggin, turn off the main road to Ravenstonedale. Proceed through the village and out along Townhead Lane to meet the A683. Turn right across Ravenstonedale Common to descend to Cross Keys at Cautley. There is a small parking area for fine views of the waterfall Cautley Spout and Cautley Crags. Proceed down the valley of the Rawthey beneath the Howgill Fells returning to Sedbergh.

*Looking north to the Eden Valley and the Pennines
from Randygill Top in the Howgill Fells*

Looking across the Mallerstang from Intake to Wild Boar Fell

2. Sedbergh to Dent and Hawes

Distance: 56 miles (89.6km)

From the centre of Sedbergh, take the road south past the church towards Dent. The meandering road crosses the River Dee and on into Dent Town. Proceed along the narrow street, bearing left at the Sedgwick Memorial. Re-cross the Dee continuing up the dale to Cowgill. From here the route closely follows the beautiful river with its many little cascades, and views of magnificent viaducts on the Settle to Carlisle railway line. Eventually, the road climbs on to the moorland at Newby Head Moss. Turn left on to the B6255, and descend Widdale to Hawes.

Pass through the town and bear left crossing the River Ure. Beyond the river turn left and then take the next turn right. The road continues to climb to the Butter Tubs Pass before dropping down into Swaledale. Turn left on to the B6270, and proceed up the dale. Beyond Keld, stretch the moorland wastes of Birkdale, to reach the summit at Lamps Moss. Descend from the limestone pavements to reach the village of Nateby.

Turn left on to the B6259 and head down the Mallerstang by Outhgill, with fine views of the escarpment edges and the sharp peak of Wild Boar Fell. At the Moorcock Inn, turn right on to the A684. This road traces a winding route down beautiful Garsdale, between the rising slopes of Baugh Fell and Rise Hill, returning to Sedbergh.

Castlehaw Tower

On the north-eastern outskirts of Sedbergh lies Castlehaw Tower, an earth mound crowning a natural hill. This perfect vantage point overlooks the whole valley and the entrances to its branching dales – the valleys of the Lune, Rawthey, Dee and Clough River.

This location may well have been used by the Romans as a look-out point or signal tower and later by Norse settlers moving up the Dales. The Normans constructed a motte and bailey castle on the hill. The motte contained a wooden tower and the surrounding bailey or enclosure was defended by a palisade. For further protection, a ditch was dug round the perimeter of the outer stockade.

Spout tumbles downwards in a dark forbidding cleft.

Sedbergh

From early times the settlement of **Sedbergh** lay at the crossing of two important routes; from Kendal to York and from Lancaster to Newcastle-upon-Tyne. This attractive, stone-built little town has more of a look of a Lakeland settlement than it has of a Dales' settlement. Grey stone and slate complement its situation at the foot of the Howgill Fells.

Prior to 1974, Sedbergh was in the West Riding of Yorkshire but now it is part of Cumbria. Both the town and the southern half of the Howgill Fells remain within the area of the Yorkshire Dales National Park. Strangely, an administrative planning decision left the northern half of the Howgills outside the boundary of the National Park. Sedburgh is easily accessible from Junction 37 of the M6 only a 5-mile (8km) drive from the town.

Recently, the narrow main street had an argumentative, short-lived love affair with cobbles but these were unpopular and the road was resurfaced. Sedbergh is the market town for the western dales, its charter dating from the twelfth century, and Wednesday is a popular market day; it is the focal point for the farming community.

The town offers a range of accommodation facilities, and there is a good variety of local shops and cafés. Car parks are situated at the end of the main street and opposite the church. There are toilet facilities nearby. The National Park Information Centre is also situated in the main street. Sedbergh is a book town for England and boasts several special interest booksellers. Its annual Festival in September offers music, poetry, local history tours and walks.

The lovely parish church of St Andrew has a west tower and a long nave with aisles. The north doorway is Norman and much of the interior is of the thirteenth century. The pulpit has a fine eighteenth-century Tester, which is a horizontal sounding board or canopy. Sedbergh, like Dent, had its knitters but in the late eighteenth century they changed to the cotton trade. An alleyway called Weavers' Yard reminds us of the old woollen industry.

Sedbergh School

Sedbergh is well known for its public school. Some of its buildings are found in the town such as Evans House in the main street. The well-proportioned early eighteenth-century building, originally the grammar school and now the school library, is situated near the car park opposite the church. The main school buildings and playing fields extend into the valley on the south side of the town.

On a summer's day, climb the fellside overlooking the town and the school playing fields. When a cricket match is in progress, watch the batsmen run between the wickets and listen carefully. Then after a momentary time lapse, you will hear the sound of the bat striking the ball.

Holme Farm, Sedbergh is a traditional Dales working animal farm that is open to visitors. There is a Nature Trail which includes a fox earth and a badger sett. A conducted tour is available with working sheep dogs, local breeds of poultry, sheep, chickens, calf-rearing, pigs and goats. Examine farm machinery, old and new and enjoy the experience of touching, holding and feeding the baby animals. Come at lambing time – mid March to mid June or for sheep shearing – mid June to late August. Evening farm tours can be arranged concluding with badger watching. Special local interests include – Roman road through farm with ancient ford, ancient settlement nearby, fishing available and fine scenic surroundings.

Sedbergh is known for its association with George Fox. At **Brigflatts**, just outside the town, (SD 641 912), the first Quaker meeting house was established. The building has an air of stillness and quiet with a very special atmosphere of its own. George Fox spent ten years travelling round the country, questioning the preaching of the church and seeking a true faith to which he and every man and woman could respond. He had received a vision from God showing a great multitude of people waiting to receive the word. He was often physically assaulted and persecuted. But on Firbank Fell on the western flanks of the Lune Valley, he preached to a large crowd of people on Trinity Sunday, June 1652. The place is known as Fox's Pulpit, (SD 619 938) and a plaque set in the rock marks the spot.

The **meeting house at Brigflatts**, dated 1675 is often considered the most beautiful meeting house in England; it originally had an earth floor and no ceiling, but with holes in the roof which had to be plugged with moss. Now the interior is handsomely fitted with fine wooden panelling and a wooden gallery. At the foot of the stairs is a pen for the farmers' sheep dogs.

Garsdale

Garsdale extends eastwards from Sedbergh with the Rawthey Valley and the valley of the Clough River separated by the great moorland mass of Baugh Fell. An interesting fact here is that both rivers rise close together, then flow in opposite directions, and join together near Sedbergh.

Garsdale is noted for its narrow winding profile and its pattern of slender intakes that run parallel with each other up the northern and southern sides of the valley. Each enclosure usually contains one of the many short-lived but lively streams. Lovely names abound such as Ringing Keld Gutter (the word *keld* is Norse meaning a spring), Church Milk Gill, Liquor Gill and Swarth Gill (from the Norse *svartr* meaning black).

The main road, the A684, wriggles its way through the dale and keeps very close company with the Clough River, crossing and re-crossing it several times. The river has a most charming aspect as it flows swiftly over its tree-lined rocky bed that is often interrupted by many attractive waterfalls. The dale is dotted with small farmsteads; many are old, such as East Rackenthwaite which has a massive chimney buttress. In the centre of the dale, a small number of dwellings form the little community of Garsdale.

Garsdale Head

At **Garsdale Head** there is a row of cottages, some scattered dwellings and a station on the scenic Settle-Carlisle line. The railway crosses over the twelve-arched Dandrymire Viaduct before entering the Moorcock Tunnel on the way to Aisgill summit and the beautiful journey down Mallerstang Dale.

Garsdale was once called Hawes Junction, where passengers changed for the route down Wensleydale. There are apocryphal tales of conditions in winter at this bleak spot; engines cab-high in snow drifts and the famous turntable

being spun round, with the locomotive standing on it, by the force of the wind. The station is a good starting point for walks in Grisedale, the Mallerstang and upper Wensleydale.

The little road past Garsdale Station climbs over Garsdale Common to reach a height of 1,755ft (535m) and eventually descends steeply past Dent Station into Dentdale.

Dentdale

The narrow road from Sedbergh to Dent winds and twists throughout its journey, as though it is avoiding every individual field boundary and hedge-row; it is not recommended for folks in a hurry. The route begins in slaty countryside and crosses the Dent Fault to reach more familiar limestone. From the north it is protected by the long whaleback mass of Aye Gill Pike and Rise Hill, by the heights of Towns Fell, Barbon High Fell and Whernside to the south, and Great Knoutberry Hill to the east. These high fells contribute much to Dentdale's attraction; this green and well-wooded dale, barely 10 miles (17km) long, is a secluded haven of great charm and beauty.

A number of the old white painted buildings in the dale were 'Statesman's or Yeoman's' farmsteads. These homesteads are often situated away from the valley bottom on sheltered sites that were favoured by the Scandinavian settlers of centuries ago. The pattern of homesteads in Dentdale is a special feature of this attractive Pennine landscape. The characteristic narrow intakes of land stretch up the slopes from the lower pastures and the dwellings are linked by a network of ancient paths

Above: Dent Village

Below: The joyous River Rawthey flows through lonely Uldale

Sedgwick Geological Trail

The Geological Trail lies 2 miles (4km) east of Sedbergh just off the A684 Hawes road. There is a convenient car park at the junction of the minor road to Danny Bridge, (SD 698 912). The trail follows the Clough River in a westerly direction along its southern bank and then a return route direct back to the car park for a distance of 1 mile (1.6km).

The Dent Fault is a major break of the earth's crust, which took place in the late Carboniferous Period some 290 million years ago. This important fault was first discovered and interpreted by Adam Sedgwick, the famous geologist of Dent. From this fascinating trail it is possible to observe the fault line and to notice how the Carboniferous rocks of the Pennines have been crumpled up against the older Silurian rocks of the Lake District. Here is an excellent example of seeing rocks at first hand that were laid down in very different environments over millions of years.

The trail is fairly rough going underfoot, so **boots are essential**. Great care is needed in wet weather. An excellent explanatory leaflet may be obtained from the Yorkshire Dales National Park Information Centre at Sedbergh, ☎ (01539) 620125.

and tracks. These rights of way offer an excellent means of exploring the area on both sides of the river.

A signpost indicates the way to the ancient settlement of **Gawthrop**, the start of an interesting scenic route that climbs out of Dentdale beneath the dark crags of Combe Scar and the sprawling grassy slopes of Barbon High Fell. This lonely road crosses the boundary of the Yorkshire Dales National Park at Short Gill Bridge and continues down Barbondale following the beck. Beyond the village of Barbon the Barbon Beck joins the River Lune.

Viewed from a suitable vantage point, you will notice how the village of **Dent** is the natural point of convergence of hill and valley roads, from Newby Head, Deepdale and Barbondale. It was once a town of considerable importance and looked on as the Capital of the Dales.

People came to trade and to attend the market and the great annual Fair. The community had its own craftsmen and tradesmen, consisting of shoemakers, tailors, colliers, marble workers, weavers and knitters. At the beginning of the twentieth century, the population of Dent stood at over a thousand inhabitants.

Lordsland was originally one of the four ancient parts of the township of Dent. In the sixteenth century it was divided into North and South Lordsland when the former manor, which belonged to the Parr and FitzHugh families, came into the possession of the crown.

As one approaches the village, or Dent Town as it is grandly known, the attractive white and colour-washed stone cottages seem to huddle closer together. Then the narrow road bends into the centre becoming a thorough-fare set with cobbles; a quaint and often admired feature particularly by the local dalesmen and women.

At the side of the cobbled street, set against a cottage, is a large wedge-shaped block of Shap granite – the **Sedgwick Memorial Fountain**. This commem-orates Adam Sedgwick (1785-1873), a renowned son of Dent who became Woodwardian Professor of Geology and Senior Fellow of Trinity College, Cam-bridge. He pioneered the new science of geology based on his study of rock strata in the Lake District, in Wales and in his native dales; he is remembered for his work on what he termed the Cambrian System. Sedgwick, whose father was vicar and schoolmaster of Dent, often wrote about the rural and social life in his own community in bygone times, including the remarkable Dent knitters (see page 35).

Mention should be made of an ancient institution in the Dale, known as the Twenty Four Sidesmen or States-men. It appears to have started in the fifteenth century as a kind of local government scheme on a voluntary basis, where the yeomen farmers and gentlemen took on parochial duties for the benefit of the community. Throughout the years they have figured in many important happenings and in local terms could be described as men of great vision and enterprise. They were responsible for the rebuilding and extension of the church, contributed a major part to the foundation of Dent Grammar School in 1604 and acted as agents for the Dent wool and knitting trade.

Today, its importance has been considerably reduced and cannot be compared with that of past times in the Dale. Many of its former functions are now statutorily provided but it holds trusteeship of certain charities.

Splendid walking country

Dentdale offers ridge walks along Rise Hill and Middleton Fell. From the Dentdale-Barbondale watershed, a track crosses South Lord's Land and contours below the glaciated scars of Great Coum. There is a linking route to Dent Town following Flinter Gill and another called Nun House Outrake into Deepdale. This old way, known as the **Occupation Road**, is thought to have been a Roman secondary road to the Bainbridge and Ribchester-Carlisle roads. Later it became an important link as one of the many old droving and packhorse routes that linked the Dales.

Between the Flinter Gill route and the Nun House Outrake track stand the **Megger Stones**. This name is given to a group of stone cairns standing below Crag Hill. Their purpose is unknown but like the Nine Standards Rigg and the Three Men of Gragareth, these grey columns keep silent watch over the surrounding hillsides and valleys – clear landmarks for shepherds and walkers alike. The Occupation Road, so named when the moorland above Dentdale was enclosed, continues with a wide sweep south and then heads east to meet the Kingsdale road at High Moss.

Selected Walks

1. Swarth Fell, Fell Tarn, Wild Boar Fell and Hanging Lund

Distance: 9 miles (15.2km). Highest Elevation: Wild Boar Fell 2,324ft (708m). Total ascent: 1,827ft (557m)

Map: OS Outdoor Leisure 19 Howgill Fells and Upper Eden Valley 1:25,000

From a small parking area by Cotegill Bridge (SD 774 970) walk along the road to Aisgill Moor Cottages. Take the start of the public bridleway to Grisedale, then immediately right up the grassy slopes of Stubbing Rigg; along the line, on paper, of the county border. The ridge is easily reached near the south cairn on Swarth Fell Pike. Bear right and follow the fence passing two more cairns. Note the circular OS Survey Plate in the ground and on the left are a cairn and trig point. From here there are fine views of the Howgill Fells, Baugh Fell and Grisedale. Continue along the right-hand side of the fence and gradually ascend the fellside to the ridge top.

The summit cairn of Swarth Fell, 2,234ft (681m) lies to the right. Descend to so named by the author, Fell Tarn, and from the col climb the grassy slopes ahead slanting to the right. The gradient levels out to reach a stile and a number of cairns on the edge of the escarpment. This fine viewpoint commands a superb panorama of the Mallerstang Valley.

The true summit of Wild Boar Fell, 2,324ft (708m) lies on a north-westerly bearing, a short walk across the flat top. There is an OS Survey Column and a stone shelter. From the summit, walk just east of north-east to reach The Nab. The route from the rash of cairns lies along the escarpment edge to arrive at The Nab.

Descend steeply following the escarpment edge to reach the angle of a wall. Turn sharp right and descend into a dip. Traverse the slope and veer towards a limestone pavement. Here the route becomes indistinct, but proceed over the limestone pasture keeping to the left and below this little plateau. Cross the boundary line beyond Little Wold and descend the grassy slope to a gate in a fence. On reaching a ruined building bear right by a wall. There is a little waterfall down below in the gully to the right.

Cross the stream and continue ahead, as the track swings to the left and passes under the Settle to Carlisle railway line. Descend to Hazelgill Farm, keep right to a metal gate in the corner and go across the meadow to a stile in the wall. Walk through a pine copse to a wall stile and proceed along the river bank. Beyond the meadow cross the bridge over the River Eden.

Looking north down the Mallerstang at Cotegill

There is a footpath sign on the far side of the road, so slant right towards a stile in the wall. Cross a farm track and walk across a pasture towards a partially blocked stile. Note, there is a gate further along the wall.

Aim for the top left-hand corner of the field towards a building and to a stile in the wall. Pass in front of the building and head half left towards a gate and a step stile in a wall. Continue on to a gap stile in a wall and across the meadow to a step stile.

From here proceed in front of Hanging Lund Farm to reach a gate. Cross the stream over a footbridge to a gate with a footpath sign. Bear left, follow the wall to a gate with a public bridleway sign and head up the walled grassy way to a gate. There is a barn ahead as the route passes a small quarry working to reach a gateway. Beyond this gate do not follow the faint grooved track up the slope but continue straight on across the grassy slope to meet a gap in a wall. Pass a spring issuing from a small limestone outcrop and follow the wall to a gate by a small clump of sycamore trees. Proceed along Slade Edge, a limestone terrace and carry on alongside the wall to reach a stile.

Walk along the access track passing a corrugated iron shed to reach Hell Gill Beck and nearby Hellgill Force. This fine waterfall plunges 60ft (18.2m) over a limestone scar. The track carries on to cross over the railway line before joining the road at Aisgill Moor Cottages. Turn right and stroll down the road to the starting point at Cotegill Bridge.

2. Across the southern slopes of Baugh Fell

Distance: 8 miles (12.8m)

Map: OS Outdoor Leisure 19 Howgill Fells and Upper Eden Valley 1:25,000

An east to west crossing of this sprawling, featureless mass may be attempted, providing you have a kind friend to pick you up at the end of the day.

From Fellgate Farm (SD 694 924) follow the direction of the right of way to Near Gill Laids. Climb the grassy slopes in an east-south-east direction to meet the stone wall ascending Ringing Keld Gutter. Follow the wall to Knoutberry Haw and continue alongside it to Tarn Hill on East Baugh Fell. Descend on a north-north-east bearing between Haskhaw Gill and Grisedale Gill to reach the path from Uldale House. Bear right and follow the route to Flust, then over Grisedale Common and a descent to South Lunds Pasture and the B6259 in the upper Eden Valley.

3. Ascent of Whernside from Dent

Distance: 11 miles (17.6km)

Map: OS Outdoor Leisure 2 Yorkshire Dales – Southern and Western areas 1:25,000

From Dent town take the minor road north to Church Bridge and then by footpaths via Double Croft to Bridge End. After a short distance along the road, bear right along Dyke Hall Lane and turn left on the track to Whernside Manor. Almost immediately take the track on the right signposted, Bridle Path to Ribblehead. This is the Craven Way, an old packhorse route and coal road. This pleasant green lane starts between stone walls and climbs gently up the fellside. Stop occasionally to turn round and admire the view down Dentdale to the Howgill Fells.

Continue to meet a gate. In the vicinity, a number of tiny watercourses have their beginnings; note the old lime kiln on the north side of the track. Almost opposite to the kiln is a gap in the wall. From this point strike off in a southerly direction, passing the sites of old coal workings and climb gradually to reach the cairns on the end of the ridge called Pike. Aim for another cairn directly ahead and then veer half left to arrive at two tarns. The Whernside Tarns are shallow stretches of dark water that are rimmed by sandy beaches with pebbles and stones.

Proceed ahead keeping slightly to the left to meet the third tarn and then ascend to the ridge of Knoutberry Hill (the hill of the cloudberry). This moorland plant found on northern hills has white flowers and edible orange-red berries. Meet a wall coming up to the ridge from the west and continue along the ridge to the OS column marking the summit of Whernside, 2,415ft (736m), one of the famous Three Peaks of Yorkshire. From the summit, head due west and descend to cairns. Then proceed northwards for a little way and continue the descent by following the wall into Kingsdale. Bear right along the road to High Moss. As the road begins to descend, take the path on the right and walk down into Deepdale. Follow the marked route via Deepdale Head and Mire Garth, then along the path that connects with Dyke Hall Lane. From the end of the lane return to Dent Town along the road.

St Andrew's Church is prominently sited in the centre of the village. Throughout the Middle Ages, Dent was in the territory of the FitzHughs of Ravensworth Castle in North Yorkshire. The spiritual needs of the area were attended to by the monks of Coverham Abbey near Middleham; a house of Premonstratensian canons.

A church was erected at the beginning of the twelfth century as a chapel to Sedbergh. The present church has an imposing tower, circa 1785 and there is a three-bay interior with circular piers and pointed arches, probably thirteenth century. However, on the north side of the church is a blocked-up doorway, surmounted by a badly-weathered Norman arch of chevron pattern, a reminder of the early church.

At one time, Dent Town had a number of inns and alehouses situated in the centre near the market place, including the King's Arms and the White Hart. Today, Dent is very much at the heart of tourism in the Dale. It offers a small range of shops, tea rooms, including the Stone House Café, an Art Gallery, a Photographic Studio, the Sun Inn and the George and Dragon, where locally brewed Dent bitter is available. For two centuries the Sun at Dent has enigmatically told its customers that it sells the 'Best Ale under the sun'. A number of local establishments offer accommodation. There is a large car park with toilet facilities situated at the western approaches to the village.

Leaving Dent, the road lying to the south of the River Dee soon meets a road junction. From this point, another route turns southwards into Deepdale. A short distance away to the east at Bridge End stands Whernside Manor. This Georgian mansion, the largest residence in the valley, was built by the Sills, an old yeoman family. The Sills engaged in trade with the West Indies and it is said that the household was served by a retinue of Negro servants. This house was also the home of Miles Mason, (1752-1822), founder of Mason's Ironstone China. In more recent times, the house served as a centre for cave and fell exploration and lately for adventure training.

Little **Deepdale**, just over 2 miles (3.3km) long, is tucked between the steep flanks of **Whernside** and Great Coum. The dale is a quiet, almost secret place, of stone barns, farmsteads, sloping fields and isolated meadows.

From Dent Town roads travel up the dale on both sides of the River Dee. The northern route via Church Bridge is more straightforward with fewer bends and friendlier gradients. From the road short lengths of track reach out to the white-washed farmsteads and their attendant barns; all snugly set on the steepening slopes of Rise Hill.

Each level of the dale has its own flora: the hedgerows with high banks support hazel, holly and hawthorn; the valley meadows containing a profusion of wild flowers rise to the sweet herbage of the limestone. Coarse grasses predominate on thinner wetter soils and on high ground, moist infertile patches support sedge, peat mosses, cotton grass and heather – the kingdom of the grouse and curlew. In the valley bottom, the course of the river is marked by an irregular line of copses and fringing trees; it is there that some of the dale's scenic gems lie hidden.

The Dent knitters

In the seventeenth and eighteenth centuries, Dent houses were mostly three floors high with an outside staircase and wooden galleries. Sedgwick records that groups of men, women and children knitted with amazing speed, often by candlelight and firelight using knitting sticks and curved needles. Robert Southey referred to them as 'the terrible knitters of Dent' ('terrible' meaning 'hard working').

On winter evenings it was the custom to have social gatherings in each other's houses for a gossip, to knit, to listen to readings and to sing knitting songs around a wood and peat fire. The finished articles consisted of quality stockings for the army; jackets, gloves, mittens and caps for general use.

Today, some local residents are fortunate to have in their possession examples of old knitting sticks. These are symbols of a once thriving cottage industry that made use of coarse worsted wool called bump. Many of these knitting sticks were finely carved and young men often gave them to their girlfriends as a token of affection.

A street in Dent and a name that commemorates its famous past

Along the road from Church Bridge footpath signs soon indicate access to the riverside footbridges. At Tommy Bridge, the river passes over water-worn pavements of limestone and sometimes disappears underground. From this bridge visitors may walk along the north bank on the line of the Dales Way, to reach the next footbridge. Paths then lead to the road on the north side of the river, or to the one on the south side. Close by, below the ruins of

Settle to Carlisle Railway

The Settle to Carlisle line, one of the most scenic in the country, was built following a dispute between two railway companies about connections at Ingleton. Here, from 1861, the Derby based Midland Railway exchanged traffic in an atmosphere of mutual distrust with its arch rival the London and North West Railway, the company running the service over Shap to Scotland. The two companies had separate stations at either end of the viaduct over the Greta, passengers being turned out of the train and forced to walk between the two points, only to see the so-called connection steaming away into the distance. This intolerable situation resulted in Midland seeking powers to build its own main line over the Pennines to Carlisle.

The Settle-Carlisle railway runs through the length of Ribblesdale, up and over Garsdale Head to Mallerstang. At Aisgill Summit, 1,169ft (356m) above sea level, the railway attains the highest altitude of any line in the country. It keeps close company with the River Eden on the long descent of Mallerstang; then runs under the shoulder of Wild Boar Fell through the Birkett Tunnel and downhill to Kirkby Stephen. The line was opened for goods traffic in August 1875, when there was only one track through Mallerstang; it was first used for passenger traffic on 1st May 1876.

Building of the line

The building of the whole route from Settle to Carlisle took six years and was a tremendous feat of engineering. Bad weather often hampered the cutting of the line through some of the wildest terrain in England. Within a comparatively small area, considering the total distance involved, the navvies building the railway line faced incredible difficulties. Large and complex viaducts had to be raised across Batty Moss (now known as Ribblehead), Dent Head, Artengill and Dandry Mire before reaching the highest point at Aisgill. Not only had they to contend with the terrain, but also the fierce Pennine weather, disease, shanty-town and overcrowded living conditions, drunkenness, brawls and frequent accidents. These feats of construction, together with the rock and drainage problems of Blea Moor and Rise Hill Tunnels must rank amongst the finest of British railway engineering achievements.

The navvies, mostly miners from Ireland and Wales, lived in hutted camps erected at intervals along the line. Not the sort of place that people would choose to live. Yet in the 1870s the area east of Ribblehead railway viaduct was a centre of great activity. Here was a shanty town of huts housing the hundreds of men engaged in the construction of the viaduct and railway. The labour force which worked on the Garsdale section of the line and the Hawes branch was based near the Moorcock Inn. In 1871, over 140 navvies, some with wives and children, lived here in nine wooden huts.

The wild behaviour of the men living in this way led to the railway company providing missionaries to try to curb some of the fighting and drinking that went on. Other specialist craftsmen accommodated here were blacksmiths, stone masons, wood sawyers and an engine driver.

Features of the line

Although the line was only 72 miles (116km) long, building it required the erection of twenty major viaducts and fourteen tunnels with very little mechanical help. Probably the most famous of the viaducts is Ribblehead with its twenty-four arches that span Batty Moss 105ft (32m) below.

The Moorcock Inn stands in an open position at the junction of the B6259 Mallerstang road and the A684, $5^{1}/_{2}$ miles (8.8km) from Hawes. This well-known hostelry, at the windswept head of the Garsdale valley, is near to the point where the Settle to Carlisle railway crosses over the Dandry Mire viaduct; this structure is 227yds (208m) long, 50ft (15m) high with twelve arches.

Garsdale station has become a well-known feature of the famous Settle to Carlisle line. Like Ribblehead and Dent, it has achieved a prominent position in the history of this Pennine railway. Hawes Junction, as it was originally designated, became Hawes Junction and Garsdale at the beginning of the twentieth century. Later in 1933, it was renamed 'Garsdale (for Hawes)'. The Midland Railway Company completed the branch line, nearby 6 miles (9.6km) long from Hawes, on a picturesque route that climbed steadily to Hawes Junction. Hawes station was shared by the two railway companies, the Midland and the North East, the latter having extended their line from Northallerton to Leyburn to Hawes.

Garsdale or Hawes Junction was unusual in the fact that it served no particular community. The station had an engine shed but no goods shed; there were cottages for railway employees but no Station Master's house. At one time the waiting room was used for church services. Unusually, there was a library of two hundred books donated by two sisters who had, on one occasion, been stranded at the station; it was available for the use of passengers and railway employees. The water tank house was used as a social centre. Just south of Garsdale, on a piece of level ground, were the highest railway water troughs in the world.

Modern times

In the early 1980s, British Rail began to remove traffic, so that it could be claimed that the line was not needed. This led to the formation of the Friends of the Settle-Carlisle line, which ultimately joined with Transport 2000 and the Railway Development Society to oppose the line's closure. In October 1984, in the face of a huge public response and the fact that the saving of the Settle-Carlisle had become a national cause; there were signs of a change in British Rail's strategy. Many observers claimed that BR was seeking a way to reprieve the line. Finally however, it was left to the then transport minister for his decision to keep the line open.

Today there is a daily diesel passenger service between Leeds and Carlisle, via Settle. Steam trains operate special services at various times and further information can be obtained from Tourist Information Centres. There are buses linking stations on the line with other places nearby. Traveline ☎ (0870) 6082608 for further details.

Guided walks from stations on the line operate throughout the year and details are available from ☎ (01729) 825454. Leaflets detailing self-guided walks based on train travel on the Settle-Carlisle line can be obtained from the same source. There is also a website: www.settle-carlisle.co.uk.

Gibbs Hall (telephone box), the River Dee flows in another deep ravine and cascades into a dark and rather sinister-looking pool beneath a heavy canopy of trees – this is **Hell's Cauldron**. In times of spate the sight can be fearsome, but even under normal conditions, it is a most impressive place.

By continuing along the road from Gibbs Hall, to a point where the dense barrier of trees ends, there is a parking space on the right. From here, a short stretch of path descends to a footbridge over the river. By walking back along the road for a short distance, a step down discloses a path high on the river bank above a deep gorge; the waterfall soon becomes visible. The cave system of **Ibbeth Peril** leads off a small opening under the overhang of the cliff. This is only for experts experienced in underground exploration.

At Ewegales Bridge, both valley roads join together and enter the hamlet of **Cowgill**. In the Cowgill part of Dentdale there were at one time thirty-nine Quaker families out of a total of fifty-six families. On different occasions a number of local farmhouses were used for their meetings. Adam Sedgwick was instrumental in instituting the church at Cowgill, the foundation stone of which he laid in 1837.

A little group of buildings clusters around the road junction at **Lea Yeat**. Here, the Cowgill Institute was once a Friends' Meeting House. During the railway building era, the tiny settlement of Lea Yeat was transformed with the construction of blacksmiths' shops, a saw mill and storehouses. On the north side of Cowgill church are many unmarked graves of the victims of the smallpox epidemic during the building of the Settle-Carlisle railway line.

The narrowing dale now turns southwards with the road and river in close company to pass the welcoming Sportsman's Arms. The river is re-crossed at **Stone House** where a few cars may be parked. Stone House was the site of a flourishing marble works from the early nineteenth century.

Dent 'vampire'

Outside the church porch is the grave of one George Hodgson, who died in 1715 aged 94. The story of the Dent 'vampire' is perhaps just a good yarn – very suitable for an old knitting village. There are accounts of the mysterious deaths of people claiming to have seen George after his burial. Nevertheless, his gravestone seems to have a hole drilled in it, where it is said, an iron stake was hammered through the stone into the coffin.

History of Dent

Adam Sedgwick's two classic works on 'the climate, history and dialects of Dent', were first privately published in 1868 and 1870 as *Memorial by the Trustees of Cowgill Chapel* and *Supplement to the Memorial*. These publications contain a wealth of information on the Dale and its inhabitants. They were reprinted as one volume in 1985 with a new introduction by David Boulton.

Here, locally obtained black and grey fossiliferous limestone was cut, dressed and polished into ornaments, fireplace surrounds, monuments, tables and staircases. The patterns in the stone are formed almost entirely by fossil crinoids (sea lilies). Look out for examples of this attractive and fascinating Dent marble in buildings throughout the locality and further afield.

Both mills had waterwheels, but that at High Mill was a remarkable 60ft (18m) in diameter. W G Armstrong, visited the dale and became fascinated by the use of water-power, with its attendant dams and system of underground culverts at the marble works. It is believed that soon afterwards he gave up his vocation and became an inventor of hydraulic machinery. He ultimately founded Armstrong's engineering works on Tyneside.

Highest station

Dent Station is situated at a height of 1,148ft (350m) above sea level and is the highest main line station in the country. After closure on the 4 May 1970, it was re-opened for the Dales Rail services in 1975.

Catching a train from Dent Station is quite an adventure in itself. Travellers who have not had the fortune to obtain a lift from the valley bottom at Lea Yeat are faced with a steep half-mile (0.5km) climb in order to reach their objective. One will be glad to rest part way and perhaps even enjoy the splendid view down the dale. From this high vantage point, it is particularly noticeable after summer haymaking, how the patchwork effect of fields varies in colour and tone from pale brownish-yellow to rich green. Dividing these colourful patches are the dark outlines of hedgerows, stone walls, copses and gills.

Places to Visit

Sedbergh

Holme Farm

Middleton, nr Sedbergh. Enjoy an educational visit to a traditional working animal farm, 11/4-mile (2km) nature trail.

☎ (015396) 20654. Guided farm tours daily, 11am–4pm. Opening dates: 1 Mar to 30 Sep (Closed Tue). Evening Farm Tours, Caravan and Camp Site by arrangement. Direct bookings or enquiries call 1–1.30pm or after 4.30pm. Special Local Interests: Roman road through farm with ancient ford. Remains of Stone Age settlement nearby. Children can touch and feed baby animals at the farm.

Brigflatts Meeting House*

Two miles (3.2km) south of Sedbergh (SD 283 773)

☎ (015396) 20005

Open: 11am–6pm Easter to Sep, 11am-dusk Oct to Easter, every day. The oldest meeting house in northern England dating from 1675.

Farfield Mill*

Located 1 mile (1.6km) east of Sedbergh, A684 Garsdale – Hawes Road. Open: end of Mar, daily 10.30am-5pm to beginning of Nov (7 days a week), Nov–Jan Wed–Sun (open New Years Day), Jan–Mar, weekends only.

Arts and Heritage Centre a unique arts and crafts journey into the past. Open: 1st April, daliy 10.30am–5.00pm Jan–Mar, Sat & Sun only. ☎ (015396) 21958. Disabled access throughout. www.farfieldmill.org, themanager@ farfieldmill.org

Craftshop and café. Resident Artists' Exhibitions. Mill Shop and Tearoom. Coaches are welcome by appointment.

Beyond Stone House Farm lies the massive **Artengill Viaduct** carrying the Settle-Carlisle line. Its huge piers built of fossiliferous limestone rise to a lofty structure of eleven arches spanning a hollow in the skyline; it stands magnificently set against a moorland background of dun-coloured slopes. A track passes through the arches and rises gradually, before continuing into Widdale and on into Wensleydale. From this route, a right of way heads northwards and then skirts round the slopes of Great Knoutberry Hill to Garsdale.

There is also a grassy climb from Artengill Moss on a north-north-west bearing to the summit of Great Knoutberry Hill, 2,205ft (672m) and thence a short moorland crossing north-north-east to the shores of Widdale Great Tarn. Return to Artengill by the same route.

With its course still overhung by trees and fringed by grasses and ferns, the Upper Dee in its narrowing valley continues to display all the characteristics of a limestone stream. The water runs smoothly over eroded rock beds

Sedbergh Book Town

Sedbergh Tourist Office, 72 Main St, Sedbergh, Cumbria, LA10 5AD
☎ (015396) 20125
Websites: www.sedbergh.org.uk
www.sedberghbooktown.co.uk

A walk around Sedbergh Town

A leaflet, obtained from the National Park Information Centre, describes a circular walk around Sedbergh. It points out some of the architectural and historical features of the town. The trail follows a route through the town centre and takes approximately one hour.

Dent

Dent Crafts Centre*

Helmside, nr Dent
Picture gallery and restaurant.
☎ (01539) 625400
Open: 10.30am–5pm (5.30pm in summer). Closed Tuesdays.

Dent Heritage Centre

'Stepping back in time' an educational and interesting theme of farm life and the history of Dentdale. Please ring for details of opening times.
Websites: www.dentvillageheritage centre.com
School & coach parties welcome.

Hill Studio*

Working studio of paintings and drawings. ☎ (015396) 25354 Please ring for details of opening times.

Stone Close Tea Room and Bed and Breakfast

Main Street, Dent
☎ (015396) 25231. 17th century listed building. Open: 12–5pm Closed Mon & Fri. www.dentdale.com

and round boulders; it tumbles, sparkles and cascades over ledges, gliding and swirling in many different ways. In flood conditions, its brown torrent of unleashed fury thunders and sprays over outcrops and rock steps, leaping from side to side as it tries to escape from its natural channel. A small stone bridge crosses the river for access to Deeside House, Dentdale Youth Hostel. The building, a former shooting lodge, is a long established port of call for hostellers, and for walkers on the Dales Way.

The winding road steepens to reach ten-arched **Dent Head Viaduct**. At this point, trains on the Settle-Carlisle railway have just emerged after their dark journey below ground in the Blea Moor Tunnel. Finally, the little road wriggles clear of the confines of the dale and crosses the barren wastes of Newby Head Gate at a height of 1,385ft (422m); the boundary with North Yorkshire. Just ahead lies the B6255, Hawes to Ingleton road.

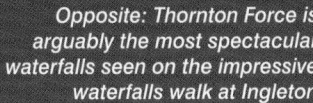
Opposite: Thornton Force is arguably the most spectacular waterfalls seen on the impressive waterfalls walk at Ingleton

In its early stages, the River Lune flows north-north-east as Dale Gill from its source high on the slopes of Green Bell in the northern Howgill Fells. The watercourse then turns westwards and becomes considerably enlarged by vigorous tributaries, including Bowderdale Beck and Langdale Beck.

Lunesdale

In the upper Lune valley, north of Sedbergh, remotely tucked away on the northern slopes of Fell Head, lies the impressive waterfall of **Black Force**. Viewed fleetingly from the nearby main railway line or the motorway, the sleek smooth-looking, steep-sided Howgill Fells appear suddenly with startling effect. They are a commanding presence that induces a rash of promises to return and explore those delightful grassy hills.

Beyond Carlingill Bridge and sinister Gibbet Hill, the **Fairmile Road** runs south along the foot of the fells and crosses Chapel Beck at the small hamlet of **Howgill**. Here, clustered together, are a few cottages the old school and schoolhouse and the lancet-windowed church of Holy Trinity built in 1838.

A footpath leads from the hamlet of Howgill and connects with the Dales Way. Further on at Beck Foot, the Crook of Lune road bridge is one of the few crossing points in the vicinity. This interesting narrow structure bears marks of vehicle contact due to the restricted approach. A vehicle that can bend in the middle has a definite advantage. A visit to Crook of Lune with its photogenic stone bridge and fine river and hill scenery is well worthwhile. This stretch of the Lune is popular with canoeists.

South of Beck Foot, the **Firbank** part of Lunesdale is very beautiful indeed. Ancient farmsteads are set amongst lush meadows and low rounded heights. Many of these are of seventeenth century origin; stone and whitewashed structures with flagged roofs, mullioned windows and rounded chimneys. The surrounding hedgerows in the valley bottom are coloured with hawthorns and rose hips; the bleating of lambs heralds the green spring and bracken glows russet in autumn. Many

Norse names

Here in the surrounding area, like Lakeland, streams are becks, ravines are gills, valleys are dales, hills are fells and clearings are thwaites, all denoting their Norse influence. In and around the Howgills are another Langdale, another Borrowdale, another Bowderdale and another Grisedale.

of the dry stone walls were built in the eighteenth century. The skilful work of the old craftsmen to be seen on fell and field, has resulted in the walls withstanding the extremes of the weather.

At the foot of Firbank Knott stands the parish church of St John built in 1842. Behind the church a track climbs steeply up the fellside, with glorious views of the dale and continues on to the little road leading to Firbank Old Graveyard and Fox's Pulpit.

The Waterside viaduct stretches across the Lune near to another old ford. Built in the latter part of the nineteenth century, this finely engineered structure carried the Clapham-Lowgill branch line over the river. Its rather unusual construction still proves a source of great interest.

South of Sedbergh

A short distance south of Sedbergh is the old Toll Bar House at **Borrett Bar**; one of a group of seven Toll Gates in the district, which were let for three-yearly periods to the highest bidder. The board bearing details of toll charges at Borrett Barr in 1826 is preserved in Kendal Museum. One entry reads 'For every Horse drawing any coach (Except Stagecoach) 6d. Every Drove of Oxen, 10d a Score'.

At Killington Bridge, the River Lune flowing through beautiful rock-girt surroundings, is a popular spot for angling. Below the bridge is Broad Raine, an early seventeenth century grain mill. At autumn time one may see the interesting sight of salmon jumping up the salmon leap close by the mill.

Across the Lune to the east is the attractive mass of the Middleton Fells which rise to the summit of Calf Top, 1,998ft (609m). This height lies on the Barkin escarpment overlooking **Barbondale**. The area is sparsely favoured for footpaths, but there is an excellent right of way that circuits around the edges.

The Roman road from Low Borrowbridge followed the Lune in the neighbourhood of **Middleton**. Evidence of this route came to light when a cylindrical stone shaft, a Roman milestone, was unearthed in 1836; it was re-erected on rising ground just south of the church, between Hawking Hall and the A683. The stone pillar is inscribed '53' miles and probably refers to the distance to and from Carlisle. Upon re-erection, a further inscription was added to it by a Dr Lingard.

Just north of Middleton Church lies Middleton Hall. The H-shaped fifteenth-century house is approached through a gate arch in a high wall, formerly the west side of a gatehouse. During the Civil War, John Middleton supported the Royalists and lost three sons fighting against the Parliamentarian army.

Barbon is a small village of grey and whitewashed cottages, formerly served by a station on the Lowgill to Clapham line. The surrounding slopes of Barbon Park are softened by woodlands. Barbon Manor, designed by E M Barry, 1862-3, is wonderfully sited high above Barbon Beck. This Victorian shooting lodge with its tall roof and high dormer windows was built in the style of an Italianate mansion. The owner, Sir James Kay Shuttleworth, was a successful physician in Manchester during the great cholera epidemic of 1852.

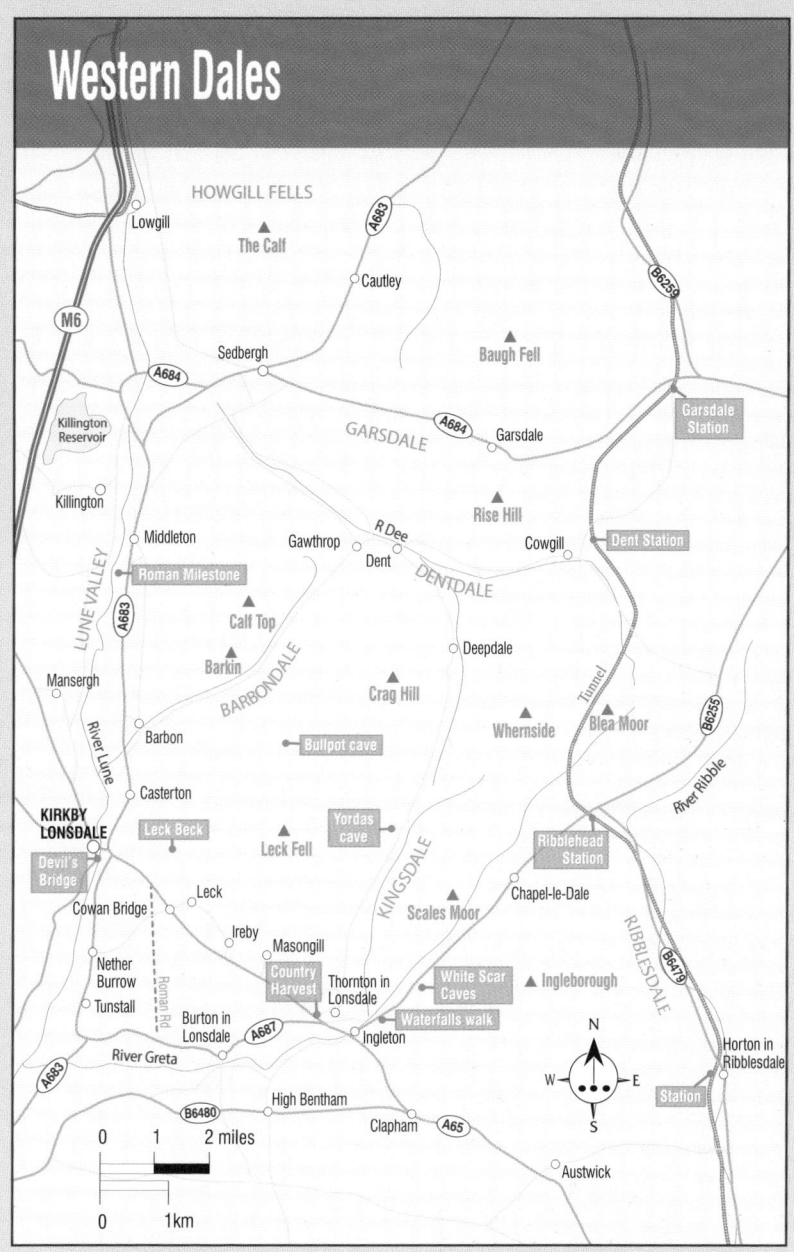

Western Dales

HOWGILL FELLS

Lowgill

A683

The Calf ▲

Cautley

M6

Sedbergh

A684

Baugh Fell ▲

B6259

GARSDALE

A684

Garsdale

Garsdale Station

Killington Reservoir

Killington

Rise Hill ▲

Middleton

Gawthrop

R Dee

Dent

Cowgill

Dent Station

Roman Milestone

DENTDALE

LUNE VALLEY

A683

Calf Top ▲

Barkin ▲

Deepdale

BARBONDALE

Crag Hill ▲

Tunnel

Mansergh

River Lune

Barbon

Bullpot cave

Whernside ▲

Blea Moor ▲

B6255

Casterton

River Ribble

KIRKBY LONSDALE

Leck Beck

Yordas cave

Ribblehead Station

Devil's Bridge

Leck Fell ▲

KINGSDALE

Leck

Scales Moor ▲

Chapel-le-Dale

Cowan Bridge

Ireby

Masongill

RIBBLESDALE

B6479

Nether Burrow

Roman Rd

Country Harvest

Thornton in Lonsdale

White Scar Caves

Ingleborough ▲

Tunstall

Burton in Lonsdale

A687

Waterfalls walk

N

Horton in Ribblesdale

River Greta

Ingleton

W E

A683

S

Station

High Bentham

B6480

Clapham

A65

0   1   2 miles

0   1km

Austwick

ton-in-Lonsdale. The church of St Oswald was rebuilt by Paley and Austin in 1869-70. Originally it had a Norman arcade before a fire in 1933 and this has now been faithfully reproduced. Opposite the church is the attractively grouped inn and barn. The Masons Arms, 1679, was once called Church

Stile Inn. In a tour of the local caves, the Reverend John Hutton when visiting Yordas Cave, procured a guide, candles, lanthorn, tinder box and provisions at the Church Stile in 1781.

From Thornton-in-Lonsdale to High Moss, Kingsdale is barely 5 miles (8.8km) long. It is a quiet, lonely dale with only two farmhouses, Kingsdale Head Farm and Braida Garth. There is an absence of running water as the stream, Kingsdale Beck, prefers to travel underground. At Keld Head, a large deep pool appears to be the resurgence point for all the streams draining into the potholes on the western side of the road. The byroad accompanying Kingsdale Beck descends into Deepdale and on into Dentdale.

Along the eastern side of Kingsdale looms the ridge of West Fell leading to the summit of Whernside. While to the west, the scars of North End and Keld Head are overlooked by the

steep slopes of Gragareth that lead on to Great Coum.

The dale is a fine example of limestone scenery, a glaciated valley with the steep scars on the western side having been gouged by the moving ice. These limestone scars on the western terrace contain some of the area's well-known potholes. These include Jingling Pot, Marble Steps Pot and Rowten Pot whose opening is a sheer fall of 213ft (65m). A delightful grassy track, the Turbary Road, winds its way along the western terrace. This was a way used by horse-drawn sledges bringing peat down from the fells. This is an exhilarating walk with open views across the valley of Kingsdale to Whernside.

Ingleton

From Kingsdale, return down the by-road to Thornton-in-Lonsdale and bear left to cross over the River Greta into **Ingleton**. A busy and popular tourist centre, it originated as a small farming community but grew into an industrial community due to the presence of local coal seams. Ingleton's narrow winding streets radiate from an ancient market place. Winding Bell Horse Gate descends in steep twists to the River Greta, and to the cottages where textile workers lived. They were once employed in mills powered by the river.

The parish church of St Mary occupies a spacious site in the centre of the village. It has a perpendicular tower but the remainder of the building is mostly 1887. However, the nave has been built more than once. The font is one of the best Norman fonts in Yorkshire. It is circular with twelve figures under in-

Yordas Cave

Yordas Cave, (SD 705 791) in Kingsdale is the legendary home of the giant Yordas. This cave has been known for a long time. In Victorian days it was a showplace, a charge for admission being payable at Braida Garth farm. A neat stone arch and a flight of steps were built at the entrance. Inside there is a fine cavern called the Chapter House, and a spectacular waterfall, also a muddy floor. A good torch is essential, wellingtons are the best footwear, and a hard hat needed to protect tender skulls.

Selected Car Drive

Kirkby Lonsdale to Ingleton

Distance: 52miles (83.2km)

In Kirkby Lonsdale, from the parking area near the Devil's Bridge, cross the new bridge over the Lune and turn left. Travel through Casterton and take the byroad on the right to Barbon. The village lies at the foot of lonely Barbondale, and ahead, the ribbon of tarmac rises between steep fellsides, followed by a sharp descent to Gawthrop in Dentdale. Proceed through Dent Town, and take the right-hand road at the Sedgwick Memorial and at the next junction. From here, a winding road climbs above Deepdale, and then ascends steeply to the summit at White Shaw Moss.

Beyond, the route is a journey through the limestone landscape of Kingsdale. Descend to Thornton-in-Lonsdale and bear left for Ingleton. Cross over the River Greta climbing up past the church to the left, and on through the village to reach the B6255 road, turn left. The route along Doedale gradually rises between Ingleborough and the slopes of Whernside to Chapel-le-Dale. Turn right at Ribblehead, and travel down Ribblesdale, through Horton-in-Ribblesdale to Helwith Bridge. Here, turn right on to a byroad that touches the village of Wharfe, and continues on through Austwick to the main A65, turn right.

Proceed for a short distance, and then take the next turn right into Clapham. Follow the B6480 to the main road, and then go straight across towards the twin villages of High and Low Bentham. In the centre of Low Bentham, turn right on to a byroad to Burton-in-Londsdale. Cross the river, and rise up to the A687, turn left. Continue through Cantsfield to the junction with the A683, turn right. Proceed through the village of Tunstall, returning to Kirby Lonsdale.

---

tersected arches. A thirteenth-century arch contains a Tree of Life and among the figures are the Virgin and Child and three Magi.

Ingleton has a wide variety of services and facilities for its visitor. There is an impressive Youth Hostel, Tourist Information Centre and Community Centre. Its cafés, shops, hotels, guest houses and caravan sites can be put into perspective against the splendour of its falls (see next page) and glens and the incomparable limestone scenery on its

doorstep. Ingleton is one of the gateways to the beautiful Craven District of Yorkshire.

Doedale to Ribblehead

The B6255 climbs out of Ingleton on its scenic way up Doedale to Ribblehead. After a short journey of 1 mile (1.6km), the well-known **White Scar Cave** is reached. There is a large parking space

Waterfalls walk

When the London and North West Railway reached Ingleton in the 1850s the village was small. It is thought that the local people were unaware of the spectacular waterfalls and deep rock-strewn gorges that existed close by, probably because the two converging valleys of the Twiss and the Doe were almost impenetrable. Joseph Carr was instrumental in bringing to local people's attention the beauties of the Ingleton Glens. In 1885, a public meeting was convened to discuss the need to open up the falls to a wider public. At the meeting, Carr suggested that steps and wooden bridges be put down and so the Improvement Company was formed.

The Joseph Carr Memorial was erected in 1900 to honour the life of a man who opened up the Waterfalls Walk. The railway company furthered the publicity angle with posters and excursions. In 1893, an estimated 100,000 visitors came to see the 'wonders of nature', in particular the $4^{1}/_{2}$ miles (7km) of the 'Falls Walk'.

Pecca Twin Falls,
Ingleton Waterfalls Walk

for cars and coaches, toilet facilities, picnic areas, café and shop.

The original cave entrance was found in 1923 by a Cambridge undergraduate named Christopher Long. Sights include waterfalls, massive banks of flowstone, galleries decorated with cream and orange-coloured stalactites and curious cave formations, including the Devil's Tongue, the Arum Lily and the Judge's Head. Battlefield Cavern, with prehistoric mud pools, is over 300ft (91m) long, its roof soaring in places to 100ft (30m). The cave has a cool 46°F (8°C) temperature throughout the year, so an extra pullover or jacket is recommended. Hard hats are provided and the interior is illuminated.

As one travels up the dale, the surrounding limestone landscape in all its starkness and beauty forcefully displays its features on both flanks of the valley. On the western side of the River Doe there are the serrated terraces of Twistleton Scars and the fine limestone pavements of Scales Moor and on the

Above: Ribblehead Viaduct

Below: Stockdale House, the hamlet of Feizor

Right: The path through Trow Gill leading to Gaping Gill and Ingleborough

51

eastern side, the higher distinctive shape of Ingleborough with its limestone pavements and scars.

Ingleborough is a fine hill and a wonderful upland height to explore. The Great Scar Limestone, 400ft (122m) thick, is well seen in Giggleswick Scar near Settle and in many other parts of the area. Originally, it was an ooze accumulating over millions of years, on the subsiding bed of a clear sea with the sediment composed chiefly of the hard parts of corals and other small creatures.

The foundations of the hills are of Great Scar Limestone and the Three Peaks of Ingleborough, Whernside and Penyghent stand on this limestone plateau. The peaks rise from it in a series of steps, short vertical sections alternating with gentler slopes. These slopes are shales and sandstones, whereas the vertical sections are narrow beds of limestone. Gradually earth movements altered the relation of land and sea. Great quantities of coarse grit were washed down from the north, producing the 'Millstone grit' that forms a protective cap to the Three Peaks.

The summit of Ingleborough is a place of legend and history. There are still traces of hut circles attributed to an Iron Age occupation. The native Brigantes people established a hill fort covering 15 acres (6 hectares) to defend the settlement. The crags which protect the encampment were reinforced by the Iron Age occupants by means of thousands of blocks of millstone grit. Three of the original entrances, on the north, south-west and east can still be traced.

In 1830, the new owner of Ingleton Manor had a tower erected on the summit made from stone pillaged from the Iron Age defences. However, during the opening ceremony, drunken visitors dismantled the building. Nearby stands a wall shelter, with a view indicator installed in 1953 to commemorate the Coronation of Queen Elizabeth II. Ingleborough is a very fine vantage point with Pendle Hill to the south, Lakeland to the north-west and Morecambe Bay to the west.

There are a number of walking routes from different directions that reach the summit of Ingleborough: from Ingleton via Crina Bottom, from Newby Cote via Newby Moss, from Clapham via Clapham Beck, from Horton-in-Ribblesdale via Sulber Nick and from Chapel-le-Dale via Souther Scales.

The roads on either side of Doedale converge at the hamlet of **Chapel-le-Dale**. The minor route below Twistleton Scars follows the line of the Roman road from Ingleton to Bainbridge in Wensleydale. It leaves Ingleton by a cleverly designed route which climbs the spur between the Doe and Kingsdale Beck and, having gained a suitable height, it continues as a very straight valley side road.

Classic walk

The **Three Peaks Walk** takes in the summits of Penyghent 2,278ft (694m), Whernside 2,416ft (736m) and Ingleborough, 2,375ft (724m), involving over 5,000ft (1524m) of ascent in a single day. Sadly, the routes involved have suffered from path erosion.

High in the narrowing dale, below the long hog's back of Whernside, nestles the tiny church of St Leonard, Chapel-le-Dale. Originally a chapel of ease for Ingleton, it has a nave and chancel in one, less than 50ft (15m) long, with a bell turret. St Leonard's churchyard was the last resting place for some 200 navvies, working on the Settle-Carlisle line between 1869 and 1875, and their families. They are all commemorated on a tablet set up in 1876 by the Midland Railway Company and their fellow workmen.

Behind the church, which is screened by trees, is a lane that passes the large pothole of Hurtle Pot and then further on the entrance to Jingle Pot. A little way beyond is the huge cleft of Weathercote Cave, once a showplace cave with a flight of steps descending into the abyss. From the depths the scene is very impressive and it is where in 1808, the artist J M W Turner portrayed the cave with its high waterfall gushing out from behind a jammed boulder known as Mohammed's Coffin.

The B6255 continues along the line of the Roman road for 2 miles (3.2km) to reach the open, windswept area of Ribblehead. The road is joined by the B6479 that has followed the River Ribble up the dale from Settle. The notable feature here is the famous twenty-four arched Ribblehead Viaduct on the Settle to Carlisle line. Both platforms at Ribblehead Station are now in use and visitors can start from here as a base for exhilarating local walks or the more challenging ascents of Whernside and Ingleborough. The huge sweep of the fells may again be enjoyed during the return journey down the valley of the Doe to Ingleton.

Clapham

The main road heads in a south-easterly direction for 4 miles (6.4km) to the village of **Clapham**, now mercifully bypassed by the busy A65. The settlement is peacefully tucked away in a narrow wooded valley below Ingleborough. The houses of the village line leafy Clapham Beck and the stream is pleasantly crossed by four bridges of different structural proportions. Clapham has the distinction of being the home for many years of the magazine, *The Dalesman*.

The church of St James has a Perpendicular tower, although possibly altered in the late Middle Ages. The interior has tall octagonal piers and the ends of old pews, Jacobean style, used as wall-panelling.

Much of the character of the village is derived from the Farrer family who settled here in the 18th century, softening the surrounding landscape by a considerable programme of tree planting; the beck was dammed creating a lake, Ingleborough Hall rebuilt and Clapham developed as an estate village.

Plant collector

Reginald Farrer, (1880-1920), the famous botanist, introduced over a hundred new plants into Europe from the far east. These included twenty-four species of rhododendron, ten of which are still to be found in Clapham Woods. Two of his books, *My Rock Garden* and *The English Rock Garden* stimulated the building of rockeries.

Left: The church of St James in Clapham set in leafy surroundings

Right: The site of the impressive entrance to the underground cave system of Gaping Gill

Gaping Gill

At Gaping Gill, a gaggle of coloured tents spread out around Fell Beck indicates that the Bradford Potholing Club or the Craven Potholing Club are preparing for a winch meet. The two clubs erect winches, one at Spring Bank Holiday, the other on August Bank Holiday. They will drop you to the bottom of Gaping Gill free of charge but they do charge however for bringing you back up again. Gaping Gill is well worth a visit; it is 364ft (111m) deep and its main chamber is 460ft (140m) long and 100ft (30m) high and wide. The descent by bosun's chair is not to be missed.

The start of the Nature Trail walk is from the National Park Information Centre and leads to **Ingleborough Cavern**. Simply follow the beck upstream passing the church and waterfall to enter the grounds of the old Sawmill. Nature trail leaflets are available here as well as the Grounds Ticket. The track leads on into woodland and passes alongside the lake. Just beyond the trees lies the cavern where tickets may be obtained for an underground visit. This takes about an hour and the attractions include a large impressive cave, underground streams and natural passages, cave coral and illuminated pools.

Ingleborough cave was first explored in 1837 when the landowner ordered a stalactite barrier to be removed. Behind it was an impounded lake which, when drained away, allowed the cave system to be explored. It was believed that the

Norber erratics

The Norber Boulders may be approached from Town Head Farm, Austwick northwards up a farm road. At a point where the farm road is crossed by an unsurfaced lane coming from Clapham, turn left where a signpost points the way to Norber.

The boulders are known to geologists as erratics, huge boulders of darker-coloured Silurian gritstone rock. At the end of the Ice Age, the glacier that once occupied Crummack-dale retreated and deposited the blocks, having swept up the Silurian gritstone from the valley floor. Now they rest quite out of place perched on slender pedestals of limestone. Over the centuries, the blocks have withstood the elements, while the softer plinths have been eroded by wind, rain, frost and snow. Grid reference SD 770 698.

Flascoe Bridge across Austwick Beck near the village of Austwick

Celtic wall

Overlooking the monastic route, but not visible, from it, is the so-called 'Celtic' wall, SD 801 675. It is evident from the weathered condition of the limestone blocks on the hill south of Smearsett Scar that the stones are very old. The most perfect example is some 65ft (20m) long, 6ft (1.8m) wide and 6ft (1.8m) high. The stones approximately point in the direction of the rising point of the midsummer sun and may thus have some religious significance. Other theories propose an ancient burial site or a settlement enclosure.

stream entering Gaping Gill eventually reappeared again in Ingleborough Cavern. This was confirmed in 1983 when an expert team of cavers and cave divers achieved a difficult crossing between the two caves.

Beyond Ingleborough Cavern the path enters **Trow Gill**, now a dry valley carved out by a tumultuous rush of water at the end of the Ice Age. It was probably a cave where the roof collapsed after the rush of water. The path continues across the open moor to reach **Gaping Gill**. From Gaping Gill the path continues across moorland to the south ridge of Ingleborough and on to the summit. The distance from Clapham to Gaping Gill and return is 5 miles (8km).

Austwick

Leave Clapham on the B6480, briefly touch the A65 and then proceed along quiet winding lanes to the village of Austwick. The village is a tranquil collection of grey stone cottages straggling down lanes or set round little greens. The ancient base of a market cross surmounted by a ne v shaft points to an early market nas an inn called the Gamecock ere are a number of sev-

enteenth and eighteenth century houses displaying elaborate and decorated lintel stones with initials and dates. The prominent local family of the Ingilbys bought Austwick Hall, a small fortified manor house in 1573. The Hall has been much altered but part of the massive wall of a peel tower that stood on the site has been kept.

In a surrounding area of such rocky nature, the areas of pasturage or 'stints' were of great importance for the grazing of sheep. These units of pasture were allocated and shared out amongst the local farmers. Many of the houses face south, looking out across fields patterned with drystone walls, many built during the enclosures in 1814. The footpath linking the southern end of the village with Clapham passes through meadows containing traces of old settlements and ploughing terraces called lynchets.

Austwick is an excellent starting point for an exploration of its immediate surroundings. Narrow walled lanes, used in earlier days by packhorse trains lead to the limestone hills of Moughton and Oxenber, Long Scar, Norber and Crummackdale.

Just over a mile north of Austwick lies the hamlet of Wharfe, on a byroad

Selected Walks

1. Barbon to Cowan Bridge

Distance: 7$^1/_2$ miles (12km)

Note, arrangements should be made for picking up at the end of the walk.

Map: OS Outdoor Leisure 2 Yorkshire Dales – Southern and Western areas 1:25,000

From the church join the bridleway alongside Barbon Beck to a point just beyond the tree line. Cross the beck by a footbridge to the road and turn right. Just beyond Blindbeck Bridge a track branches off and climbs steadily with the Aygill stream on the left. The track crosses the depression to Bullpot Farm, now a caving club.

From the area of the farm a vast expanse of rough moor grass and heather rolls away to the heights of the Gragareth skyline. But below the surface is an extensive network of channels, narrow passages and caverns, all carved in the limestone by the action of running water. Close to the track south to Ease Gill lies the pothole called Bullpot of the Witches. This frightening hole descends to a depth of 175ft (53m) into which a stream tumbles.

The passage systems in the Ease Gill area are of great interest to the caving and pot-holing fraternity including Bull Pot of the Witches, Cow Pot, Lancaster Hole, Top Sink and County Pot. The great gash of Ease Gill, tracing a serpentine course, descends from Great Coum to join Leck Beck. Its twisting journey is for the most part a deeply gouged dry channel in the limestone.

From Bullpot proceed south alongside the wall to reach Ease Gill. The impressive ravine of Ease Gill Kirk is a mass of boulders piled up together below towering walls. As the beck travels underground until Leck Beck Head, walk some way up Ease Gill for an easy crossing. Now follow the beck downstream passing a series of stunning little gills and waterfalls. Continue on the right of way through a wooded green valley to emerge at the hamlet of Leck. Finally, there is a beckside path to Cowan Bridge on the A65.

2. Ingleton Waterfalls Walk

Distance: 4$^1/_2$ miles (7.2km)

Map: OS Outdoor Leisure 2 Yorkshire Dales – Southern and Western areas 1:25,000

The walk begins in the car park on the west side of the River Twiss, SD 693 733 and then follows a well laid and well maintained footpath. There is a charge for admission. Two deep and rocky glens accommodate the River Twiss from Kingsdale and the River Doe from Doedale, the rivers combining at Ingleton to form the Greta which flows a further 5 miles (8km) to join the Lune.

Selected Walks

The walk begins at the abutments of a former railway. At Manor Bridge, the walker crosses the South Craven Fault and enters an area where Ordovician shale is exposed. Steps lead to a point that offers a view of Pecca Falls. Here water flows over bands of vertical green sandstone and fine-ground slate. The surroundings open out and into view comes Thornton Force. To geologists it is a classic example of an unconformity, representing 150 million years of missing strata. The water pours 45ft (14m) from a horizontal lip of Carboniferous Limestone, below which is a bed of near vertical Lower Ordovician slates. At the base of the limestone is a thin layer of boulders and pebbles of Ingleton slate; this represents an ancient beach deposit.

The grassy area beyond is Raven Ray, a terminal moraine formed by the Kingsdale glacier. Cross a metal bridge and follow the track to Beezley Falls, beyond a minor road and a farmstead. At Beezley, the River Doe thunders through a ravine with dark pools shaded by trees.

After the triple spout of Beezley come the Rival Falls, followed by the Baxenghyll Gorge where the river is hemmed in by dark sheer cliffs. A metal bridge provides a splendid viewing point. Snow Falls completes the circuit with the fine contrast of Quarry Wood carpeted in due season with bluebells and wood anemones.

The track leaves the wood and the view opens out across the river to the former quarrying area. This site is now grassed over and forms part of an attractive riverside scene. The track continues into Ingleton.

3. Circular walk from Austwick to Moughton

Distance: 8 miles (13.6km)

Map: OS Outdoor Leisure 2 Yorkshire Dales – Southern and Western areas 1:25,000

From Austwick a steep narrow road runs for 2 miles (3.2km) as far as the one habitation, Crummack Farm. Continue along the lonely green dale enclosed by Norber and Moughton and on to Austwick Beck Head. Here, the stream issues from a cave, one of those slits in the Great Scar Limestone which are a most common sight in Craven.

Pass through some traces of old settlement patterns and ascend via Beggar's Stile, an extensive semi-circular cliff; beyond is an area of clints. Limestone is soluble in the weak acids of rainwater and throughout time the water has gouged out and dissolved away the stone. As well as the resulting passages and potholes, the clints and grykes of limestone pavements have been formed. The clints are the wedges of limestone left standing and the grykes are the crevices and hollows.

Turn right at a crossroad of paths and walk through Sulber Nick to where a path aims south-west and then south towards Moughton. The ridge of Moughton is an extensive area of limestone pavement. After following a wall, a stile gives access to the path now on a westerly heading, to a point where the rim of the cliffs dips to a hollow. The path, which becomes a track, curves round the western base of Moughton and enters the hamlet of Wharfe. Bridleways continue via Wood End, where a footpath leaves Wood Lane to Flascoe Bridge and a return to Austwick.

Thornton Force on the Ingleton Waterfalls Walk

to Helwith Bridge in Ribblesdale. The tiny settlement is approached by footpaths and and the impression is one of peace and tranquillity that should not be disturbed by the intrusion of motor vehicles. This secluded community lies against the limestone of Moughton Scar; a huddle of mellowed buildings hidden by trees. A local point of interest is the style of the gateposts, fashioned from slabs of Horton flagstone quarried at Helwith Bridge.

Just to the south of Wharfe, beyond Oxenber Wood, lies the tiny settlement of Feizor, pronounced Fazer. This small farming community was originally a place where people took their livestock to graze in summer. The hamlet is snugly hidden under the wooded slopes of Oxenber and the scars, crags and pavements of Pot Scar. Ash is always present in the scar woods, being a tree of the limestone, together with hazel, hawthorn, mountain ash and blackthorn.

Feizor lay on a monastic route used by the monks of Fountains Abbey on journeys to their granges in Lakeland. Feizor Hall, originally a monastic property is now a farmhouse. Stockdale House with a water pump and trough before it, was the home of the Clapham family who once owned Austwick Hall.

Feizor was also a staging point on an important packhorse route between the north of Lancashire and Yorkshire.

Many footpaths cross this lonely stretch of countryside, a landscape study in grey and green. It is the best way to explore its inner recesses using the narrow walled lanes and tracks, its clapper bridges and wandering paths. Feizor hides its sequestered situation very well indeed; just a couple of narrow winding roads north of the A65.

From the village of Austwick, Graystonber Lane leaves the village, crosses the A65 and reaches Lawkland. Lawkland Hall is an Elizabethan house with an earlier south front and tower dating from the reign of Henry VII. It was built of sandstone, set in a formal garden with land sloping down to the beck and home to the Ingilbys, whose coat of arms appears on a shield over the entrance on the north front.

The surrounding area is a different-looking landscape with scattered communities of farmsteads, old barns and isolated cottages. The byroad wriggles its way via the back door, so to speak, to Giggleswick and Wigglesworth in the Ribble Valley.

Places to Visit

Kirkby Lonsdale

Kirkby Lonsdale Victorian Fair

Events, activities, stalls, costumes and music. Join in the fun by taking part in the Victorian Fair. First week in September

☎ (01524) 271261

Finestra Gallery*

Main Street, Kirkby Londsdale. Prints, originals and exhibitions.
☎ (015242) 73747

Ingleton

Ingleton Waterfalls Trail

$4^1/_2$-mile (7.2km) walk from centre of Ingleton. Scenic beauty, spectacular waterfalls, geological features, ancient oak woodland.
Suitable footwear advised, admission charge.
☎ (015242) 41930
Open: all year.
www.ingletonwaterfallswalk.co.uk

White Scar Cave*

$1^3/_4$ miles (2.8km) from Ingleton on the B6255 road to Hawes.
Underground streams and waterfalls, large cavern, stalactites.
Large car park, café and shop.
LA6 3AW, ☎ (01524) 241244
Open: 10am daily, Feb–Oct,
Weekends, Nov–Jan.
www.whitescarcave.co.uk

Country Harvest*

Situated 1 mile (1.6km) west of Ingleton

Gifts, books, clothing, coffee shop, foodhall with over 100 varieties of cheeses.
☎ (01524) 242223

Ribblehead Viaduct

Settle-Carlisle Railway. The famous 440 yard (402 metres) long viaduct has 24 arches, and is 100 feet (30 metres) high.

Clapham

Ingleborough Cave

Go underground in the outlet caves of the famous Gaping Gill System. Natural large cave passages all floodlit. Magnificent displays of cave coral, calcite deposits, flowstone. Guided tour of the Cavern; no steps, accessible for perambulators; dogs allowed on lead. Christmas Grotto on weekends in Dec.
LA2 8EE, ☎ (01524) 251242
Open: daily Feb half-term to early Nov. During the winter months the Cave is open at weekends and mid-week visits are by appointment only.
www.ingleboroughcave.co.uk

Reginald Farrer Nature Trail

From Clapham village to Ingleborough Cavern, via woods and lakeside. Distance, there and back $2^1/_2$ miles (4km).

Ingleton Pottery

Bank Bottom, Ingleton
☎ (015242) 41363
Open: Daily; Summer 9.30am–5.30pm. Winter 9.30am–5pm.
www.ingletonpottery.co.uk

The area of the central Pennines is known as Craven. It has a particular charm of its own, an attractiveness largely the result of the Great Scar Limestone which occupies much of the surface of the district. The actual region can be thought of as extending from Ribblehead in the north-west to Long Preston in the south-west and from Great Whernside in the north-east to Barden Fell in the south-east. Craven is chiefly renowned for its prominent, isolated hills, its extensive pothole and cave systems, the starkly beautiful limestone pavements and their wealth of flora.

Giggleswick and Settle

The A65 descends towards the valley of the River Ribble beneath the impressive bastion of Giggleswick Scar. A bypass now takes this busy road to the south and west of Settle and Giggleswick. This leaves the original route a much more peaceful and safer road leading to the two communities. Compared with Settle with its busy atmosphere of tourism and commerce, the village of **Giggleswick** lies quietly to one side and escapes the major effects of traffic and the influx of visitors.

The attractive old dwellings exhibit features of mullioned windows, square dripstones and decorated door lintels of the seventeenth and eighteenth centuries. From here there are glimpses of woodland slopes and the green copper-covered dome of the chapel of Giggleswick's famous public school.

The architecture of the church dedicated to St Alkelda, one of the Saxon martyrs, mainly covers the period from 1335-50 to 1530. It is Perpendicular

Giggleswick School

The school was founded in 1512 and granted a Royal Charter in 1553. The school is a co-educational boarding and day school. The buildings grouped together to the west of the village are mostly in the sixteenth and seventeenth century style; a little grey and austere but softened by the green surroundings. The School Chapel was designed in 1897 by Sir Thomas Jackson and completed in 1901. The donor was Mr Walter Morrison of Malham Tarn House.

throughout and important interior features include: a handsome panelled pulpit with signs of the twelve tribes and reading desk, 1680, a communion rail of 1676, a poor box of 1684 and a brass candelabra of 1718.

Settle is one of those satisfying little market towns, a popular stopping place for local people and visitors alike. The town received its market charter in 1249 and has always been a busy place astride the main route from Yorkshire into Cumbria. Its location is dramatic, lying in a restricted area between the River Ribble and the grey-white hills of Craven, in Settle's case, at the foot of the 300ft (91m) high limestone crag of Castlebergh.

The market square is the focal point of the town, where one building in particular catches the eye. The arcaded seventeenth-century building, with a later Victorian top floor, was the old Shambles with six arches formerly occupied by the butchers and the slaughter house. Prominent on the opposite side of the square is the Naked Man Café, which was once an inn. No one seems to know why the carved figure is there but it is said to have been a form of protest against the colourful fashions of the seventeenth century. At the present time, Tuesday is Market Day in Settle.

On this restricted site, the town has had to use all the available space. As the ground rises towards the crags there are a number of alleys and courtyards behind the main streets. The predominant theme of the town buildings is late Georgian but scattered among them are structures from the previous century. Identifying features are decorated lintels and date stones.

High Street leads to 'Preston's Folly' built in 1675, so named because its first owner ran out of money before it was finished. This building is a large three-storey town house with a recessed centre and two wings. The splendid doorway has a fantastic columnar surround and a lintel with arched gothic forms. The house has an interesting window going right round the corner. The main staircase is a tower at the back of the house.

For railway enthusiasts, Settle means the Settle-Carlisle Railway; from here begins the long climb over the Pennine hills. The station is a well-tended place, clean and inviting with interesting tourist information. During the summer months, flower beds and potted plants glow with colour adding to its attractions.

Edward Elgar

The composer Edward Elgar, when a young musician, became friendly with Dr Charles William Buck who lived in Ribblesdale. Elgar often visited Settle and stayed with his friend. The two men enjoyed walking in the surrounding limestone countryside and particularly enjoyed its scars and waterfalls. In 1884, Elgar dedicated a Gavotte in the form of a violin solo to Dr Buck. While visiting Settle, Elgar completed the work 'Salut d'amour'.

Ancient cave

In May 1838, a local man was walking with companions near Langcliffe Scar when their dog disappeared into a foxhole. This turned out to be a massive cave, its entrance blocked by scree. An organised excavation of the cave, Victoria Cave, uncovered evidence of the creatures that once roamed the Craven hills – straight-tusked elephant, woolly rhinoceros, hippopotamus and ox. They ended their days in the Victoria Cave, a hyena's den, probably during the tropical climate of the Great Inter-Glacial period.

After the retreat of the glaciers at the end of the Ice Age, a layer of clay covered these remains. Next came the fauna of a cold period – reindeer, arctic fox, badger, horse, dog and sheep. Eventually man arrived – Mesolithic hunters who left a harpoon in the cave; and lastly, Iron Age man, who used the caves in Langcliffe Scar as a refuge in Roman times. They left behind silver and bronze brooches, armlets, rings, Roman coins, spearheads, daggers and spindle whorls.

Upper Ribblesdale

Stackhouse is a picturesque scattering of old stone buildings reached from Settle by turning off the main road just after crossing the Ribble. Its layout around a maze of narrow lanes is delightfully haphazard and its situation in the shelter of wooded limestone scars is beautiful. Stackhouse is a little-known hamlet, the roads within it being private. There is a seventeenth-century hall, a few large houses and a number of majestic chestnut trees.

Take the B6479 road from Settle following the River Ribble towards Ribblehead. About a mile away from Settle, **Langcliffe** is a peaceful village with a broad green and a cobbled area with a war memorial cum fountain.

Langcliffe Hall has a doorway of two dates, the outer surround no doubt by the same workmen as The Folly at Settle. The lintel stone has the date 1602. Near the back gate of the hall is a carving with a seventeenth-century datestone. The building, formerly the Naked Woman Inn, replaced the house of the Swainson family on which the 'woman' was first displayed, together with the date 1660.

Below the village, in a crook of the river, a cotton mill was opened in 1783. **Langcliffe High Mill** was situated at the southern end of the mill reservoir. Salmon move up the river to their spawning grounds usually in August if there is a good flow of water. A number of concrete-sided pools have been constructed to help the fish to negotiate the obstacle of the weir. This is an advantageous place to watch the salmon leap.

A footpath leaves the main road where it crosses the railway and heads down to the mill cottages and a footbridge over the Ribble. This path, part of the Ribble Way, follows the west bank of the river to the beautiful **Stainforth Force** and Stainforth Bridge. Here the river cascades joyously over a number of limestone ledges before plunging into a dark, sinister-looking pool. The narrow, single span packhorse bridge was built by Samuel Watson of Knight Stainforth Hall and it is now under the guardianship of the National Trust.

The village of **Stainforth,** mentioned in Domesday, also lies just off the B6479. There is a parking area off the northerly approach road to the church from the B6479. The tree-shaded church of St Peter, 1842, was remodelled later.

Silverdale

A byroad leaves the village and follows Stainforth Beck at first before heading into the hills. Some roads have an immediate appeal to cyclists and drivers and this route is certainly one of them. In its early stages, it is known as Goat Lane which then becomes Silverdale Road. Climbing briskly it soon reaches Rainscar and the lonely farmsteads of Dale Head and Rainscar House.

This remote valley head is set between the peaks of **Penyghent** and **Fountains Fell**, 2277ft (694m) and 2192ft (668m) respectively. The two hill farms are dwarfed by the magnificence of crisp, green meadows, tawny pastures and the long, lean Pennine ridges. The sprawling upland mass of Fountains Fell takes its name from the Cistercian abbey of that name in Skelldale near Ripon. Dale Head en-route for the summit of Penyghent was once an old packhorse hostelry at the junction of routes from Ribblesdale, Littondale, Malham and Stainforth.

As the upland pastures stretch away on both sides of the narrow strip of

Jaggers

In the seventeenth and eighteenth centuries, men and horses that travelled these local routes were very much bound up with the day to day existence of the scattered rural population. A packhorse train often comprised twenty to forty ponies of the wiry strong Galloway breed, or the Jaeger (hunter) pony imported from Germany – the man in charge was often called a 'jagger'. Packhorse loads were carried in two panniers slung over a saddle, or on a wooden frame, on which sacks or baskets rested. The lead horse had a harness of bells that rang out as it trotted along.

The approach of a packhorse team sent a surge of excitement through the isolated farmsteads, hamlet or village. The arrival of the jaggers meant that news could be exchanged, messages taken from people in other settlements and replies returned. The packmen took on the role of postmen, merchants and bearers of news for the surrounding communities.

tarmac, the descent begins alongside Penyghent Gill. This gill cuts a deep trench in the limestone before entering Littondale as Hesleden Beck. Stand at the head of the gill in the first enclosed pasture for an impressive panorama. There is Fountains Fell and Plover Hill on either hand and Penyghent rearing abruptly at one's back. Admire the brilliance of the green fellsides and the limestone in sunlight.

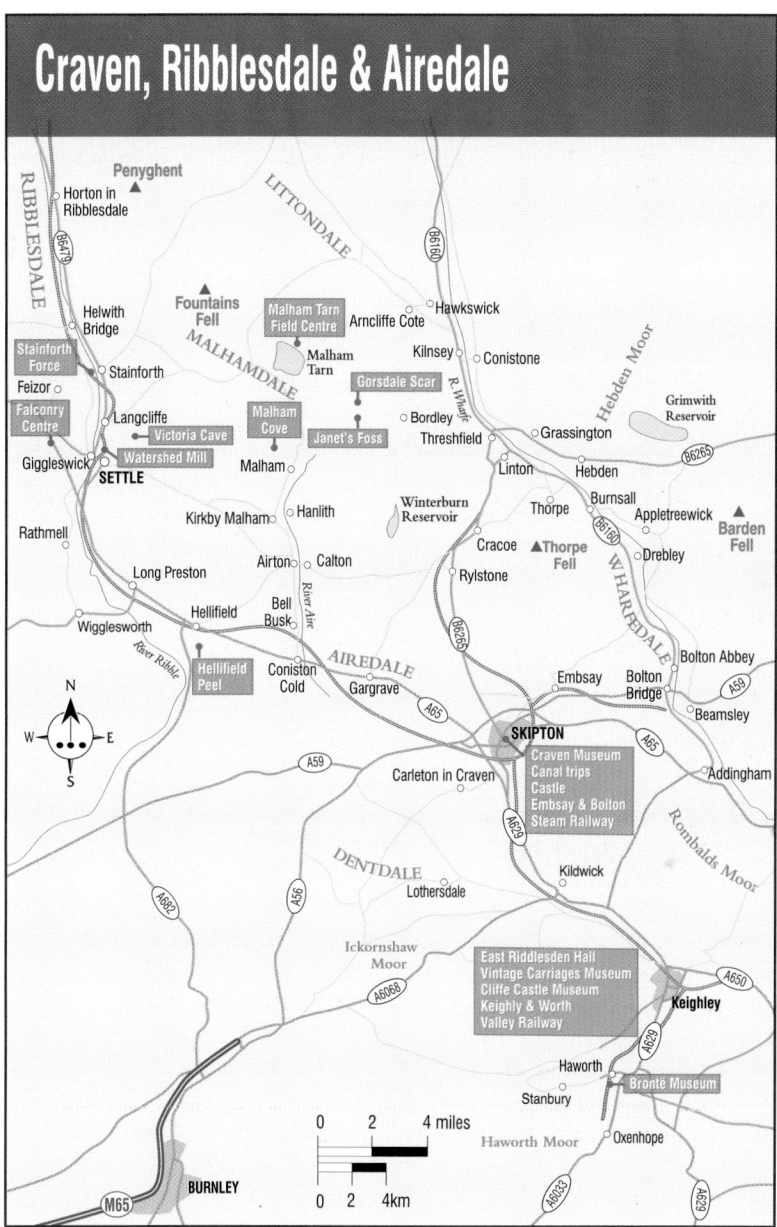

Craven, Ribblesdale & Airedale

Penyghent
Horton in Ribblesdale

RIBBLESDALE

LITTONDALE

B6160

Helwith Bridge
Fountains Fell
Malham Tarn Field Centre
Arncliffe Cote
Hawkswick

MALHAMDALE
Kilnsey
Conistone

Stainforth Force
Stainforth
Malham Tarn
Gorsdale Scar
R. Wharfe

Feizor
Falconry Centre
Langcliffe
Victoria Cave
Malham Cove
Bordley
Grassington
Grimwith Reservoir

Watershed Mill
Janet's Foss
Threshfield

Giggleswick
SETTLE
Malham
Linton
Hebden
B6265

Rathmell
Kirkby Malham
Hanlith
Winterburn Reservoir
Thorpe
Burnsall
Appletreewick
Barden Fell

Cracoe
Thorpe Fell
Drebley

Long Preston
Airton
Calton
Rylstone

WHARFEDALE

Wigglesworth
Hellifield
Bell Busk

River Aire
B6265

River Ribble
AIREDALE
Bolton Abbey
A59

Hellifield Peel
Coniston Cold
Gargrave
Embsay
Bolton Bridge
Beamsley

N
W E
S
A65
SKIPTON
A65
Addingham

A59
Carleton in Craven
Craven Museum
Canal trips
Castle
Embsay & Bolton
Steam Railway

A56
DENTDALE
Lothersdale
Kildwick
Rombalds Moor

A682

Ickornshaw Moor
East Riddlesden Hall
Vintage Carriages Museum
Cliffe Castle Museum
Keighly & Worth
Valley Railway
A650

A6068
Keighley
A629

Haworth
Bronte Museum

Stanbury
0 2 4 miles
Haworth Moor
Oxenhope

BURNLEY
0 2 4km
A6033
A629

M65

Perhaps these incomparable surroundings touched early man's inner
soul and became the inspiration to con-
struct a passage grave in this place for
their dead chieftains. **Giant's Grave** is a
late Neolithic long barrow, although the
circular mound, about 50ft (15m) across
has been greatly disturbed. However, two groups of large limestone
blocks mark the position of the burial

chamber.

From Dawson Close a green track terraces the hillside on its descent into **Littondale**. It is a route that invites the walker, as it crosses a number of becks coming briskly down from Fountains Fell. To the west of the green road are the remains of tumbled walls and foundations of roughly circular huts. These are situated along a grassy terrace following the lines of natural outcrop and are of Celtic origin.

Returning down the Silverdale Road to Stainforth, the route from the village to Catrigg Force is to the left. Follow a rough walled track for about a mile and, as one ascends, a glorious panorama is unveiled – Smearsett Scar, Ingleborough, Penyghent and Fountains Fell. **Catrigg Force**, a feature on Stainforth Beck, is a double waterfall largely hidden in summer by foliage. Special care should be taken.

Helwith Bridge to Horton

From Stainforth, the road, railway and river accompany each other up the dale. The area around the hamlet of **Helwith Bridge** is known for its quarrying operations with the old flagstone quarry at its peak of activity in Victorian days. In former times, large pieces of stone were sawn by a piece of metal without teeth, the abrasion being produced by sand fed to it by water. Limestone and slate were quarried near Helwith Bridge, the slate being put to a multitude of uses – to pave cottage floors, doorsteps, cisterns, tombstones, gate posts, porches and partitions in byres.

From Helwith Bridge the Ribble winds along the bed of a post-glacial lake. The approach to the village of **Horton-in-Ribblesdale** features the long slopes of pasture land rising to Penyghent. The church of St Oswald has a Perpendicular tower and some Norman features. The west window contains a few fragments of medieval glass. The village straggles on for half a mile to a second cluster of houses and an inn near two bridges, one over the beck and one over the Ribble.

Just beyond is the location of Horton station and, whilst waiting for a train, one can enjoy a splendid view towards Penyghent which forms a grand back-cloth to all the buildings in the village. The village houses reflect the development of the dale – fine old farmhouses built by yeomen. There are dwellings of 1679 and 1731 with lintels decorated in the traditional Craven pattern. With ample accommodation facilities to cater for visitors, Horton is a centre for landscape studies for geologists, potholers and for walkers doing the Pennine Way and the Three Peaks Walk. There is a large car park at the northern end of the village; Grid Reference SD 807 726.

Seen from any direction except the north, **Penyghent** is a most shapely and attractive mountain; it is a landmark for miles around with a commanding prospect. Penyghent exhibits markedly the geological characteristics mentioned earlier that are common to the Three Peaks of north-west Yorkshire. Its compelling attraction for walkers has so denuded the soft peat of the upper slopes, that various methods have been employed to try and combat path erosion.

From Horton-in-Ribblesdale, the

Pot-holing country

The numerous great holes eroded in the Great Scar Limestone of Craven by centuries of surface drainage include in Ribblesdale, Hunt Pot and Hull Pot. The former, which lies on the open western flanks of Penyghent, is a long narrow opening only 6ft (1.82m) wide but 200ft (61m) deep. Hull Pot, which lies a short distance to the north of Hunt Pot, is a much larger opening, 330ft (91m) long, 60ft (18m) wide and 60ft (18m) deep. This immense hole which straddles a geological fault, has an attendant stream which pours over its northern lip.

dale widens, becoming broad and expansive, with views over to Cam Fell to the north-east and Simon Fell to the west. **Selside** is a cluster of houses round a bend in the road. The hamlet was once a lively place, where navvies working on the Settle-Carlisle Railway caroused and fought with each other. The building, Hill Foot, was formerly the Red Lion Inn.

Footpaths leave Selside for the limestone pavements and scars of Sulber and Moughton and on to Wharfe, Feizor and Austwick. Selside is the nearest and most convenient starting point for a short walk to **Alum Pot**. Within a walled enclosure, the beck disappears into the overgrown abyss of Alum Pot. This is a huge hole that descends to a depth of 340ft (104m). Visitors should be aware of the danger; it is wise to give it just a single fearful glance.

The head of the dale, **Ribblehead**, is an open tract of rough ground; it is 1,000ft (305m) above sea level and completely open to the extremes and vagaries of the weather. The austere feature of Ribblehead is the 165ft (50m) high, 24 arched viaduct.

Following the B6255 road beyond the viaduct, one may be unaware of the presence of earlier routes established before transportation depended on the wheel. This is the network of routes seen today as bridlepaths, overgrown lanes or green tracks. Their courses are marked in the valleys by packhorse bridges and fords and on the hills by ancient crosses or markers. A road over Cam Fell, known to the Romans, came over to Gearstones from Bainbridge. Gearstones was once a drovers' inn, where Scottish cattle were gathered for sale twice a year.

Returning down Ribblesdale to Horton, travellers on foot may leave by Horton Scar Lane. The route continues past Hull Pot, crosses the open moor, descends to the isolated farmstead of Foxup and on to Halton Gill at the head of Littondale. From here, a high level walking route crosses Horse Head Moor towards Langstrothdale. For car drivers, Ribblesdale may be left at Stainforth and Langcliffe and a climb out of the dale along delightful moorland roads with the surroundings decorated by outcroppings of limestone. Both routes converge on Malham Moor and continue past Capon Hall to Malham Tarn and the village of Malham.

Mining on Malham Moor

For centuries man has explored the Dales for signs of mineral reserves. A little over a hundred years ago, there was mining for lead, copper and calamine (carbonate of zinc) on Malham Moor. When 't'owd man', as the miner was called, travelled on foot or on horseback across the moor to work, he would pass some signs of human activity of times gone by; these would take the form of Iron Age settlements, field systems, enclosures, a Roman camp and a wayside cross.

On the moor, just to the south-west of Malham Tarn stands a prominent smelt mill chimney, 1815-1860; this was restored between 1965 and 1969. Until about 1780, large quantities of lead were lost because the lead fumes were exposed to the air too soon. It was discovered that if the fumes were passed through a long horizontal flue, lead would sublimate on its inner surfaces. A vertical chimney at the end of the flue ensured a good draught.

Calamine was hauled from the Grisedale and Pikedaw mines; it was washed and calcined (roasted) on the surface and then taken to Malham village. At the depot it was packed into casks and carried by packhorses to Gargrave for the long journey by canal. The calamine was sold to make brass in Lancashire, Staffordshire and in Birmingham.

Ribblesdale

*The market town of Settle; an attractive town
at the foot of the grey-white hills of Craven*

Malham

The monasteries extended their influence over the landscape, in particular the Cistercian monks who brought with them great sheep-breeding skills. They ran their pastoral activities through granges and regular routes developed between them and their religious centres. One such example is Mastiles Lane across Malham Moor, now a splendid green track for walkers. A few of these monastic outposts survive and the words grange and cote can be found

by studying a large scale map.

To the east and south of Malham Tarn, the area of Great Close was a vast pasturage for livestock. In the eighteenth century, this was used for cattle fairs and for the grazing of the thousands of Scottish cattle brought here by drovers.

Malham Tarn at 1,200ft (369m) above sea level, lies along the North Craven Fault; its bed is of a durable Silurian slate impervious to water. In a predominantly limestone area, where normally water is swallowed up by a

---

Malham Tarn House

Overlooking the lake, the house was built in the middle of the nineteenth century on the site of a former shooting lodge owned by Lord Ribblesdale. It became the home of a wealthy businessman and MP for Skipton, Walter Morrison. His house was visited by eminent Victorians and influential friends, including Charles Darwin, Charles Kingsley and John Ruskin. Charles Kingsley, perhaps inspired by the area, wrote his classic *Water Babies* after a stay here. The house is now leased to the Field Studies Council.

71

surface of clints and grykes, it is strange to find a fairly large stretch of surface water. This highest lime-rich lake of its size in England holds a rich variety of plant and animal life.

Most of the woods around the tarn were planted early in the nineteenth century to provide shelter around the big house. They comprise a mixture of sycamore, beech, Scots pine, ash and larch. There is an area of fen by the lake and this National Nature Reserve contains a raised bog rich in wild flowers.

Malham Tarn forms the focal point of a large estate owned by the National Trust and the area is one of their most important conservation sites. In fact, most of the estate is within the large Malham-Arncliffe Site of Special Scientific Interest. Many varieties of bird life frequent the tarn and a hide has been erected to enable visitors to observe great crested grebe, coot, mallard and other birds which visit this lovely stretch of water.

The source of the River Aire was generally thought to have been in Malham Tarn. The tarn's outlet, which runs towards Malham Cove, now vanishes underground at Water Sinks. In times past, a considerable torrent of water created the Dry Valley and undoubtedly flowed on to pour over the lip of the 300ft (91m) high limestone face, in what would have been a waterfall higher than Niagara. However, over the ages, the limestone surface became eroded, fissured and jointed and the water in the valley disappeared into underground channels.

The stream that emerges from the foot of the Cove was thought to be the infant Aire; but it has been proved by experiments with dyes that the water diverted at Water Sinks emerges at Aire Heads springs south of the village. Some people believe that there is a considerable underground lake locked away behind the face of the Cove. The water issuing from the base of the cliff is thought to have its beginnings high on Malham Moor.

Malham Cove is a wonderful visitor attraction. Pathways begin from the village to follow the beck and with each step the object ahead becomes more and more imposing. This magnificent natural feature is a curved cliff of limestone, 600ft (183m) across, falling to a green amphitheatre. A path climbs around its western edge to bring the visitor above the Cove. Here, the limestone pavement displays a wonderful example of jointed and fissured rock; it is obviously dangerous to go too close to the edge.

Another of Malham's impressive natural attractions is **Gordale Scar**, which lies a mile (1.6km) to the east of the village. The narrow canyon choked by boulders, descends between towering rock walls hundreds of feet high. The sides of the ravine, sheer and in parts overhanging, are quite intimidating. Then, round a corner, appears the spectacle of Gordale Beck plunging down in great leaps, the final section cascading over solidified lime deposits known as tufa.

Whilst **Malham** is counted as one of the most popular villages in the Yorkshire Dales, it is not the village particularly which visitors come to but the surroundings which embrace landscape features of compelling beauty. Nevertheless, its collection of grey and

Selected Car Drive

Skipton, Keighley, Haworth, Malham

Distance: 64 miles (102.4km)

Skipton is a town to explore with its castle, fine parish church and busy market. Take the Keighley road, the A629 following the valley of the Aire, past Kildwick's long church, and through Steeton to Keighley. Continue along the main street of the town, the A629, and proceed for $2^1/_2$ miles (4km) to take the A6033 Hebden Bridge road. After a short distance as the main road swings away, proceed straight ahead, and ascend the steep hill into Haworth. Pass the Brontë Museum and follow the road to Stanbury. Here, and beyond, is a bold landscape of parallel gritstone walls on the edge of this moorland village.

Travel along the line of the old packhorse and drove way by the reservoirs of Ponden and Water Sheddles to reach Laneshawbridge. Cross over the main A6068 and take the byroad opposite. Go on ahead and take the next turn to the right. Proceed to the pub at Black Lane Ends, but keep straight on and take the next turn right. Do not deviate from this route, which then descends steeply. Turn right into the village of Lothersdale.

Travel ahead passing Stone Gappe House to a crossroads, turn left. Continue to another crossroads but keep straight on and descend towards Elslack. Take the right turn, Church Lane, just before the village, which descends to meet the A59, turn right. Take the next turn left to Gargrave, then cross over the A65 to a byroad, which crosses the canal, and on to a road junction, turn left.

After a short distance, turn left to Airton and on to Kirkby Malham, a compact village with a fine church. Proceed to Malham with its large car park and fine information centre. Leaving the village, keep straight ahead to climb steeply past the impressive Malham Cove and on to Malham Moor. For Malham Tarn, turn right at the first intersection, otherwise, bear left past Capon Hall, and beyond, turn left again. This delightful route past Cowside Farm then descends steeply to Langcliffe and joins the B6479, turn left.

From the interesting market town of Settle, continue along the A65 through Long Preston and Hellifield returning to Skipton.

whitewashed buildings, its lively stream and village green make it an ideal base to explore the locality. There is a large car park, an excellent Tourist Information Centre, inns, tea-rooms and accommodation facilities.

Malham is a popular resting place for Pennine wayfarers and a purpose-built youth hostel designed by John Dower, a Malham man, was constructed in the village. John Dower compiled the Government Report that led to the

Selected Walks

1. The caves around Settle

Distance: 4 miles (6.4km)

Map: OS Outdoor Leisure 2 Yorkshire Dales – Southern and Western areas 1:25,000

The caves north-east of Settle in Langcliffe Scar and Attermire Scar may be reached by footpaths from the town. A circular walk may be accomplished by climbing up the track beneath Castlebergh and then heading east below Blua Crags to Attermire Scar and cave. A right of way continues below the foot of Attermire Scar passing Victoria Cave and on towards Jubilee Cave. Return on a path via Clay Pits Plantation and then by bridle way and track back to Settle.

2. The Three Peaks Walk

Distance: 24 miles (38.4km) long, though 'short-cut' routes can be taken

Map: OS Outdoor Leisure 2 Yorkshire Dales – Southern and Western areas 1:25,000

The Three Peaks Walk is a classic marathon walk, and takes on average from 12 to 14 hours to complete. Many walkers start at the Three Peaks Café in Horton, which has a clocking-on machine, and walk the route anti-clockwise. The recommended route is via Brackenbottom Farm, Penyghent, Nether Lodge Farm, Ingman Lodge, Ribblehead, Gunnerfleet Farm, Winterscales Farm,

establishment of National Parks – the hostel bears his name.

Two rough-stone buildings are village hostelries. The Buck Inn, rebuilt by Walter Morrison in 1874 has the interesting features of hood mouldings over mullioned windows. The Lister Arms is plain Georgian with a three-storey façade and ashlar window surrounds. The inn has an unusual datestone above its door, an oval bearing the letters R and RA, 1723 and a wineglass motif.

The southerly road from Malham passes near to the location of Aire Head. This is the point where Malham Beck and Gordale Beck join forces together with the reappearance of the stream that vanished at Water Sinks, they all now combine to form the River Aire.

Kirkby Malham to Long Preston

The village of **Kirkby Malham** nestles in a shallow valley midst lovely sur-

Whernside, Bruntscar Farm, Chapel-le-Dale, Ingleborough, Horton-in-Ribblesdale. Detailed route guides may be purchased in Horton.

3. Janet's Foss & Gordale Scar

A footpath leads to the impressive limestone crags of Gordale Scar

Distance: 3¹/₂ miles (5.6km)

Map: OS Outdoor Leisure 2 Yorkshire Dales – Southern and Western areas 1:25,000

From the car park in Malham, cross the clapper bridge, bear right and follow the Pennine Way route for a short distance. Turn left on the field path to New Laithe following the beck. Janet's Foss is a pleasant diversion, a lovely leafy setting where Gordale Beck creates a picturesque waterfall. Turn right along the road for a little way then bear left on to the Gordale Scar footpath. A path follows the stream towards the awe-inspiring cleft in the limestone. To get a little closer requires a scramble over the rough rocky ground. Return by the same route.

Those wishing for a longer and more strenuous expedition could return to the road and take the footpath on the right across Cawden Flats. Turn right on the next lane and almost immediately left on to a path climbing Sheriff Hill. This path meets the Pennine Way path. Take the left hand branch and head for the top of Malham Cove. The route on the west of the Cove can then be followed back to Malham. (4¹/₂ miles/7.2km).

roundings. Pleasant footpaths connect with Malham on either bank of the river. From the centre of the village a byroad strikes west to join a route to Settle.

The village was founded by Anglian colonists in the seventh and eighth centuries. The historic church of St Michael the Archangel dates from the fifteenth century, but built on the site of an older structure. With the houses of the village settled comfortably around the church, the impressive tower can be seen from some distance away. Oliver Cromwell is said to have signed the church register in 1655, when acting as a witness at a marriage. That page from the register has disappeared, presumed stolen. General John Lambert, an important figure of the Parliamentarian forces in the Civil War, was born at Calton Hall, Airton.

Walter Morrison of Malham Tarn House, donated monies for the restoration of the church in 1879. His grave lies in the churchyard. The interior contains a 12th-century circular font; box pews, late Georgian and panelling in the chancel (Morrison Memorial).

The peaceful hamlet of **Hanlith** lies on the opposite bank of the river; the quiet lane is a cul-de-sac leading to a track over Hanlith Moor. The riverside walk from Airton Bridge passes through beautiful surroundings, parkland in appearance. There is a good view of stylish Hanlith Hall from the Pennine Way footpath. Although remodelled three times, the original building was erected in 1668.

From Kirkby Malham the road follows the Aire to the village of **Airton** with its spacious triangular green surrounded by houses; in the middle is a squatter's cottage with a stone-walled garden. One of the houses is dated 1666 and a plain two-storey building, dated 1700, is a Friends Meeting House. Down by the river is a Quakers' burial ground.

A winding rural road leaves Airton and heads for the isolated hamlet of **Otterburn**. This scattered community lies on an ancient pre-turnpike highway which can be traced to Langbar Lane and Settle. The southerly route from Airton passes through Bell Busk, under the railway viaduct to meet the A65 at Coniston Cold.

The byroad from Otterburn reaches the outskirts of **Hellifield**; the A65 likewise west of Coniston Cold. Hellifield was formerly an important railway junction and distribution centre. At one time it had two railway stations – one on the line south to Clitheroe and the other on the line from Skipton. Today, it is well known to visitors using the Settle to Carlisle line. Hellifield developed

into an important cattle market.

This lovely triangle of countryside between the Ribble and Aire and contained by the A65, A682 and A59 is well worth exploring using a 1:25000 map. It is a landscape of drumlins, small hillocks of boulder clay that were deposited by receding glaciers of the final Ice Age.

Take the A65 westwards for $1^1/_2$ miles (2.4km) to **Long Preston**; it is as long and straggling as its name suggests. The site of the Roman fort, no doubt linked to the Roman road up Ribblesdale from Ribchester, lay east of the churchyard. There were two forts, one inside the other, defended by a double ditch except on the south where there is a stream.

On the way eastwards to Gargrave the A65 passes over the River Aire and, just before entering the village, over the Leeds-Liverpool Canal. Gargrave marks the most northerly point of this waterway and the start of **Airedale**.

Gargrave to Skipton

Sitting astride the busy main road, **Gargrave** is well remembered as a refuelling and resting stop for leisure craft and Pennine Way walkers. The latter find comfortable accommodation here and enjoy the softer surroundings of river valley, pastures and woodland. In the eighteenth and nineteenth centuries the settlement was a busy depot for the loading and transportation of minerals, particularly lead, zinc, copper and calamine. These ores were carried on barges to Lancashire and the Midlands.

It is $4^1/_2$ miles (7.2km) along the A65 to Skipton, as the road and railway follow the River Aire beneath the rising ground of Flasby Fell. **Skipton** lies in the Aire Gap, a natural break in the Pennines. Early travellers followed the river through the gap between West Yorkshire and the Lake District.

After the Norman Conquest, Skipton was given to Robert de Romille and his successors who built a castle beside the Eller Beck. The original settlement grew up beside the castle. In 1204, Skipton was granted a charter for a Saturday market and two fairs each year. **Skipton Castle** assumed its present form in the early fourteenth century, in the time of Henry VIII, and in the seventeenth century.

The site is well fortified to the north where there is an almost perpendicular fall to the Eller Beck. The entrance from the town to the Outer Bailey is by a mighty fourteenth-century Gatehouse with fat semi-circular projections to the north and south. The upper parts, including the handsome ornamental parapet with the motto *Desormais*, are mid seventeenth-century work of the Lady Anne Clifford, who reconditioned the castle after its partial demolition in 1649. The castle had been partly destroyed by Cromwell but Lady Anne Clifford was determined to build it up again. Despite the potential threat of the building being pulled down again, the castle was rebuilt and completed in 1657. The castle is open to the public and its courtyard is extremely attractive with an old yew tree standing in its centre.

Near to the castle entrance the church of Holy Trinity stands in a

Ghostly inn

The inn at Long Preston, the Boars Head, was originally built as stables and became an inn in 1752 when it serviced passengers, provided food, accommodation and fresh horses, on the toll road. The inn is reputed to have the ghost of a former landlord; it is said he hung himself in the cellar. A photograph, claimed to be of the man's mother, hangs in the bar; as long as it remains there he will not return.

commanding position at the head of Skipton High Street. The church contains a very fine Jacobean font cover of two tiers, a rood screen originally dated 1533 and a reredos designed by Sir Gilbert Scott in 1874. The monuments include Clifford memorials. Lady Anne Clifford built a black marble tomb for her late father.

The importance of the Leeds-Liverpool Canal faded with the coming of the railways and motor vehicles. This impressive waterway was engineered by James Brindley and built between 1770 and 1815. The route made a wide detour north to avoid the high land. After a period of neglect, the canal is now thriving with a busy traffic in leisure craft. Boats can also be hired for long or short holidays.

The Red Lion, in Skipton's main street, dates from 1205, the oldest pub in Craven. The Black Horse stands opposite and is mainly seventeenth century. It is built on the site of the Royal Mews of Richard III when he was Lord of the Honour of Skipton between 1483 and 1485.

The woollen industry has always been important in this area and Skipton has a famous sheep market. Most of the textile mills, both wool and cotton, are no longer operating but today there is a busy general market not only on Saturdays but also on Mondays, Wednesdays and Fridays. Skipton caters for holidaymakers and sports enthusiasts, with an indoor swimming pool and facilities for golf, football, tennis, cricket and local horse riding and angling.

Railway facilities include the famous Leeds, Settle, Carlisle line and connections are available to Lancaster and Morecambe. For steam train enthusiasts, there is the **Embsay and Bolton**

The splendid doorway to Preston's Folly in Settle

Abbey Steam Railway, just $1^1/_2$ miles (2.4km) east of Skipton. There are steam trains every Sunday with summer services up to five days a week. The line has now been extended to Bolton Bridge.

Around Skipton

The pleasant village of **Rylstone** lies 5 miles (8km) north of Skipton on the B6265 road to Grassington. Rylstone Hall once stood behind the church and the hollows of its fishponds can be seen in the field.

The house was the home of the powerful Norton family who participated so tragically in the Rising of the North in 1569. For this involvement, certain members of the family were accused and either banished or executed. Wordsworth's poem, '*The White Doe of Ryleston*' tells the legend of Francis Norton who was murdered and buried at Bolton Priory. His sister took her pet doe to the grave and even after her death, it still came to the tomb.

To the east of the village lies a large area of gritstone moorland called Barden Moor. A right of way leaves the village, ascends High Bark and continues across Rylstone Fell to Halton Moor and thence by path to Bolton Priory. Along the escarpment edge to the north at Watt Cragg is a memorial cross which commemorates the Paris Treaty of 1813.

The church of St Peter in Rylstone, 1853, is a pleasing building. In 1876, the large parish of Burnsall was divided with a new parish created that was based on Rylstone. It is known that a chapel-of-ease had been here since the twelfth century. Visitors out for a stroll

Malham National Park

should note that the bridleway running north from the village is descriptively called 'Mucky Lane'.

South of Rylstone, near Scale House is a famous Bronze Age burial site. A celebrated nineteenth-century antiquary, Canon Greenwell, discovered a tree-trunk coffin under a small barrow or burial mound. The tree trunk had been split in two halves and hollowed out. The body had been wrapped in a woollen cloak or shroud.

From Rylstone, a byroad soon reaches the small compact community of Hetton, where after a right turn, a lane branches left over Boss Moor to Lainger House. A bridleway follows the valley of Bordley Beck towards the lovely green route of Mastiles Lane. Bordley Beck flows down the dale to Winterburn Reservoir, which becomes Eshton Beck before joining the Aire just

Clifford Family

Interesting and eventful tales surround the Clifford family throughout their long history. 'Butcher Clifford' was killed at the Battle of Towton in 1461 during the Wars of the Roses. His eight year-old son, Henry, was removed from danger and brought up in the house of a shepherd in Cumbria. He was restored to his inheritance after some years of humble life. Henry Clifford fought with distinction at the Battle of Flodden in 1513, when he was sixty years old.

The name of Lady Anne Clifford is well known in the north of England. Born in 1590, the estates should have come to her as the only surviving child but her father had willed them to his brother. Lady Anne's mother began a lawsuit to regain the estates. These proceedings were continued by Lady Anne and she finally won her case thirty-eight years later.

east of Gargrave.

Bordley was a Saxon settlement and then another possession of Fountain's Abbey who pastured horses here. It now consists of two farmhouses. On closer inspection, there are barns with seventeenth-century dates that show that they had been dwellings. Between 1490 and 1670, there were nearly sixty families living in this part of the dale. Just to the north-east of Bordley a lane crosses Malham Moor to Threshfield in the valley of the River Wharfe.

South to Keighley

From Skipton to Keighley, the A629 passes down Airedale and the traveller is aware of attractive higher land on either side of the valley. On the eastern side there is the heathery mass of Rombalds Moor, sprinkled with woodland and pierced by sharp outcrops of gritstone. To the west lies a wedge of countryside rising to Pinhaw Beacon; a landscape of small rolling hills and twisting brooks in quiet valleys.

The main road crosses the Aire at

Kildwick, a village set between the river and the Leeds-Liverpool Canal. Its dark stone buildings emphasise the sturdy nature of the place and complement the beauty of its church. The 'long church of Craven' is 165ft (50m) long with a broad embattled tower. Kildwick was part of the territory of the Canons of Bolton Priory; it is recorded that the nearby bridge over the Aire was rebuilt in 1305.

South of the river, a byroad climbs on to Steeton Moor and passes through the large straggling village of Sutton-in-Craven. The upland country westwards to the Lancashire border is a fine walking area, with the bold gritstone edge of Earl Crag topped by two monuments, one called Wainman's Pinnacle and the other named Lund's Tower.

The town of **Keighley** grew up in the narrow valley of the River Worth near to its confluence with the Aire. Attractive hillsides rise in all directions with buildings and roads extending up the slopes. Keighley is a town with a typical West Yorkshire blend of industry, textiles, engineering and countryside.

Most of the town is nineteenth century in character, its old centre is by the church. North Street is a wide, straight street with the town's principal buildings on, or just to the side of, this main thoroughfare; these include the Mechanics' Institute and Public Library.

The church of St Andrew is a large church of Perpendicular style. The R.C. church of St Anne in North Street was designed by A W N Pugin and opened in 1840; it was much altered and enlarged in 1907. To the north is the lodge of Cliffe Castle, a mansion on the hillside begun in 1878 – now the **Cliffe Castle Museum**. Here there are displays telling the story of the Aire valley set in rooms still furnished in the lavish style of the 1880s.

The town's railway station lies on the Leeds, Settle to Carlisle line and the Airedale line to Leeds and Bradford. It is cheek by jowl with the station of the **Keighley and Worth Valley Railway**. Here, every weekend of the year and daily in summer, one can take an interesting steam train journey on a complete branch line. The trains call at

East Riddlesden Hall

East Riddlesden Hall, Keighley stands on ground above the River Aire. It was built in the mid-seventeenth century for a wealthy clothier James Murgatroyd. A main architectural feature is a two-storey entrance porch in Gothic and Classical styles.

The interior contains panelled rooms, fine plasterwork and mullioned windows. There is a good collection of oak furniture, pewter and textiles. In the grounds is a fishpond fished by the Canons of Bolton in the fourteenth century and an impressive oak-framed barn, one of the finest in the north. The house produces a strong sense of its mysterious past, as the house and pond both have incidents of hauntings connected with a number of murders and unexplained deaths.

Brontë Country

Although not strictly part of the Yorkshire Dales the moorland area, familiarly known as the Brontë country, spreading out from Haworth and Keighley offers visitors a fascinating day out. It is a bold landscape with much of the local stone millstone grit, greatly in evidence. Water-powered mills in the valley bottoms were built of the dark, grey stone and the moorland sides were liberally scattered with stone-built cottages and farmsteads.

Haworth is a straggling, sinewy village, approached up its steep main street from the valley below. The Reverend Patrick Brontë brought his young family here in 1820, to a rough moorland village, whose inhabitants frequently succumbed to the outbreaks of tuberculosis and typhoid. The borrowed horses toiled up the steep cobbled way pulling a cart containing the new parson's family and effects.

Just round the corner of the 'Black Bull' stands the church, the parsonage and the graveyard, where the gravestones crowd in on each other. The Parsonage is a plain Georgian house dating from 1779, except for the tall gable end that was added in 1872. Much of the church was rebuilt in 1872 by Patrick Brontë's successor.

The Parsonage, now the Brontë Society's Museum, has been much altered since the Reverend Patrick Brontë's time but remains a place of pilgrimage for all admirers of his daughters' novels. In the Parsonage, one can see the dining room where the children marched round the table reciting some of their tales and poems and the nursery, later Emily's bedroom, where some years ago many tiny drawings were found on the plaster surface.

Patrick's wife, Maria, died in 1821 at the age of 39 and his daughters Maria, Elizabeth, Charlotte and Emily were sent to the infamous Clergy Daughter's School at Cowan Bridge. The harsh conditions led to Maria and Elizabeth becoming ill and, aged 12 and 11 respectively both died in 1825. Charlotte and Emily rejoined Anne and Branwell to be cared for at home by their aunt, Elizabeth Branwell and Tabitha their servant.

little attractive stations, including Oakworth, which is a splendid example of Edwardian times – authentic advertising signs, gas lighting and coal fires. This station and the line in general played starring roles in the well-loved family film, *The Railway Children*.

It is worthwhile alighting at the first station out of Keighley, Ingrow. Here is **The Vintage Carriages Trust Carriage Museum** housing a fine collection of coaches and three small locomotives dating back to the nineteenth and early twentieth centuries. It

The fanciful world created by the Brontë children was greatly influenced by their surroundings. The panelled library room at nearby Ponden Hall was reputed to contain many important literary works, to which Emily Brontë had access. Certain family details were known to her and quite probably inspired much of the plot of *Wuthering Heights* (1847), Ponden Hall being the likely model for Thrushcross Grange.

From Ponden Hall there's a stiff climb over peaty slopes to Top Withens, a now derelict house that most literary enthusiasts associate with *Wuthering Heights*. A plaque states that the farmhouse has been associated with the Earnshaw home in Emily Brontë's novel. However, the description goes on to say that the building bore no resemblance to the house she described – but its situation may have been in her mind.

The secluded village of Lothersdale, about 4 miles (6.4km) south-west of Skipton is included in Brontë country. Here will be found an attractive Georgian house named 'Stone Gappe'. It was at Stone Gappe in 1839 that Charlotte Brontë worked as a governess for Mr John Benson Sidgwick. This was an unhappy period in her life that led to the writing of *Jane Eyre*. The description of the house was the original for the Gateshead Hall of the novel.

Charlotte had often heard her father reminisce about the Luddites who consequently provide some exciting scenes in her novel, *Shirley*, published 1849, together with her lively portraits of Oakwell Hall and Kirklees Hall.

Ann's first novel, *Tenant of Wildfell Hall,* was also published in 1847 but tragically within two years she, Emily and Branwell all died. Branwell, who had once had ambitions as a painter, caused his family great anguish with his dissolute ways, eventually succumbing to his addiction to drink and opium. His sisters Emily and Anne did not live long enough to appreciate the success of their novels and Charlotte was left alone to care for her father. Later, after considerable hesitation, Charlotte married her father's curate, the Reverend A B Nicholls, in June 1854 and enjoyed a brief period of happiness. She died in March 1855 of an illness probably associated with pregnancy.

Although Haworth is chiefly known for its Parsonage and the three famous sisters, it is a place that still preserves a hardy character of its own. Despite its busy main street and trappings of tourism, Haworth draws on the strength of the Brontës and the beauty of its moorland landscape.

is also the Trust's workshop and visitors can watch restoration in progress.

The Haworth station shop is open 364 days of the year for books, magazines, videos, souvenirs and model railway items. Passengers should alight here for a visit to the famous **Brontë Parson-age and Museum**. The Parsonage is a mecca for Brontë lovers from all over the world. The displays give a fascinating glimpse into the isolated world of this family and there are regular special exhibitions of Brontë material from elsewhere.

Places to Visit

Settle

Watershed Mill & Visitor Centre*

Langcliffe Road, Settle
A former 1820s cotton mill which contains speciality shops – woollens, pottery, woodwork, leatherwork, fashion knitwear, paintings, prints and textiles. Rock and fossil shop, café.
☎ (01729) 825539
Opening times: 10am–5.30pm Mon–Sat, 11am–5pm Sun.

Yorkshire Dales Falconry and Conservation Centre

Crows Nest Barn, Nr. Giggleswick
☎ (01729) 822832
Free flying demos, hawking holidays, handling courses, tea room and shop.
Open: Summer 10am–4.30pm. Winter 10am–3.30pm. All year, everyday except Christmas Day.
www.falconryandwildlife.com.

Horses Health Farm

Rathmell near Settle
☎ (01729) 840284
www.horseshealthfarm.co.uk

The Folly; Museum of North Craven Life

Settle
An impressive Grade I listed 17th century house close to the centre of Settle.
Open: 1st Jul–30 Sep, Tue–Sat, Sun 10.30am–4.30pm. And all bank holiday weekends.
Limited diabled access. Toilet accessible for wheelchairs. Party visits by appointment.
Bookings: ☎ (015242) 51388 or (01729) 822361
www.ncbpt.org.uk/folly

Malham

Malham Tarn Field Centre

Courses: details from Tarn House – Rambling, Natural History, Arts and Crafts, Archaeology, Fly Fishing etc.
Conference venue
☎ (01729) 830331
www.field-studies-council.org

The Cove Centre*

Malham
Outdoor clothing, accessories, maps, books, buttery.
☎ (01729) 830432. Open: Daily 9.30am–4.30pm. Sunday 10.30am–4.30pm.

Gordale Gifts

Malham
Outdoor clothing, wine and beers.
☎ (01729) 830285

Skipton

Craven Museum*

Town Hall, High Street.
Fascinating exhibits, artefacts, costumes models.
☎ (01756) 706407
Open: 10am–5pm daily (except Tue), 2-5pm Sun, Apr–Sep; 1.30pm-5pm daily (except Tue and Sun), 10–12 noon; 1–4pm Sat, winter.
www.cravendc.gov.uk

Skipton Castle*

Finely preserved castle
☎ (01756) 792442
www.skiptoncastle.co.uk
Open: Mon-Sat 10am–6pm. Sun
12noon–6pm. (Oct–Feb 4pm).
Closed 25th Dec. www.skiptoncastle.co.uk

Embsay and Bolton Abbey Steam Railway*

Bolton Abbey Station. Embsay
Station, 2 miles (3.2km) east of
Skipton on A59
Steam trains every Sun, summer
services up to 7 days a week.
Talking timetable ☎ (01756) 795189.
Enquiries (01756) 710614. www.embasyboltonabbyrailway.org.uk

Country Publications – Dalesman Magazine*

The Water Mill, Broughton Hall,
Skipton BD23 3AG
To try Dalesman free of charge,
please write to the above address.
☎ (01756) 701381. www.dalesman.co.uk

Canal Trips

Pennine Boats of Skipton

Waterside Court, Coach Street,
Skipton. ☎ (01756) 790829 Talking
timetable ☎ (01756) 701212

Keighley

East Riddlesden Hall*

Bradford Road, Keighley (NT)
Seventeenth-century West Yorkshire
manor house. Garden and herb
border. ☎ (01535) 607075
Open: 5th Apr – end of Oct, 1st week
in Nov.

Cliffe Castle Museum*

Spring Gardens Lane, Keighley
Original furnishings of the hall,
natural history and geology.
☎ (01535) 618230. Open: 10am–
5pm Tue–Sat, 12–5pm Sun. Open
bank holiday Mon.

Vintage Carriages Trust Carriage Museum*

Station Yard, Ingrow, Keighley
☎ (01535) 680425, website: www.bradford.gov.uk/tourism
Open: 11am–5pm (dusk in winter)
daily, all year.

Haworth

The Keighley and Worth Valley Railway*

The Railway Station, Haworth
Steam trains from Keighley to Haworth.
Enthusiasts' Weekends; Vintage Trains;
Heritage Diesel; the Railway Children
Walk.
☎ (01535) 645214. www.kwvr.co.uk
Open: All year, weekends and public
holidays. Tue-Thu, mid Jun to early Jul,
then daily until begining of Sep.

The Brontë Parsonage Museum*

Haworth
☎ (01535) 642323, website: www.bronte.info
Open: Everyday of the year except 24–
27 Dec and 3-31 Jan. 10am–5.30pm
Apr-Sep. 11am–5pm Oct–Mar.

Townend Mill*

Brontë Weaving Shed, Haworth
☎ (01535) 646217, Open: 7 days
a week, except Christmas Day &
Easter Sun. Mon–Sat 10am–5.30pm.
Sun 11am–5pm.

4. Wharfedale

Wharfedale and its feeder dales, Littondale and Langstrothdale reach into the very centre of the Yorkshire Dales. In the south Rombalds Moor is a large wedge of moorland that separates the valleys of the Aire and Wharfe and the towns of Keighley and Ilkley. There are a number of walking routes across the rough moorland and adventurous motorists can tackle the narrow by road from Riddlesden, over Whetstone Allotment and Ilkley Moor. Otherwise, main roads circle all round the moor.

Ilkley

Ilkley is a pleasant unassuming town in a leafy, attractive setting at the foot of its gritstone moor. Well-tended gardens and flowery borders are a feature of the place. It has a mixture of fine houses and gentleman's residences; a legacy of the new prosperity due to the building boom at the end of the nineteenth century. Ilkley became known as the Heather Spa, as visitors arrived to take the water cure.

The railway speeded up the town's expansion but although the line now terminates at Ilkley, there is a regular and convenient service to Leeds and Bradford. This Wharfedale town is less well known than the famous stretch of moorland to the south, Ilkley Moor, where as all discerning Yorkshire folk know, it is unwise to go without a hat. Ilkley Moor is but a part of the extensive Rombalds Moor.

The Romans established a fort at Ilkley which was known as Olicana. It was an important base guarding the supply roads – a route following the Wharfe and continuing to Long Preston and a route from Hampsthwaite on the Nidd to Littleborough and Manchester. The site of the Roman fort, now obliter-

Rombalds Moor

There is an ancient prehistoric way crossing the moor, a route used by settlers from Ireland who first brought the early bronze weapons to Yorkshire. They also brought the practice of rock carving in the form of cup and ring markings. As the engraving of the rocks would involve a very laborious and lengthy operation, it is fair to assume that the symbols held some very special meaning for the Bronze Age people.

Some patterns consist of cup-like depressions picked out of the surface of the stone. Some of these cup-like hollows are surrounded by a number of broken or continuous concentric rings. Cup and ring markings may be linked together and other variations in design include circles, half-circles, arches, grids, ladders and spirals.

Rombalds Moor also contains cairns, burial mounds and stone circles of late Neolithic and Bronze Age period. The stone circles consist of circular, almost circular or oval settings of spaced standing stones. The structures may be integrated with banks, ditches, single stones, rows of stones and vary greatly in diameter. Some monuments on Rombalds Moor: Twelve Apostles stone circle SE 126 451; Great Skirtful of Stones SE 141 445; Swastika Stone, Woodhouse Crag SE 094 470; Badger Stone, Ilkley Moor SE 110 460; Barmishaw Stone SE 112 464; Pancake Stone SE 133 462; Willy Hall's Wood SE 115 465; Piper Stone SE 084 471.

ated, partly lies where the parish church now stands.

It is believed that the original fort was of the Emperor Agricola's time and evidence has confirmed that it was garrisoned by detachments of the Ninth Legion. There was probably a Roman presence at Ilkley for nigh on 300 years. At the rear of All Saints Church is a small section of the fort, while two of their altars are built into the basement of the church tower.

The church of All Saints has a thirteenth-century south doorway to admire with a decoration of continuous mouldings and dog-tooth patterns. Inside, the ninth century is recalled in the form of three Anglo-Saxon crosses. These fine examples, which for many centuries stood outside, are now sensibly located inside. The taller of the three portrays the four Evangelists, Matthew, Mark, Luke and John with the figure of Christ and beasts. The sides are decorated with vine-scrolls; it is one of the most important Anglian crosses in the North.

On the north-western side of the church stands the Manor House, a large sixteenth-century building with gables and mullioned and transomed windows. This is now **Ilkley Museum and Art Gallery**. Regular exhibitions of paintings, sculpture and art-work are held here, and there are local history collections.

Visitors find Ilkley an ideal place for shopping and browsing. The Victorian Arcade, built in 1895, has an imposing towered entrance on Church Street. The arcade has been attractively restored as a shopping centre and tearoom. One of the favourite places in Ilkley, **Bettys**

Café and Tea Room, is famous for its cakes and pastries.

The gritstone edges on the moor, such as the **Cow and Calf Rocks**, are a considerable attraction to visitors. The location is a focal point for the start of longer moorland walks and the car park is often busy. The group of white buildings on the moor edge called **'White Wells'** played an important role in the past during the rise of Ilkley as a spa town. The old stone bath-house dates from about 1690 and the buildings were rebuilt and enlarged in 1780. At the rear of the building one can taste the cold, fresh spring water.

The **Dales Way** long distance footpath begins its 81 mile (130km) journey at Ilkley Bridge. This is not the modern bridge at the bottom of Brook Street but the seventeenth-century structure, now closed to vehicular traffic. The footpath continues on the south bank of the river. Soon the view is one looking out above the wide river; a panorama of pastures, woods and distant hills – a promise of scenic delights to come. The Dales Way takes the walker right to the head of Wharfedale, over the fells into upper Ribblesdale and Dentdale to the Kent Valley, terminating at Bowness-on-Windermere.

Ilkley to Bolton Abbey

The former mill working community of **Addingham** is situated by the River Wharfe between the rising gritstone slopes of Addingham Moorside and the prominent summit of Beamsley Beacon. In the early nineteenth century, Addingham was the scene of riots. Luddites, who saw their livelihood threatened by machines, smashed equipment and threatened to burn down the factory.

At Bolton Bridge, a byroad leads to the small pleasant village of **Beamsley** sitting below the steep slopes of Beamsley Beacon. In medieval and Tudor times a beacon was lit on the summit to signal major events. Just to the north of the village on the A59 are a small number of almshouses founded in the late sixteenth century by Margaret, Countess of Cumberland and developed by Lady Anne Clifford. The quaint central stone building has a chapel with seven rooms for destitute women radiating from the centre.

The B6160 road travels north from Bolton Bridge for three quarters of a mile through an avenue of ash and sycamore to reach the hamlet of **Bolton Abbey**; this tiny settlement was named after the twelfth-century Priory Church founded by the Augustinians. The Priory sits in a magnificent situation on a slight rise in a bend of the River Wharfe. This house for Augustinian canons first had its beginnings at Embsay near to Skipton but after thirty years, the order moved to Bolton and stayed there for nearly 400 years.

Seen from almost any viewpoint, Bolton Priory looks venerable and splendid. A particularly good aspect of the site can be enjoyed from the top of the cliff on the other side of the river. The adventurous may cross on the stepping stones but in times of flood the footbridge is a better option.

In troubled times, the canons of Bolton Priory were afforded protection by the Cliffords of Skipton Castle. This relationship continued in complete harmony, as at least two Clifford lords slain in battle were buried at Bolton.

When the religious houses were forced to close, by order of Henry VIII, Bolton Priory was the last to go. Many of the abbeys and monasteries were demolished, but in Bolton's case something was saved. Here, religious services were allowed to continue in the nave; so this building has been used for worship for over 800 years, a very grand parish church.

The church of the Blessed Virgin and St Cuthbert was apparently begun shortly after the establishment of the Priory. Twelfth-century work exists in the west half of the chancel, such as late-Norman blank arcading with round-headed arches. The nave was not continued until the mid-thirteenth century, when the south wall received its upper storey with six tall narrow-set windows. The west front is a highly decorated piece of mid-thirteenth century design, with much dog-tooth ornamentation. After 1325 there was substantial rebuilding and the chancel was lengthened.

The west tower was begun in 1520 by Prior Richard Moone, but the Priory's surrender meant that the masons had to cease their work. A wall was built at the east end of the nave where the rood screen had stood and the eastern parts of the Priory were allowed to decay. The church was restored, 1875-80, by George Edmund Street.

The Rectory was built from Priory stones and incorporates the infirmary's original six-light window. Bolton Hall, together with the estate, parkland and surrounding woods belongs to the

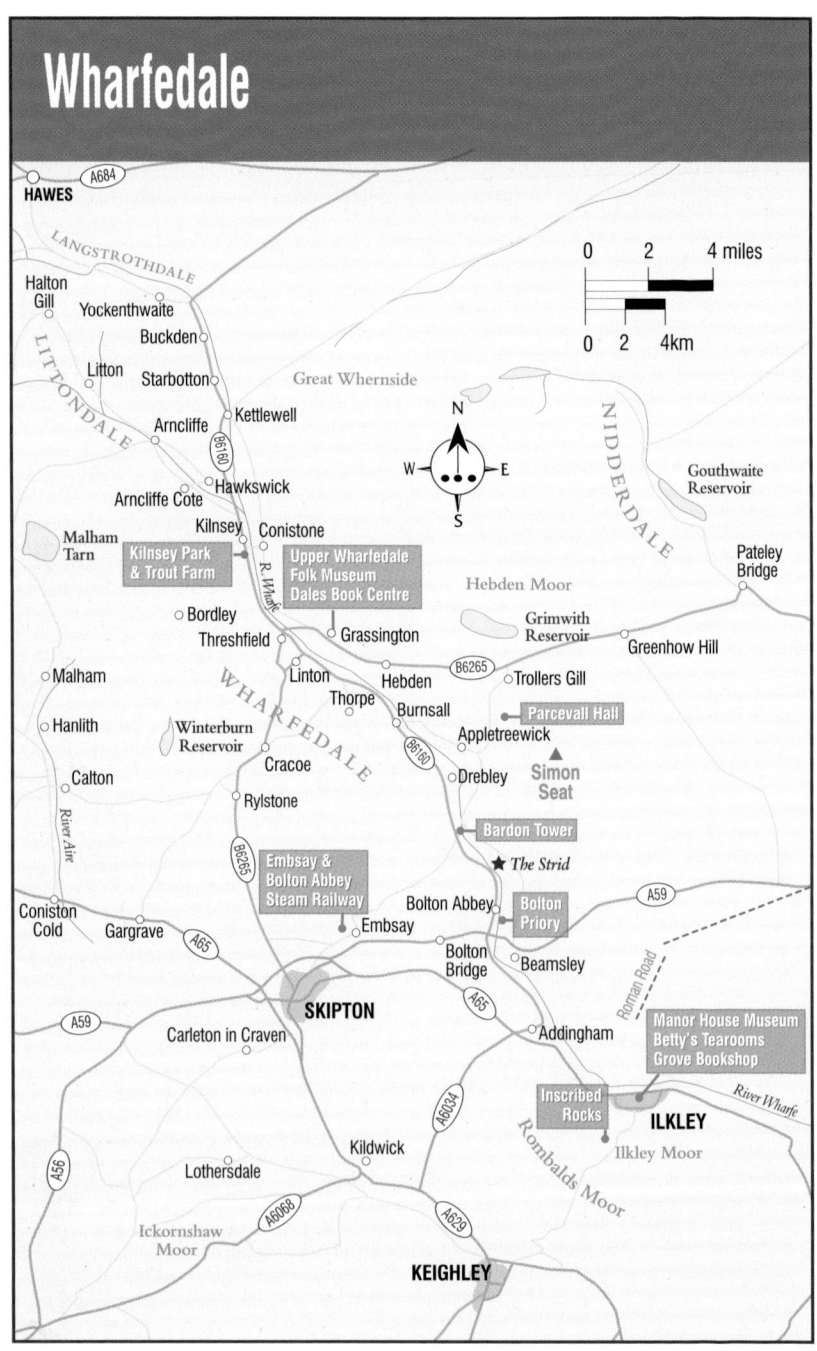

Wharfedale

HAWES
A684

LANGSTROTHDALE

Halton Gill
Yockenthwaite
Buckden
LITTONDALE
Litton
Starbotton
Arncliffe
Kettlewell
B6160

Great Whernside

0   2   4 miles

0   2   4km

N
W   E
S

NIDDERDALE

Gouthwaite
Reservoir

Arncliffe Cote
Hawkswick
Kilnsey
Conistone
Malham
Tarn
Kilnsey Park
& Trout Farm
Upper Wharfedale
Folk Museum
Dales Book Centre

Pateley
Bridge

Hebden Moor

Bordley
Threshfield
Grassington
Grimwith
Reservoir
Greenhow Hill

Malham
Linton
Thorpe
Hebden
B6265
Trollers Gill

Hanlith
Burnsall
Parcevall Hall

WHARFEDALE
Winterburn
Reservoir
Cracoe
B6160
Appletreewick
Drebley
Simon
Seat

Calton
Rylstone
Bardon Tower

River Aire

B6265
Embsay &
Bolton Abbey
Steam Railway
★ The Strid

Coniston
Cold
Gargrave
A65
Bolton Abbey
Bolton
Priory
A59

Embsay
Bolton
Bridge
Beamsley
Roman Road

SKIPTON
A65
Manor House Museum
Betty's Tearooms
Grove Bookshop

A59
Carleton in Craven
Addingham

Inscribed
Rocks
River Wharfe

ILKLEY

A6034
Ilkley Moor

A56
Kildwick

Lothersdale
A6068
A629
Rombalds Moor

Ickornshaw
Moor

KEIGHLEY

Steam Railway

Within comparatively recent years, visitors to Bolton Priory came by train to Bolton Abbey Station. Now, enthusiasts of the **Embsay and Bolton Abbey Steam Railway** have recently completed their track extension from Embsay near Skipton, together with the opening of the award winning Bolton Abbey Station so that today's visitors can do the same. The station is a reconstruction of the original building that offers visitor facilities including a shop and refreshments with plenty of parking nearby.

At Embsay several of the original station buildings are still in use, augmented by a ticket office transported from Barmouth in North Wales in 1992 and now fully restored. Here too there is ample parking and other facilities. Along the line at Holywell Halt there are two picnic areas offering a 'surprise view' and a children's trail. There are steam trains every Sunday and a summer service up to seven days a week.

Duke of Devonshire. The hall, also constructed from Priory stones, lies across the lawn to the west of the Priory; it was built as a hunting lodge in the seventeenth century.

Wordsworth, Landseer and Turner were all inspired by the area around Bolton Abbey. The Duke of Devonshire's estate, with its beautiful and varied landscape, has been superbly maintained. There are extensive woodlands containing ash, sycamore and beech with the river powering through **The Strid**. The whole canvas of moss, ferns, trees, rocks and water is magnificent but none more so than in a colourful autumn, when the woods are afire with russet, gold, copper and crimson.

The estate has provided over 75 miles (121km) of footpaths, including Nature Trails and Children's Trail. The Strid is best seen when the flow of water is not too high. As the Wharfe surges through a narrow gorge, the river has carved, smoothed and gouged out the bed and sides of the rocky channel. This can be a dangerous place especially when the rocks are wet. On no account attempt to jump the river. It is wider and deeper than it looks and has claimed many lives over the years.

A pathway climbs steeply behind the Strid, with attractive views of the river and continues to a point where the river valley has broadened out. Proceed on the path through the woods to reach **Barden Bridge**, a lovely seventeenth-century stone bridge.

Just above the bridge is **Barden Tower**, a hunting-lodge of the Clifford family. Henry Clifford, the shepherd lord, inherited his estates when Lancastrian fortunes improved and lived in the tranquil surroundings of Barden. Later the building became ruinous, to be restored by Lady Anne Clifford in 1658. Afterwards, it soon fell into disuse and disrepair. It now stands, an imposing ruin, alongside the B6160 road to Threshfield.

Burnsall to Kilnsey

From Bolton Abbey the road passes Barden Tower and wanders alongside sloping green pastures and large patches of woodland to descend gently to the village of **Burnsall**. This settlement is a fine example of a Dales village; so delightfully situated in a green bowl close to the river. This landscape is a beautiful and complete contrast to the dark gritstone heather-clad Pennine moors of the Brontë country.

The Red Lion Inn, beside the graceful five-arched bridge, is backed by clustered cottages of mellow stone, many dating back to the seventeenth and eighteenth centuries. The church was founded in the twelfth century by the de Romilles of Skipton. The entrance is through an interesting and unique lych-gate. Some restoration took place in 1612, according to an inscription stating that in that year the church was 'butified'. This was carried out by Sir William Craven, who also endowed the Grammar School next door. This old building which is similar in style to a manor house, is on two floors with mullioned windows. Sir William Craven became Lord Mayor of London in 1598.

Burnsall celebrates its annual sports day on the Saturday following the first Sunday after the 12th August. Amateur athletes compete in the sports events and also in the classic fell race, the oldest in England.

A secondary road crosses Burnsall's photogenic bridge and heads for the interesting village of **Appletreewick** whose steep main street climbs up from Low Hall at one end to High Hall at the eastern end. The manor of Appletreewick was acquired by the canons of Bolton Priory for the value of its grazing and lead mines. A charter was granted in 1311 for the holding of a fair known as the Onion Fair. It is interesting to note that those far-off medieval days are recalled by the local name, Onion Lane.

High Hall is a house on three floors, rebuilt by Sir William Craven. Monk's Hall or Mock Beggar Hall was possibly a monastic grange. It has three bays, the doorway reached by an outer staircase and was mostly rebuilt at the end of the seventeenth century. The church of St John is a small church converted from two cottages.

From Appletreewick the minor road continues straight on and descends into the valley of Fir Beck. The scattered community of **Skyreholme** is divided into three settlements, Skyreholme, Middle and High.

Just north of Middle Skyreholme is the site of **Parcevall Hall Gardens**. Open to the public, these hillside and woodland gardens offer dramatic views over beautiful countryside. There are terraces, rock gardens, streams and quiet pools. There is an orchard for summer picnics and glorious views of Simon Seat and Wharfedale. The gardens have year round interest.

Trollers Gill is a splendid limestone gorge just a short walking distance from Parcevall Hall. A footpath accompanies Skyreholme Beck beyond Middle Hill to reach New Road. According to legend, Trollers Gill is the haunt of the mythical 'Barguest' – the dreaded phantom dog. Beyond Burnsall the B6160 continues to follow the Wharfe, and with one's attention drawn to the expanding vistas ahead, a small byroad climbing steeply away on the left to **Thorpe** could go unnoticed.

Another lane from Thorpe joins the main road to a junction with the B6265 and round the corner is the village of **Linton-in-Craven**. This pretty settlement can claim its accolades quite rightly when it comes to competing for the Most Attractive Village in the North awards. The old village green surrounded by interesting architectural features, is crossed by a high-arched bridge and an old clapper bridge. Indeed, if one is looking for other ways to cross the beck, there is also a modern road bridge, stepping stones and a ford.

Cottages and dignified old houses complete the picture: the Old Rectory, a Youth Hostel, has recently been closed. It had catered for the spirit of the hostelling movement for many years. At the end of the village green is the hospital, seven almshouses founded by Richard Fountaine in 1721 for poor men or women. The range has a grand façade, a central part with a square tower and projecting wings. The central doorway leads to a chapel. No less a personage than Vanbrugh is said to be the designer.

The church of St Michael lies a little distance away from the village on the banks of the River Wharfe. This delightful little church has a handsome, short square bell-cote; it was probably built to replace an ancient pagan shrine some distance from the neighbouring settlements of Linton and Grassington. The interior contains a Norman arcade and splendid roof bosses. One of these knobs shows the 'Green Man' – an ancient fertility symbol.

Lovers of good food may care to make a slight detour before visiting the next village, Threshfield. A short way south on the B6265 is Jacksons of Cracoe farm shop. At least twelve different kinds of sausages are made on the premises and visitors may watch the process. Other local foods are also on sale here.

The scattered village of **Threshfield**

Secret village

The tiny hamlet of Thorpe is secreted away above the valley of the Wharfe. It is one of those odd, but delightful places in the dales of which local people are very proud. One can readily believe that during Scots' raids men, women, children and cattle from the valley were hidden here and never discovered. The monks of Fountains Abbey trekking across the fells were grateful to the inhabitants of Thorpe because it was a settlement of shoemakers, employed to make and mend shoes.

The collection of houses and cottages lies in a fold of the hills, protected by two encircling limestone reef knolls, Elbolton and Kail. There are several small shapely hills in the area and all these green mounds are rich in limestone fossils. It is thought that they were formed in the same way as coral reefs, when the present limestone country was the bed of a shallow sea.

Lead mining

This is documented on Grassington Moor from the thirteenth century and no doubt was carried on in earlier times. The wide area of Grassington and Hebden Moor is crossed by numerous faults and veins of lead were associated with most of these faults. The ore has been found mainly with barytes, calcite and fluorspar. Galena, sulphide of lead, is the main lead ore; the silver content of the galena would average some 4-6oz per ton of smelted ore.

The mineral rights passed into the possession of the Devonshire family after the marriage of the fourth Duke of Devonshire to Charlotte heiress to the third Earl of Burlington. By the middle of the eighteenth century, the free miner was replaced by the formation of small mining companies. Winding and pumping machinery and a smelt mill were erected by 1755 and by the end of the eighteenth century, most of the miners were employed by the Duke of Devonshire.

At the Cupola smelt mill in 1793, the old hearths were removed and replaced by reverberatory furnaces fired by locally dug coal. Still seen today on the moor, are the long, horizontal flues and one remaining 40ft (12m) high chimney. However, towards the end of the 1870s, the market for English lead collapsed due to cheaper foreign imports. By 1874, very few mines were working on Grassington Moor.

Warning: Visitors are warned to take special care in an area of old mine workings. Keep away from disused shafts and do not enter the adits. Children should be kept under strict control.

is set around a busy crossroads and has a number of seventeenth-century houses and barns. Probably Threshfield's most interesting building lies outside the village on the Bow Bridge minor road. The Free Grammar School, an attractive building with a prominent porch and mullioned windows, was founded in 1674 by Matthew Hewitt, a Rector of Linton.

From Threshfield the road crosses the Wharfe via a four-arched bridge and enters the village of **Grassington**. The village was a small settlement until the seventeenth century, forming part of the parish of Linton. The discovery of lead ore on the high moor, north and east of the village, no doubt contributed to its growth.

The main street, narrow at first, opens out into an attractive cobbled square, now a Conservation Area. Motorists can drive to the north end of the village and then out on to the moor. However, there are also excellent parking facilities at the large car and coach park next to the Yorkshire Dales National Park Centre on the B6265 Hebden road.

During the heyday of lead mining, many cottages were built to house the increased population. In the centre of the village there are a number of attractive buildings, including Church House, with a dated lintel of 1694 and Grassington Hall, part of which is of the late thirteenth century. **Upper Wharfedale Museum** is housed in two former leadminers' cottages in The Square at Grassington. An interesting collection of exhibits portrays life in Wharfedale over the last two centuries.

Soon after the decline in the lead mining industry, the Yorkshire Dales Railway from Skipton opened in 1901. This brought in an influx of people from the industrial towns to enjoy the clean air, a beautiful river valley and the wide expanses of hill and moor. The railway opened out this strip of dale and the development of services to cater for the visitors grew rapidly.

Today, it has become an attractive village set in beautiful countryside. Though the railway closed long ago visitors still come to enjoy the countryside and visit the unusual and individual shops that provide designer goods, craft items, gifts, greetings cards, paintings and clothing. Grassington provides an ideal base for outdoor enthusiasts to enjoy the many walking routes on the surrounding limestone uplands and

Foxup Beck at the head of Littondale

Above: An example of a long, horizontal smelt mill flue

wild moorland.

Historians can trace and examine sites of ancient settlements and field systems. Commencing just north of Bank Lathe there are fine impressions of rectangular fields and circular hut enclosures including at the northerly part of the Lea Green area, clear evidence of stone hut foundations within an enclosing wall. This points to the site of an Iron Age village settlement that probably existed into Roman times.

The natural assembly of flora can be seen to its best advantage in Grass Wood and Bastow Wood north-west of the village of Grassington. The area remains a wildwood, natural, self-seeded and uncultivated. In the middle of Grass Wood is a limestone hill, which for the lover of wild flowers is always an exciting experience.

Bastow Wood, in the main, is a scrub wood on limestone, with smaller trees such as hawthorn, hazel, birch and bird cherry. Wild roses carpet the woodland. Bastow Wood is a delightful place, with many grassy clearings that were used by lead miners grazing their ponies. There are sections of limestone pavement. The area may be approached by paths running from the north end of the village of Grassington. The OS Outdoor Leisure map 2, *Yorkshire Dales – Southern and Western areas* is an essential guide.

There is much to see from the byroad running north from Grassington following the River Wharfe on its eastern bank; the seemingly impenetrable slopes of Grass Wood, views of the sylvan Wharfe and the limestone pastures on the opposite side of the valley. The compact village of **Conistone** lies at a road junction leading to Kilnsey on the western side of the Wharfe. It looks across to the bulk of **Kilnsey Crag** but its real joy is its sheltered position under the lee of a succession of limestone escarpments.

The high-level route of the Dales Way travels through a magnificent landscape of limestone ridges, scars and pavements, interspersed with patches of pasture. The rock terraces, castles and scars are a sheer delight and the walker can count it as a privilege to be amongst such delectable scenery.

From Conistone, with its tiny central green and ancient church, one of the oldest in the Dales, travel over the old bridge to join the westerly road to Kilnsey and its crag. This spectacular limestone cliff is topped by a bulging overhang, providing a considerable challenge to rock climbers. In the shadow of the crag stands the Tennants Arms Inn and a row of cottages. Nearby, is the added attraction of **Kilnsey Park and Trout Farm** with something for all the family. Ponds of rainbow trout for fly fishing and a children's fun fishery are offered, as well as a herb centre, nature trail, restaurant and coffee shop.

For a considerable period the whole Manor of Kilnsey, together with Conistone, was in the possession of Fountains Abbey. A large grange was established here, and the old hall, now used as farm buildings, was built with stone from the medieval grange. Mastiles Lane, the fell road taken by the monks, now provides an excellent route for walkers heading for Malham.

Littondale

Just a short distance to the north of

Kilnsey, the River Skirfare joins the Wharfe from **Littondale**. There is a road on either side of the river, running parallel up the dale to meet at Arncliffe. The first village in the dale, **Hawkswick**, is snugly situated between the river and the steepening fellsides of Knipe Scar.

A linking byroad, Out Gang Lane, crosses over Hawkswick Bridge and joins the other valley road. Opposite the junction are the former monastic granges of Hawkswick Cote and Arncliffe Cote. At this point, a beck descends a deep limestone gorge – a miniature canyon. The village of **Arncliffe** lies $1^1/_2$ miles (2.4km) ahead. Arncliffe is the chief village, the 'capital' of Littondale. It lies in a most beautiful situation, nestling amid trees, watered by the Skirfare and sheltered on both sides by rising slopes pierced by limestone outcrops.

The large village green is ringed by a variety of houses, cottages and barns; one of the buildings is an inn, The Falcon. Brightened by wild flowers, or daffodils in due season, this open area whose outline of grey roofs fits so naturally beneath the enclosing fells, is a prime location for artists and photographers – especially television people. Arncliffe was the chosen setting for a wedding in the TV series *Emmerdale Farm*.

At the end of the eighteenth century, industry came to the village in the form of a cotton mill which employed fifty local workers.

The church of St Oswald has a fifteenth century tower, but now has little architectural interest due to Victorian 'restorers' in 1841. A memorial lists the names of the Arncliffe men who fought a the Battle of Flodden in 1513.

Continuing past the green, the road crosses Cowside Beck and turns sharply westwards. Brootes Lane climbs steeply up this hill highway towards Darnbrook House and Malham. There is a tremendous view down into the deep valley and the awesome craggy sides of Yew Cogar Scar. At a cattle grid, with a stroll down the grassy flank a notice reminds the visitor that it is a Nature Conservation area.

Returning to Arncliffe, the road crosses the bridge by the church and continues up the narrowing dale. Old Cotes stands by the road and is a good example of a traditional dales' dwelling dated 1650. Across on the other side of the Skirfare stretches the two-mile length of Skoska Wood, one of those ancient strips of woodland that became a feature of the upper dale.

The little community of **Litton** is a pleasant huddle of stone cottages, farms and the Queen's Arms Inn. Walkers have the choice of climbing over Old Cote Moor and down to Buckden in Wharfedale or climbing high above Penyghent Gill en-route for Penyghent, or following paths by the Skirfare.

Beyond Litton and particularly past the confluence of Penyghent Gill and the Skirfare, Littondale opens up into a green grassy bowl amongst the surrounding hills. At this point, the road is joined by another that has descended the slopes of Penyghent Fell to meet at the hamlet of **Halton Gill**. Stone houses with dated lintels and initials look out across the valley. The small stone church of St John, 1848, is now closed and is a private residence. The church is built on to a cottage two

Ascent of Great Whernside

Initially this is over the limestone and the white rock is thrust out in a series of stepped escarpments. Suddenly, there is an abrupt change as the limestone is overlaid with gritstone. The hill walker then enters a sombre yet still exciting world of tussock grass, pools of rich peaty-coloured water and tufts of cotton grass. Eventually, the gritstone outcrops appear and then the trig-point marking the summit. The long boulder-strewn ridge affords expansive views to the east of the Nidderdale moors and westwards across Wharfedale.

centuries its senior.

Looking towards the bend in the road at the north end of the hamlet, one cannot fail to notice a magnificent 'porch' barn. This outstanding building has a huge entrance and a protruding porch dated 1829. This completes the picture, a lovely little community in a magnificent setting.

Just beyond the barn a track zig-zags up the hillside to the Horse Head Pass, a bridleway climbing over the high land to Yockenthwaite in upper Wharfedale. The route was followed by A. Wainwright on his Pennine journey. Years ago, little Halton Gill was a busy place, where packhorse trains rested awhile before climbing into the hills.

About half a mile higher up the valley, the road ends at **Foxup Bridge**. Here, the Foxup and Cosh Becks join together to form the Skirfare. From Foxup a track follows the beck towards the lonely former farmstead of Cosh. Over the grassy ridge northwards lie the large forested areas of Green Field Beck. Before returning down the dale, a look at the map indicates two names, which to the local dalesfolk seem quite natural titles, but to other may elicit a smile, namely, Cosh Inside and Cosh Outside.

Upper Wharfedale

Returning down Littondale to Skirfare Bridge and resuming the journey northwards along Wharfedale, the B6160 crosses the river and enters the large village of **Kettlewell**. Like Grassington, Kettlewell has always been a busy village. Much of the surrounding land was once in the possession of the monks of Fountains Abbey and Coverham Abbey. Paths and trackways trodden by the monks were later used by lead miners and packmen. The village was an important stopping point. Those who make the journey by car from Coverdale will appreciate the old coaching and posting days when travellers from the wild country beyond would be glad to see the comforting lights of the inns.

Charity auction

An ancient local custom is enacted at the George Inn each New Year's Day, when a committee, called the Hubberholme Parliament, meets to auction off the tenancy of a field, the monies raised going to charity.

Water running over the weir in the evening at Grassington

Upper Wharfedale village of Kettlewell

Selected Walks

1. Bolton Abbey to Simon Seat

Distance 8 miles (12.8km)

Map: OS Outdoor Leisure 2 Yorkshire Dales – Southern and Western areas 1:25,000

The Cavendish Pavilion (SE 077 553) is the start of a walk to Simon Seat. Cross over to the far side of the river, turn left and follow the route to Waterfall Cottage. Proceed up the path leading to the Valley of Desolation, so-named because of mid-nineteenth century landslip. The route emerges on to the open moorland of Barden Fell; this a concession path open to the public except on days when grouse shooting takes place.

The clear track leads to the rocky summit of Simon Seat, 1,591ft (485m), an outstanding landmark and superb viewpoint of Wharfedale. From the summit follow the cairned track below Earl Seat then descend steeply through coniferous woodland to Howgill. Take the riverside path past Drebley stepping stones to the road near Barden Bridge. From the bridge there is a choice of routes, on either side of the river, for a return to the starting point.

2. Grassington to Hebden

Distance: 5¹/₂ miles (8.8km)

Map: OS Outdoor Leisure 2 Yorkshire Dales – Southern and Western areas 1:25,000

From Grassington there are a number of paths and tracks for a circular walk taking in the village of Hebden. From Bank Lane, follow Moor Lane to Yarnbury. Take a path on the right heading across to walk alongside Hebden Beck in a southerly direction to Hebden with its attractive old stone bridge. There is much evidence of mining activity amongst grand scenery, with pretty cascades along the stream. The waterfall of Scale Force is the local beauty spot. Return to Grassington via path and High Lane track.

3. Short walk from Conistone

Distance: 2 miles (3.2km)

Map: OS Outdoor Leisure 2 Yorkshire Dales – Southern and Western areas 1:25,000

For a flavour of this limestone landscape, a path leaves Conistone opposite the road over the river, heading east to enter Gurling Trough, a narrow water-carved passage through resistant beds of limestone. The route then opens out into the wide grassy valley of Conistone Dib, which climbs upwards to meet another narrow cleft and on to a crossroad of paths. Bear left and return to Conistone via Scot Gate Lane.

4. Ascent of Buckden Pike

Distance: 8$^1/_2$ miles (13.6km)

Map: OS Outdoor Leisure 30 Yorkshire Dales – Northern and Central areas 1:25,000

From Buckden take the track northwards climbing through Rakes Wood and then bear right climbing the grassy slopes of Cow Close. The route is overlooked by outcrops of limestone before it reaches the ridge. Turn right and walk to the summit of Buckden Pike 2,303ft (702m). Continue along the ridge to the southern end to reach a white stone cross, which commemorates the death of five Polish aircrew, whose Wellington bomber crashed here during a snowstorm in January 1942. Only one survivor managed to stagger down the fellside to Cray following the paw prints of a fox. Look for the head of a fox on the memorial.

Gently descend and join the path from Walden Head. Follow this route to the right and descend the clear track above Cam Gill Beck to Starbotton. Bear left through the village and take a track to the right down to the River Wharfe. Cross over the footbridge, turn right and follow the Dales Way path to Dubb's Lane Bridge. Turn right along the road into Buckden.

Grassington Moor lead mining Cupola works

Kettlewell occupies both banks of the Cam Beck near to its confluence with the Wharfe. Two important inns face each other by the bridge over the beck, The Bluebell, 1680 and the Racehorses, an enlarged Georgian inn dating from 1740.

The moorland height of **Great Whernside**, 2,310ft (704m) dominates the skyline to the east. The steep hillside slopes immediately begin to close in on the two streams, Cam Gill Beck and Dowber Gill Beck. Their swiftly flowing waters issuing from the flanks of Great Whernside have carved out deep valleys before joining forces above Kettlewell.

As the road continues up the dale, the sculptured landscape of neatly spaced villages linked by a fret-work of green pastures with grey-stone walls epitomises magnificent Wharfedale.

Starbotton lies at the foot of another Cam Gill Beck, where in 1686, a terrible flood overwhelmed the village. The line of cottages, including the inn, wriggle round a kink in the road in a gesture of solidarity.

The village of **Buckden** lies at the head of Wharfedale and at the foot of high-level ways out of the valley. There is a choice here of exhilarating routes for both motorist and walker alike; to Wensleydale, Semerdale and Bishopdale.

Buckden is a Norman foundation established for the foresters on the edge of the chase. It became the centre of the Langstrothdale hunting preserve. Walk down the road towards Starbotton for just over three-quarters of a mile (1.2km). At a point where the wall following the parish boundary reaches the road, there is an old stone base and

'The Road to the Dales'

The B6160 road that has been followed from Addingham in Wharfedale to the A684 in Wensleydale, is a road to savour. This beautiful route 32 miles (51km) long, is full of surprises for those people who are not in a hurry. The surrounding countryside is the key. There are wooded river valleys opening out into sheep-dotted pastures with farmsteads and barns anchored by a network of stone walls. The magnificent grey-white limestone edges and scars lean out over the valley sides.

Every so often, the road wriggles through attractive, mellow stone-built villages with greens and a bridge or two. Small notices in cottage windows announce some local activity or other and there is a sense of community spirit that invigorates the quality of rural life. Towards the end of its journey, the road climbs high out of long Wharfedale for a fleeting liaison with moorland at the Kidstones Pass, before descending into shy Bishopdale. The B6160 is like a good friend that one looks forward to visiting time and time again. It is a fine journey through a landscape of exceptional variety and interest; a route whose accolade should be, 'The Road to the Dales'.

Selected Car Drive

Skipton to Wharfedale and Wensleydale

Distance: 79 miles (126.4km)

From Skipton, join the A59, and proceed to Bolton Bridge. Turn left for Bolton Abbey and follow the Wharfe to Burnsall. Cross over the bridge to Hartlington, turn left and left again, then along the lane to Hebden. Turn left for Grassington for a car park and the Yorkshire Dales National Park Information Centre.

Proceed almost straight ahead on the byroad that passes Grass Wood to Conistone, and on up the dale to the village of Kettlewell, an attractive walking centre. Join the B6160 for its route to Starbotton and Buckden. Bear left for Hubberholme and enter Langstrothdale. Beyond Beckermonds, the little road climbs over the moorland wastes of Fleet Moss to meet the line of the Roman road, turn right. Take the next turn left and descend the slopes overlooking Sleddale to reach Gayle and Hawes. There is a convenient car park just before entering the town.

From Hawes on the A684, take the B6255 road on the western edge of the town, and ascend Widdale to Ribblehead, turn left. Travel down Ribblesdale to Horton-in-Ribblesdale, and continue on to Stainforth, which lies just off the main road, turn left.

An exciting and scenic byroad leaves the village and ascends the fellsides, with fine views of Penyghent and Fountains Fell. This splendid route overlooks Penyghent Gill as it descends into Littondale, turn right at Halton Gill. The fine scenery persists as the road passes through the attractive settlements of Litton and Arncliffe. As an alternative route from Arncliffe, there is an enjoyable fell road to Malham Tarn and Malham.

Bear right, cross over the bridge at Arncliffe and keeping left, continue down the dale following the River Skirfare to meet the B6160, turn right. Almost immediately, the great bulk of Kilnsey Crag rises above the road. At Threshfield, turn left and then right in the village. Travel for a short distance, and take the next right turn to the appealing village of Linton. Continue on this road through Cracoe and Rylstone, returning to Skipton.

short shaft; this marks the boundary of the ancient forest of Langstrothdale. Map reference SD 946 759.

In the village, the appropriately named Buck Inn occupies a prominent position, the last hostelry where in former times there were three. In and around the village, visitors have the choice of farmhouse, guesthouse or cottage accommodation. Buckden Pike commands an extensive view of upper Wharfedale, Langstrothdale Chase and the wild peaty wastes of Fleet Moss.

Langstrothdale

From Buckden, the secondary road

Places to Visit

Ilkley

Manor House Museum*

Castle Yard, Ilkley
Local history, archaeology and local artefacts.
☎ (01943) 600066
Open: Tue 1–5pm, Wed–Sat 11am–5pm, Sun 1–4pm.

The Grove Bookshop*

10 The Grove, Ilkley
Antiquarian and collectable books, CDs and cassettes.
☎ (01943) 609335

Bolton Abbey

Wharfedale
Picnic or stroll by the river. Wander around the ruins of the Priory, or follow the nature trails in Strid Wood. Permits for fly fishing are available from the Estate office. Tearooms & gift shops.

☎ (01756) 718009
tourism@boltonabbey.com
www.boltonabbey.com
Open: all year. Ample parking. Disabled visitors; electric & manual wheelchairs available.

Appletreewick

Parcevall Hall Gardens

Skyreholme
Magnificent hillside and woodland gardens. Pools, streams, rock gardens & terraces. Listed site of special historic interest. ☎ (01756) 720311
Open: Daliy 10am–6pm. Good Fri–Oct 31st.
www.parcevallhallgardens.co.uk

Cracoe

Jackson's of Cracoe*

On B6265, 4 miles (6.4km) from Grassington

---

follows the Wharfe into the small hamlet of **Hubberholme**. The stone bridge across the river is a favourite spot for discerning visitors, who like to watch the water gurgling and chuckling as it passes underneath. The church lies on one side of the river and the inn on the other.

The church of St Michael contains a rare polygonal font and a fascinating rood loft, dated 1558. This remarkable piece of church furniture is one of only two to survive in Yorkshire, the other is at the church of St Oswald, Flamborough. Other interesting items are

modern pews made by Robert Thompson of Kilburn. Look for the little carved mouse, his signature, which is to be found on each piece of woodwork. The well-known writer J B Priestley, (1894-1984) is buried here.

The valleys and fells of Langstrothdale Chase were colonised by Anglian settlers in the seventh century. Later, the Norsemen moved into the higher reaches of the Chase. In Norman times, many Norse settlements remained as tiny isolated farms within the hunting forest and were not allowed to expand because of the Forest Law.

Specialist sausage makers. Also sell range of local produce.
☎ (01756) 730269
Open: seven days per week.

Grassington

Upper Wharfedale Folk Museum*

The Square, Grassington
Exhibits of lead mining, minerals, craft tools, dales farming, folk lore.
☎ (01756) 752604
Open: 2-4.30pm daily, Apr– Sep (plus 10.30am–12.30pm Jul and August), 2–4.30pm Sat and Sun only, Oct–Mar.

The Dales Book Centre*

Main Street, Grassington
Local books, gallery with paintings and prints of the Dales.
☎ (01756) 753373. Open: daily Sun 11am–5pm.

Grassington Summer Festival

Wide ranging programme of arts, music, drama and local events including celebrity recitals.
☎ (01756) 753093, Festival Box Office, Festival Tickets, Grassington.

Kilnsey Park and Trout Farm

B6160 between Threshfield and Kettlewell
Trout farm with farm shop, restaurant and coffee shop. Activities include feeding giant fish, seeing the red squirrels. Nature trail, fun fishing.
☎ (01756) 752150
Open: Low 9am–dusk. High 9am–5.30pm, 7 days a week. www.kilnseypark.co.uk

Kettlewell

Scargill, Conference and Retreat Centre.
☎ (01756) 760234

Up the dale from Hubberholme, lie the attractive farm buildings and stylish packhorse bridge at **Yockenthwaite**, a perfect picture. This lovely river setting is ideal for walking, for picnicking and paddling for the children. A short distance along the river bank is a small Bronze Age stone circle. At Beckermonds, a strip of tarmac ventures along Green Field Beck to finally come to a halt surrounded by acres of dense conifer afforestation. The northerly road remains unfettered alongside the Oughtershaw Beck and climbs above lonely Nethergill and Fleet Moss at a height of 1,932ft (589m). The Roman road, Cam High Road, is touched briefly before this stalwart route descends into the sheltered narrow valley of Sleddale and on towards Gayle and Hawes in Wensleydale.

If one returns to Buckden and the B6160, it now leaves the pastoral, sylvan valley of the Wharfe and turns north to tackle the wilder landscape of the Kidstones Pass. A rough track bears left to Stake Moss and on to Semer Water whilst the main road begins the descent into Bishopdale.

5. Wensleydale

The River Ure starts life on Abbotside Common to the north-west of Hawes trickling out of the peat and rank grasses and slowly creeping down through rushes and mosses to a small rock cleft, now a dry stream bed. In winter, surface water freezes and icicles drape the sides of this eerie spot. The infant Ure emerges after a little way underground and makes its winding way down the slope. Then, in a sharp turn, it proceeds down the valley south-east of Aisgill. Quickly the stream is fed by other fellside watercourses, as it turns again to flow through Wensleydale.

Cotterdale

Eastwards beyond the Moorcock Inn, the A684 from Sedbergh crosses the Ure by Thwaite House Bridge. It then climbs to a point where a little road creeps off to the left opposite Collier House Farm. The narrow lane leads to a half-hidden little dale, and the hamlet of **Cotterdale**. There is a collection of stone-built houses that huddle together along the lane and the beckside.

This small settlement stands at the head of its own little valley and is sheltered by the broad ridges coming down from Lunds Fell, Cotterdale Common and Great Shunner Fell. The road, which passes the former Methodist chapel, leads no further than the last house. It is recorded that this remote valley was favoured by Catholic families fearing persecution in the sixteenth and early seventeenth centuries.

Up until the turn of the twentieth century, coal had been mined for some considerable time from the neighbouring fells. Galleries were driven into the fellsides to work thin seams of coal. The Pennine Way passes some of these disused workings on its route up Great Shunner Fell. This route may be reached by paths made by the miners from Cotterdale.

About half a mile from the Cotterdale lane, the A684 road crosses Cotterdale Beck at Holme Heads Bridge. There is just a short riverside walk to view **Cotter Force**, a charming stepped waterfall set in a wooded limestone gorge. The cascade is seen to best effect in springtime through the light tracery of ash trees.

The upland slopes bordering Wensleydale emphasise its green fertility. The fells do not overshadow the valley, but form perfect boundaries that are breached by side valleys linking up with the parent dale. Some join in secretly like Snaizeholme, Sleddale and Raydale; others confidently, like

Widdale, Bishopdale, Waldendale and Coverdale. There are a number of fell tops that are easily recognised as friends, when resident or visitor returns to the dale; these include Cotter End, Rottenstone Hill, Wether Hill, Addlebrough and Penhill.

In great contrast, limestone scars protrude like the gaunt white ribs of some enormous skeleton along the northern rim of the dale. This escarpment is dissected by a number of streams that descend to the main valley. Their progress is interrupted by a necklace of waterfalls, namely, Hardraw Force, Nelly Force, Eller Beck and Skell Gill.

Widdale

Leaving Cotterdale Beck behind, the tree-lined road divides, one continuing on to Hardraw, the other crossing the River Ure. Before entering the hamlet of **Appersett**, the road bends sharply over Widdale Beck. Just to the south of Appersett, a five-arched railway viaduct strides over Widdale Beck. The structure remains in restorable condition, as the viaduct is critical to the possible future restoration by the Wensleydale Railway Association of the line between Hawes and Garsdale.

From Appersett, a narrow road runs beside stony Widdale Beck to join the B6255 road from Hawes to Ingleton. **Widdale** is a quiet, lonely dale with no hamlets or villages, only a handful of farmsteads and barns. In times past it was well-wooded but the valley slopes are now covered by two areas of regimentally planted conifers.

The old road up Widdale, now a track, starts from Widdale Bridge, passes through the afforestation of Ranley

Gill and climbs steadily up to **Arten Gill Moss**, 1,726ft (526m). Widdale Fell rises to the highest point of **Great Knoutberry Hill**, 2,205ft (687m). A short distance north-east from the summit lie two lonely high-level tarns, **Widdale Great Tarn** and **Widdale Little Tarn**.

From Arten Gill Moss, the track descends alongside Arten Gill to pass beneath the famous viaduct and on to meet the Dentdale road. There is accommodation for members at the nearby youth hostel, Deeside House.

The Dentdale road twists and climbs to the moorland wastes of Newby Head. At one time, Newby Head Farm was an inn popular with drovers. Outside, large numbers of cattle, sheep and horses would be gathered and penned ready for the journey to the stock fairs.

On the way back down Widdale tracks lead up into the tiny green dale of **Snaizeholme**, no more than 3 miles (4.8km) in length. Farmsteads are dotted about this snug valley, whose steepening grassy slopes rise to Snaizeholme Fell and Dodd Fell. Meadows lie in the dale bottom and a long block of mixed wood-land along the western side of Snaizeholme Beck.

The Roman road route from Ribblehead, the Cam High Road, was the main road from the west until the Widdale turnpike was constructed. At Kidhow, the Cam Road track bears left, whilst the Roman road heads unerringly for Bainbridge and the site of a Roman fort.

Sleddale

At Ten End, the Pennine Way leaves the Cam Road and descends Rottenstone Hill. From the path, walkers will observe another narrow dale on the right-hand side of the ridge, Sleddale, a green dale merging to brown on the upper slopes. The head of the dale is split by two vigorous watercourses, Little Ing Gill and Duerley Beck, which rise from the flanks of Dodd Fell, 2,192ft (668m); both streams combine to form Gayle Beck. Three-quarters of a mile (1.2km) south of the village of Gayle lies **Aysgill Force**, which drops 30ft (9m) over a mass of curving rock. This shy waterfall may be visited by a beckside path, or approached from the Beggarmans Road at West Shaw.

This hill road climbs up the valley side to meet the Roman road, and on to Fleet Moss, at a height of 1,929ft (588m). From Sleddale it leaves all habitations and all signs of cultivation behind, until the scattered dwellings at Oughtershaw appear and another dale starts.

The village of **Gayle** lies at the foot of Sleddale just south of Hawes. The beck is the centrepiece of the village; here the houses cluster round its banks with narrow alleyways dividing them. The stream tumbles over rock shelves making a waterfall. When the water level is low, villagers can walk across the bedrock, which is open to the road on one side – a pleasant diversion for watchers on the little stone bridge and for the resident ducks.

Gayle was famous for its hand knitting in Wensleydale, with this cottage industry going back to the sixteenth century. As in Dentdale, men, women and children knitted. A manufacturing industry came to Gayle in the eighteenth century, namely 1784 when a cotton spinning mill became established. Later, there followed a short period of flax spinning. Through much of the nineteenth century the mill spun wool for the hand-knitting industry. In 1878 the water wheel was replaced by a turbine and the mill was converted to a saw mill.

Gayle Mill took part in the BBC 'Restoration' series and has greatly benefited from the resulting publicity. Phase I in the building restoration was completed in 2005. Phase II included the refurbishment of the mill's interior, and Phase III involves the restoration of the leat and reinstallation of the old turbines and the installation of a new turbine with a modern alternator. .

Hawes

On the road from Gayle to Hawes lies the **Wensleydale Creamery** with its visitor centre and restaurant. From here **Hawes** is very quickly reached and a convenient car park will be found on the edge of town. Pedestrians can take the excellent footpath beyond Gayle that leads into the middle of the town. Hawes is a popular centre for the upper dale with a dual role as an important market town and a holiday base for tourists. Traffic entering from the east has to negotiate a narrow winding street leading to the broad market place.

Small alleyways lead off the main street, which has a pattern of houses wedged between shops. Gayle Beck enters the centre of the town as a waterfall by a bridge; an impressive cascade of white water in wet weather. The town is cradled between the hills at an altitude of 787ft (240m) above sea level and is one of the highest market towns in Britain. Like Gayle, Hawes was a busy centre for the knitting industry carried out in the town's houses.

Hawes was granted a market charter in 1705 and its wide main street must have experienced a great deal of commotion as livestock was sold there on market days. This continued until 1887 when the auction mart was built. Nowadays, market day is on Tuesday.

The church of St Margaret, 1851, is a large church in the Decorated style with a tower. It stands in a commanding position overlooking the houses. A chapel of ease existed here in 1480 and was part of the parish of Aysgarth. The present building was built to replace a smaller church that stood lower down the churchyard. A programme of restoration was begun in 1930, with the pleasing inclusion of good memorial woodwork – partly dated 1932-9.

The final day of the full passenger rail service along Wensleydale was April 24 1954. The passenger service between

Ancient craft

Ropemaking is another traditional craft carried out in Hawes at W R Outhwaite and Son. Traditional products, such as halters and cow ties, continue to be made, together with a wide range of rope and twine-based craft items, dog leads, skipping ropes and plant hangers. Visitors can observe the modern ropemaking processes from a walk-in viewing corridor. Particular products that catch the eye are church bell ropes with coloured wool sallies and decorative bannister ropes.

Garsdale and Hawes survived until sixteenth March 1959. The station yard at Hawes was acquired by the Yorkshire Dales National Park Authority for use as a car park. The station building in the Derby Gothic style, now houses the Tourist Information Centre and the National Park Centre.

The former goods warehouse is the location of a very special museum. The **Dales Countryside Museum** received a boost from a collection of bygone implements and utensils donated by the well-known local authors and historians, Marie Hartley and Joan Ingleby. The museum has gone from strength to strength, increasing its collection to a fascinating array of implements and an absorbing insight into traditional Dales crafts and occupations. The exhibits include: a timewalk, a farmhouse kitchen, an activity area, local industries – mining, textiles, hand knitting, craftsmen – carpenter, bootmaker, tailor, blacksmith, farming past and present, butter and cheese making.

A variety of scenic routes invite the motorist to explore the neighbouring remoter dales and hill passes, namely: Widdale, Sleddale, Raydale, Bishopdale, Butter Tubs, Oxnop Scar, Kidstones, Fleet Moss and The Fleak.

Hawes caters well for residents and visitors alike, with a range of individual shops and services – country clothing, foodstuffs, outdoor gear, books and maps, crafts and tearooms. Accommodation facilities include a modern youth hostel on the edge of town and a number of hotels, inns, guesthouses and bed and breakfast establishments.

Just over the bridge in Hardraw, a

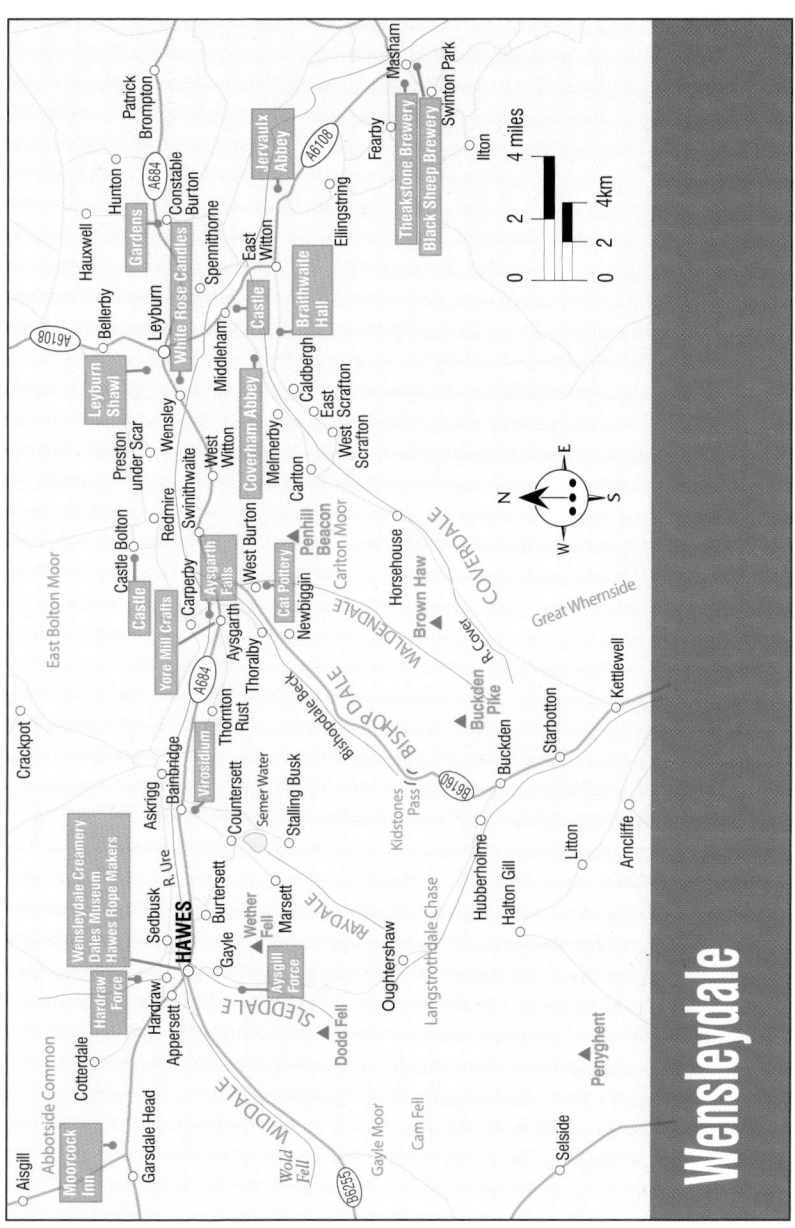

track bears right, now the route of the Pennine Way, and climbs to the summit of Great Shunner Fell, 2,349ft (716m). Along the fellside, other routes lead to Cotterdale and Fossdale. On these open rugged moorland slopes, numerous pits were established in the eighteenth and nineteenth centuries for the extraction of coal.

Along the road east of Hardraw, there

England's highest waterfall

From Hawes a minor road crosses the Ure at Haylands Bridge and meets a secondary road running along the north side of the valley to the tiny village of **Hardraw**. Out of sight behind the Green Dragon Inn is the highest waterfall in England; a spectacular leap of almost 99ft (30m). It lies in a magnificent setting at the head of a wooded limestone gorge and is reached through the inn itself (admission charge).

This sheltered amphitheatre was found to have remarkable acoustic properties and round about 1881, a band concert was organised. Soon an annual event, it drew famous brass bands from far and wide, even Besses o' th' Barn and the Black Dyke Mills bands and attracted train loads of visitors. Then in 1929, the competitions finished and the narrow valley fell silent. Happily, the last few years have seen a revival and each September the sound of silver and brass band music can once more be heard.

is a left turn to Simonstone and High Shaw. The route, one of the ways from Wensleydale to Swaledale, climbs up to the Butter Tubs Pass at 1,726ft (526m). The **Butter Tubs** are two groups of potholes on either side of the road. These striking fissures have fluted sides something like a butter tub and have been created by the action of water dissolving the limestone.

Bainbridge

Returning to Hawes and travelling eastwards along the A684, a narrow lane bears right to the hill-slope shieling of **Burtersett**. The houses of the village huddle tightly together before a sharp bend all overlooked by the prominent crest of Yorburgh, 1,686ft (514m).

In the nineteenth century, Burtersett was a busy and industrious place due to its stone quarrying. Levels were driven deep into the hillside and ponies brought out large slabs on a tramway.

The stone was rough dressed in sheds and then taken to Hawes Station in wagons pulled by horses. From the ancient heart of the village, the lane climbs steadily up to the line of the Roman road from Bainbridge and then descends steeply to the hamlet of Countersett in Raydale.

From Burtersett, another byroad snakes down to the A684, which continues into **Bainbridge**, one of the most spacious and pleasant villages in the Dales. The first element of the name is probably derived from the Old Norse being 'straight' and may refer to the short, but direct course of the River Bain. This watercourse, just two miles long, is the shortest river in England and enters Bainbridge with a flourish of falling water. From Bain Bridge there is a view of limestone shelves or terraces down which the river cascades.

The Rose and Crown Inn sits at the edge of the extensive village green with its ancient stocks. The inn dates from 1445 and is recorded in the parish

Horn blowing

The tradition of blowing the forest horn is part of an ancient custom that dates from the thirteenth century. From September to Shrovetide, three long notes were blown at 9 o'clock in the evening, to guide travellers making the difficult journey through the dark, intimidating depths of the Wensleydale Forest.

The present instrument, a great buffalo horn, dates from 1864 and is kept at the Rose and Crown Inn. The original horn is now at Bolton Castle. Many of the horn-blowers have come from the Metcalfe family of Wensleydale.

register in 1500 – 'the housewives of Bainbridge were tippling on the Sabbath at the Rose and Crown instead of attending Divine Service'. Narrow byroads, one on each side of the River Bain leave the village at its southern end on winding journeys towards Semer Water and secretive Raydale.

Brough Hill rises above Bainbridge, and although only of modest elevation, is in the right spot for a commanding view along the dale. One sees a landscape of hay meadows, cattle pastures and the smooth lines of lynchets brought into sharper focus by the evening sunlight. Running across them are the resolute lines of stone walls tying the fields together. Dotted here and there are the stout, warm-coloured stone barns capped with Yoredale flags. Between these features, peep the gables, roofs and church tower of the village

Roman remains

Brough Hill was once the site of a small, but strategically important Roman fort of **Virosidum**. The first fort was founded by Agricola, and was followed by a succession of stone forts. It was constructed in the typical Roman playing card shape, that is of a rectangular design with rounded corners; it had accommodation for a cohort of 500 men. Evidence records that the site was occupied from 2000 AD to the end of the fourth century.

The line of the outer walls, four entrances and a chapel have been located. Details have been recorded of several headquarters buildings, and two third-century building inscriptions have been found inside the camp – one relating to the construction of an annexe wall to the east by the sixth cohort of Nervians, 205-8 AD. It would be courteous to enquire locally for permission to walk on the site of the Roman fort.

This remote fort in Wensleydale was the focal point for Roman roads running out of the dale. There is the stirring sight of Cam High Road striking south-westerly in a straight course over Wether Fell to Ribblesdale, and two roads to the south, High Lane and Busk Lane, combine to form a route over the wastes of Stake Moss towards Wharfedale.

of Askrigg – all combined to form a perfect and characteristic picture of the Yorkshire Dales.

Raydale

The westerly byroad from Bainbridge, following the River Bain into **Raydale**, runs initially along the line of the Roman road. It turns off passing Semerdale Hall to the village of **Countersett**. This settlement is situated in a hillside hollow at the northern end of Semer Water. It is a quiet hamlet of old stone houses set back from the road.

Countersett Hall, 1650, is a fine house with a large porch. It has a three-sectioned window with the middle light raised higher than the others. Its most famous occupant was Richard Robinson, who in the seventeenth century established the Quaker faith in Wensleydale. Boar Inn Farm, as its name implies, was once an inn.

A road then continues up the dale passing Carr End Farm, the birthplace in 1712 of John Fothergill, a Quaker and influential physician. The road passes over Marsett's old stone bridge to reach Raydale Grange and Raydale House. The latter dwelling, which occupies a fine position looking down the valley, was largely rebuilt in the nineteenth century, but still retains some seventeenth-century parts. In 1617, it was besieged for four days by Sir Thomas Metcalfe over a dispute of ownership. Help came for the occupants and the Metcalfes were routed.

Returning to Countersett, a road descends to **Semer Water**, where there is a parking area, and continues to the hillside hamlet of Stalling Busk – 'the stallion's bush'. This ancient settlement is a quaint place, with no natural centre, where ways cross at various angles. In recent times, dilapidated dwellings have been restored and refurbished. The tiny church of St Matthew, 1908-9, is an architecturally modern building with its roof supported by scissor-beams.

From the hamlet a track continues to climb following the contours of Cragdale Water, with a comprehensive view of Raydale. Looking westwards beyond the massed ranks of conifers, distant Bardale Beck eventually emerges after a long moorland journey. The rough track continues its ascent to the heights of Stake Moss 1,831ft (558m) from where it descends to the Kidstone Pass separating upper Wharfedale from Bishopdale.

There is a direct return to Bainbridge down the dale, where a side turning to the right only leads to Carpley Green. This lane climbs beneath the scar-rimmed hill of Addlebrough, 1,562ft (476m) – a miniature Table Mountain. Bronze Age people built their homes and enclosures on the southern slopes of the hill. Two other items of interest are the Devil's Stone and a summit burial mound – from the top there is a splendid view along Wensleydale. A right of way starts at Carpley Green, passes across the southern slopes of Addlebrough and descends to the village of Thornton Rust. There are many examples of early settlements across the wide area of upland south of Addlebrough, between Wensleydale and Bishopdale.

Askrigg

From the north end of the green at Bainbridge a byroad passes Yorebridge

House and crosses the Ure at Yore Bridge to meet the road running along the northern side of the dale. Clues to the existence of an abbey in the vicinity are found on the map, namely, Grange and Abbey Head. A little higher up Grange Beck lies Coleby Hall, a manor house dating from 1633. This old house may well contain some of the stone from the abbey.

Close by at the hamlet of Bowbridge is an ancient bridge with ribbed arches, which by tradition is attributed to the monks of Fors Abbey. This Cistercian house was established hereabouts in 1145, but the land was infertile and the weather inclement. After eleven years the place was abandoned in favour of Jervaulx.

It is only a short journey from the Bainbridge road junction to the distinctive village of **Askrigg** which was an ancient market and trade centre. Its market charter was granted in 1587 by Queen Elizabeth I but its importance declined when the turnpike was constructed through Hawes. From Askrigg's point of view it was a blessing, as it is now quietly settled away from the main A684.

Up to the mid-eighteenth century, the village was known for knitting, dyeing, brewing and lead trading. Agriculture was important then as it is today. Knitting was first done by hand and then later in mills. The hand-knitters used two needles and a knitting sheath, a hollow, carved piece of wood fixed in a belt and used to support a third needle. One mill, Low Mill, is now an Outdoor Pursuits Centre and includes an extension designed to suit the needs of disabled people. At the end of the nineteenth century, clock-making was introduced using mainly German movements. The production was chiefly grandfather clocks, notable for their curious designs and the odd tools used.

A survivor of the market days is the stepped market cross set in a cobbled area outside the church. Close by, near

Herriot connection

The King's Arms in Askrigg has appeared as 'The Drovers Arms' in the TV series, *All Creatures Great and Small*, based on the stories by James Herriot. TV viewers will recognise the house opposite the market cross as 'Skeldale House', used as Herriot's home and surgery in the series. Filming was often done in Askrigg and in the neighbouring dales of Coverdale and Swaledale.

James Herriot was the pseudonym of Alf Wight, who grew up in Glasgow and qualified as a veterinary surgeon. His first post was as an assistant in a Thirsk practice, where he remained with the exception of war-time service in the RAF. Herriot's literary success was based on his ability to capture the spirit of a place, the traditional everyday life in the Dales and his love of its landscape in all seasons.

Museum: **The World of James Herriot**, 23, Kirkgate, Thirsk.

Selected Car Drive

Leyburn to Wensleydale and Upper Wharfedale

Distance: 62 miles (99km)

Leave Leyburn westwards on the A684 to the village of Wensley and on entering the village, turn right towards Redmire. At an extended crossroads continue ahead to meet another road. Proceed straight on to Castle Bolton. Turn left by the castle, descend to a junction, turn right and travel on to Carperby. At the end of the village turn left down to Aysgarth Falls. Return towards Carperby and turn left.

The road continues along the northern edge of the dale through Woodhall to Askrigg, which was often featured in the Herriot TV series. Travel on to Hardraw for a view of Hardraw Force. Beyond Hardraw, the road meets the A684, turn left, and continue through Appersett to Hawes. Proceed through the town on the main road to Bainbridge affording an opportunity to enter into secret Raydale and enjoy quiet Semer Water, return to Bainbridge.

The A684 heads on to Aysgarth. On entering the village, take the second turn on the right. This byroad descends to Thoralby, and continues on to meet the B6160, turn right. Travel on up Bishopdale, with its scattering of farmsteads, to reach the summit of the Kidstones Pass. Descend into Buckden and follow the dale down to Kettlewell. Turn left past the Bluebell Hotel, and then take a sharp left turn at the start of the steep ascent out of Wharfedale up Park Rash. From Tor Dike the road descends into lonely Coverdale. Pass through the villages of Horsehouse and Carlton, not deviating, but with an opportunity to visit Coverham Bridge and Braithwaite Hall by taking a byroad to the right. Otherwise, keep straight on across the racing gallops to the ancient market town of Middleham with its impressive castle. Turn left on to the A6108, cross Middleham Bridge, returning to Leyburn.

to the village pump, is preserved the iron ring, where bulls were tied for the once popular entertainment of bull baiting. The church of St Oswald, which dates from about 1446, is a large stately building occupying a prominent position. Two fine features are the vault of the tower with its bevelled ribs stretching across like a porch, and the splendid nave ceiling with strong moulded beams. Some restoration took place in 1770 and 1853.

Some houses around the church have decorated door lintels, one dated 1687, another 1694. The attractive, gently climbing main street of tall, handsome eighteenth and early nineteenth-century houses, contains the King's Arms dated 1767. One of the great characters in Wensleydale lived in what is now the hotel. John Platt built it as a private house and stables

Wensleydale Railway

The Wensleydale Railway Association was established in 1990 to investigate the reinstatement of a passenger rail link between Garsdale on the Settle – Carlisle line and Northallerton on the East Coast Main Line. At present, the only remaining track on the 40 mile route is the 22 miles linking the East Coast Main Line with a railhead at Redmire. Services run 7 days a week throughout the year between Leeming Bar and Redmire, with station stops at Bedale, Finghall and Leyburn.

Information Line: ☎ 08454 505474

Websites:www.wensleydalerailway.com/

www.wensleydale railwayassociation.com

and lived there until his death in 1785. A great racing man, he started life as a jockey at Newmarket and later became a successful breeder.

Askrigg is now well-known for its annual art exhibition held in the village hall during the second week in August. Most of the artists actually live in or near the village, and the event has become a significant feature of the cultural life in the upper part of Wensleydale.

At the east end of the village the tall town houses have given way to cottages. At a sharp bend, a byroad continues straight on climbing steeply with a most pleasing view looking back over the roof tops of Askrigg. For many visitors, this attractive route with bends and sharp gradients is the preferred route into Swaledale. In fact, the road divides into two ways, the westerly approach past Oxnop Scar towards Muker, and the easterly route, which crosses The Fleak moors towards Healaugh and Grinton.

Oxnop is a spectacular limestone scarp, and the heather moorland eastwards contains Summer Lodge Tarn, and numerous disused lead mines, tips, disused shafts, pits, shake holes, swallow holes and grouse butts.

On the Woodhall road from Askrigg, $1^{1}/_{4}$ mile (2km) eastwards, lies Nappa Hall. This is a fortified manor house of 1460, with a single floored hall flanked by battlemented towers, one high one low; it was probably built by Thomas Metcalfe. The building is now a farmhouse and is not open to the public. A right of way passes the Hall from the Woodhall road en-route to Nappa Mill and Worton Bridge.

Aysgarth

From Askrigg, a minor road runs south to cross the Ure at Worton Bridge and into the hamlet of Worton. Crossing the A684, the byroad climbs up to Worton Scar, and travels along the edge of a wooded scar to Thornton Rust. This quiet village looks out on the dale, and the fells climb up from the main street. The byroad continues along the fellside terrace before descending to join the A684 and the village of Aysgarth.

Cheese Making

Wensleydale cheese was first made by the Cistercian monks of Jervaulx Abbey from ewes' milk using a special recipe brought with them from France. Following the Dissolution cheese production was carried on by the local farmers' wives. In the late nineteenth century a local cheese factor, who travelled the dale buying the farm cheeses, decided to purchase the milk instead. He wanted to produce a cheese of consistent quality and so a dairy was established in Hawes to make the cheese on a more commercial scale.

Twice since then the factory has been threatened with closure, first in 1935 when a consortium of local farmers, led by Kit Calvert, staged a rescue bid so successfully that the Milk Marketing Board bought the business back. Then in 1992, surprisingly, history repeated itself. A management buy-out was agreed and once again Wensleydale cheese was being made in Hawes. Since then Wensleydale Creamery has been very successful with help and support from those great enthusiasts of Wensleydale cheese, Wallace and Gromit.

Today Wensleydale cheese is noted for its creamy smooth texture and

delicacy of flavour – made from the milk of cows grazed on the local limestone pastures. Every day 6,000 gallons of fresh local milk are delivered to the dairy. The milk is poured into vats and a starter culture added to sour the milk and produce the curds. Salt is added to enhance the flavour and help preserve the cheese while also expelling excess moisture. The curds are cut by hand, a very skilful process, to give the cheese its own particular characteristics. After draining, the cheese is wrapped in muslin and stored to ripen and mature. At the end of the day 3 tonnes of cheese will have been produced.

The original white Wensleydale cheese is a lightly pressed cheese with a fine cut curd and high moisture content. It takes about three weeks to mature. Blue Wensleydale, on the other hand, is matured for six months. From the original two varieties, 'white' and 'blue' Wensleydale, production has expanded to include smoked cheeses and those with added ingredients such as fruit and herbs.

The dairy has been developed to include a visitor centre where one can tour the dairy and view the cheese being made, learn something of its history and, after sampling the finished product, purchase a favourite to take home.

Above: A view eastwards down Wensleydale from Woodhall

Opposite: Cheesemaking at the Wensleydale Creamery, Hawes

The village of **Aysgarth** itself lies on the A684 but its many visitors take the byroad on the east side of the village. The Palmer Flatt Hotel takes its name from the practice of pilgrims returning from the Holy Land during the Crusades bearing the palms, and seeking sanctuary at a hospice that was on the present site. This road leads past the church, and descends a minor hairpin bend to reach the River Ure and its famous waterfalls.

The church of St Andrew is a large, mainly Victorian church of 1866; only the lower part of the tower is medieval. The interior contains a very fine rood-screen, thought to have been given by the monks of Jervaulx Abbey, and to have been executed by the Ripon Carvers. A reading desk with decorated ends, note the poppy heads and little animals, is also thought to have been connected to Jervaulx.

The ancient stone bridge across the river was originally a narrow pack-horse way, said to date from 1539 but widened. Yore Mill by the bridge has had an interesting and varied history. Originally built as a worsted mill in 1784, it was converted into spinning cotton, rebuilt in 1850 after a fire, and then utilised as a wool mill. Amongst its output were bolts of red cloth to make shirts for Garibaldi's army and Balaclava hats for soldiers in the Crimea. Later on it became a flour mill and remained in use until 1967.

The byroad from Aysgarth Falls gradually ascends from the wooded valley of the Ure to reach green pastures bounded by drystone walls. Away to the north-east rises unmistakably the tall keep of Bolton Castle nestling against the hill slopes. **Carperby** is a long village stretched out along the Redmire road. It was long ago in 1303 that the village was granted a market charter, but all that remains of those bygone days, is the impressive seven-stepped market cross, inscribed 1674.

The village contains a large Meeting House of the Society of Friends, 1864, a rather plain chapel-like building. There is a Methodist Chapel, 1820, and the Wheatsheaf Inn of Herriot fame. Returning to the A684 at Aysgarth,

Aysgarth Falls

There are three separate cascades, the Upper, Middle and Lower Falls. The Upper Falls lie on the western side of the bridge and can be viewed from the footpath. Here, the River Ure tumbles over an impressive broad semi-circle of rock. The Middle and Lower Falls can be approached by paths through Freeholders' Wood. This ancient area of woodland is a remaining part of the Forest of Wensleydale, a protected and delightful stretch of woodland full of hazel trees, oaks, brambles, whitethorn and wild flowers.

As the byroad ascends from the river, the National Park Centre and car park lie on the left and just beyond on the right-hand side is the former Aysgarth Falls Station. The latter has recently been purchased by the Wensleydale Railway Association with a view to opening the line from Redmire to Aysgarth, with a stop at Castle Bolton.

two byroads twist southwards, one over a shoulder of land descending to the village of **Thoralby**, and the other crossing Bishopdale Beck towards the village of West Burton at the foot of Waldendale.

Bishopdale

There is a fine view of Bishopdale from the top of the hill before the descent into Thoralby, set on a hillside terrace above Bishopdale Beck. Attractive stone houses line the street to Town Head before it becomes a track. The inn is situated on the street to Town Head and the village shop lies opposite the road junction. This splendid emporium stocks all manner of things and will also bring one up to date concerning the local teams in the Wensleydale Football League.

Bishopdale is a pleasant, lush green valley, approximately 7 miles (11km) long from Hestholme Bridge to the summit of Kidstones Pass. It is a long straight dale, with a flat valley floor containing Bishopdale Beck. The only other settlement, apart from Thoralby, is Newbiggin on the southern side of the dale. A consistent scattering of farmsteads lies on the lower slopes, some like West New House, which is a fine example of a Pennine long house. This farmstead built in 1635, has mullioned windows, and the house and barn form a continuous unit under one roof

As one progresses up the dale, the steepening sides are well covered with blocks and strips of woodland and in the valley bottom trees overhang the beck. A procession of parallel streams drain both flanks of the glacially formed U-shaped valley and enter Bishopdale Beck. The dale road is the splendidly scenic B6160 that climbs over Kidstones and down into Wharfedale – 'The Road to the Dales' (see page 102).

Two lanes lead off the B6160 to the village of **Newbiggin**. Opposite one of the lanes is the Street Head Inn established in 1730 and a relic of the coaching days; a hostelry of oak beams and charm. From the village there are rights of way leading to Wasset Fell, Waldendale and West Burton. Thoralby is also an excellent walking centre, where paths and tracks lead to Aysgarth Moor, Stake Allotments, along Bishopdale to Dale Head, Aysgarth and Thornton Rust.

Waldendale

West Burton stands just off the B6160 Bishopdale road at the junction of Bishopdale and Waldendale and lies at the foot of the Height of Hazely, the higher western end of Penhill. It is a beautiful village with houses climbing up both sides of an almost oblong hilly green. West Burton was once an important market town formerly meriting an ancient market cross. However, the present village cross of 1820 was restored in 1889.

The Walden Beck flows along the eastern confines of the village. Here waterfalls formed when melting glaciers deepened the valley. At the north of the village, a packhorse bridge crosses the beck, and leads on to a track that continues along the lower slopes of Penhill to Middleham Moor.

Waldendale is a smaller version of Bishopdale; it is a shy, secret valley unused to crowds. The dale belongs to those who love quiet places and lonely ways. Apart from West Burton there is no other village and the valley road divides, with the shorter eastern route becoming a track and then a footpath. From this side of the dale, a track and bridleway turns off at Cote, climbs above Thupton Gill and descends to Carlton-in-Coverdale. Further on up the dale another bridleway leaves the valley and crosses Fleensop Moor to Horsehouse and Braidley in Coverdale. Fleensop Colliery on the moor top was once the centre of an extensive area of coal mining. This desolate spot has numerous shafts and tips dotting the bleak wastes.

Both valley roads link the sprinkling of isolated farmsteads with the westerly route eventually crossing Walden Beck and terminating at Kentucky House Farm, Walden Head. From here a right of way climbs the dun-coloured moorland slopes of Deepdale Head. Amongst this wide expanse of moor grass, rush, cotton grass and peat, a number of gills drain the eastern flanks of Buckden Pike, 2,303ft (702m), before combining as Walden Beck. The path continues over Starbotton Fell and down into Wharfedale, with an alternative route over Buckden Pike and a descent to the village of Buckden.

West Witton and Wensley

Returning to the A684 the large village of **West Witton** is soon reached. Originally, there was a Norman church, but this church of St Bartholomew was built in 1875-6. The village lies at the foot of Penhill and in past times many of the dwellings were inhabited

The River Ure near Hawes, National Park

Left: 14th century Bolton Castle dominates the Wensleydale village of Castle Bolton

Below: Cowslips in Wensley Park, Wensley, Wensleydale

Bottom: Ivy Scar near Woodhall, Wensleydale

Templar's chapel

Just east of Aysgarth, on the main road lies the hamlet of Swinithwaite. A track leaves the hamlet and climbs to a line of trees. Bear right along the edge of the woodland to the location of the Templar's Chapel with the remains consisting of a few courses of masonry. In the interior are some steps to the sanctuary, the base of an altar, a stone piscina and two small stone coffins. The structure itself dates from the early thirteenth century, and larger coffins, now outside the walls, held skeletons when they were discovered. Another path to the Templars' chapel starts just to the west of Temple Farm. Follow a farm track to the top end of the field. Beyond a gate the way climbs through trees and further on a stile to the left gives access to the site.

by miners.

A byroad leaves West Witton and climbs up to Middleham High Moor, where a right of way to the west leads to **Penhill Beacon**, 1,686ft (514m) and an OS survey pillar at 1,726ft (526m) on the summit of Penhill Scar. This prominent hill is well known as a shapely barrier commanding extensive views across Wensleydale and dividing Waldendale and Coverdale. The beacon was chosen for the lighting of a fire forming one of a chain throughout England.

The main road crosses the River Ure over the four-arched Wensley Bridge, and enters the village of the same name. **Wensley** was once an important market town that was granted a market charter by Edward I in 1306; it was influential enough to give its name to the whole valley. Sadly, as recorded in the church register in 1563, the community was struck down by a disastrous plague. The place never recovered and its market trade eventually went to Askrigg and Leyburn.

The settlement is a charming estate village for Bolton Hall. From the en-trance gates the drive passes into park-land, and indeed, is a right of way that continues beyond the Hall to Redmire. Bolton Hall is a handsome house, roughcast with stone dressings; it faces out across the valley with fine views. The Hall was first built in 1678 taking the place of ruined Bolton Castle. The house was rebuilt in 1902 after being destroyed by fire.

The church of Holy Trinity in Wensley is of considerable architectural interest. The earliest part is the chancel 1245, Norman, with lancet windows and dogtooth designs. The church is very rich in furnishings with a two-decker eighteenth-century pulpit, a font and cover of 1662 and a wooden box with a Gothic panel. The poppy heads and little animals on the old pews and chancel stalls may have been executed by the Ripon carvers. There is the Scrope family pew, late seventeenth century, and a splendid rood screen, said to have come from Easby Abbey.

Redmire and Castle Bolton

A byroad leaves Wensley for the village of Redmire, with a lane branching off towards **Preston-under-Scar**. It passes the former Wensley station, and the site of the Keld Head Mine smelt mills in Gillfield Wood. The lead mines on the moors to the north were some of the richest in the dale and the last to be exploited. Levels, shafts, tips and chimneys are spread over a wide area of moorland, a scene of desolation now softened by natural growth.

Preston-under-Scar lies under a rocky crag, a former mining village that occupies a splendid position on a hillside shelf with magnificent views of the valley. Paths leave this pleasant unpretentious village heading in all directions.

Below Preston-under-Scar, the road continues to the charming village of **Redmire,** tucked under the hill and lying close to the wooded course of Apedale Beck. Many old stone houses surrounded the green on which proudly stands the venerable Redmire oak. Redmire, like the neighbouring villages, was home to many of the miners who worked the rich veins of lead that criss-crossed the moorland to the north.

The church of St Mary stands alone half a mile (0.8km) south-east of the village. It is a small plain structure with a bellcote, but has Norman masonry. Just to the west of Redmire, a byroad turns north to the village of **Castle Bolton**. The settlement grew up at the same time as the castle, and everything fits beautifully into place – the impressively outstanding castle, the attractive church, cottages and green.

Bolton Castle, which was used for

Burning ceremony

In West Witton, each year on the first Saturday after St Bartholomew's Day, in late August, is enacted the ceremony of 'Burning Owd Bartle'. At dusk a life-size effigy of 'Owd Bartle' is carried at the head of a procession along the whole length of the village. The crowd chants the following rhyme:

At Pen Hill Crags he tore his rags;

At Hunter's Thorn he blew his horn;

At Capplebank Stee he brake his knee;

At Grisgill Beck he brake his neck;

At Wadham's End he couldn't fend;

At Grisgill End he made his end.

The crowd stops at intervals, where the rhyme is said, followed by a loud shout. At the end the effigy, of sacking stuffed with straw and with a painted face, is placed on a pile of wood and set on fire. This is the signal for fun and jollity that continues for some considerable time.

History of Bolton Castle

Bolton Castle was built in 1379 for Richard le Scrope, Lord Chancellor of England to Richard II. Even from a distance the castle influences the valley and does not have the look of a ruin. It is an imposing type of fourteenth-century military architecture that was certainly intended to guard Wensleydale. There are four mighty corner towers and four sections of living quarters surrounding an enclosed courtyard. The castle stands nearly to its full height, except for the north-east tower, and still conveys a sense of strength and power.

The great halls and galleries supported by massive oak beams, transported into the dale, have walls nine feet thick. The medieval atmosphere lingers everywhere, for it was here that Mary Queen of Scots was imprisoned from July 1568 to January 1569.

The castle was garrisoned for Charles I against the Parliamentarians and held until November 1645. Afterwards, the castle was made untenable, resulting in the collapse of the north-east tower in 1761. The chapel, consecrated in 1399, lies on the second floor of the south range.

the location of the film *Elizabeth,* is open to visitors and can be explored from dungeon to battlement. The very large fourteenth-century Guest Hall is utilised as an inviting tea-room. The present owner, Harry Orde-Powlett has restored two of the castle gardens along medieval lines. There is a herb garden and a walled garden stocked with grape vines.

The church of St Oswald is of the late fourteenth century, small and unpretentious. It has a small tower and a nave and chancel in one. The seats for the priests, the sedilia, are divided by cross walls.

Leyburn

From Castle Bolton, a byroad crosses Apedale Beck, and continues straight ahead towards Wensley. It is then a short journey along the A684 to reach **Leyburn**, an important road junction

and meeting place, with the A684 joining for a short distance with the A6108. It has become the main town of Wensleydale and its houses and shops ring the wide market square.

Leyburn's market charter was granted by Charles I and market day is on Friday. There is also an important auction mart in the town. Two buildings of note grace the Market Place; one is the Town Hall, 1856, now turned into shops and the other is the Midland Bank, 1875. The church of St Peter and St Paul, RC, 1835, is situated at the north end of the town. The interior contains an altar with large framing, box pews and a west gallery. The church of St Matthew, 1868, has a tower and lies east of the square.

Two houses worthy of note are Thornborough Hall (Council Offices) and Leyburn Hall. The former building was originally the home of the Roman Catholic Thornborough family, and

*Above: Looking eastwards down Wensleydale
from Penhill Beacon*

Left: Mill Gill Force, Askrigg

Below: In a Yorkshire garden

Famous residents

Middleham is famous for the memory of the great people of England, kings, queens and barons who lived in the Middleham Castle. In 1270, Ralph Fitz Randolph's daughter married into the Neville family, and her son became the first Lord Neville. One of the many great men in the Neville family was Richard, Earl of Warwick, known as 'The Kingmaker'. Warwick, who lived at Middleham in regal state, was killed at the Battle of Barnet in 1471.

Edward IV gave the castle to this brother, Richard Duke of Gloucester, who became Richard III. After the death of Richard III at the Battle of Bosworth in 1485, the reign of the Plantagenets ended and the power and position of Middleham waned.

still contains a priesthole and hidden cellars.

Leyburn Hall lies just off the Market Place with open views to the south. The façade is attractive, with a five-bay centre. The one-bay pavilions are probably early nineteenth century, but the remainder of the house is 1740-50. Frances l'Anson, the 'sweet lass of Richmond Hill' was born in Leyburn.

Middleham

From Leyburn, the A6108 descends Mighten's Bank and crosses the River Ure by the Middleham Bridge. The castellated framework points to an earlier suspension bridge. A tablet records the architects, Hanson and Welch, and the bridge was built in 1829.

Beyond, the road climbs into the little town of **Middleham**, where the houses are ranged mainly round two squares. This used to be the capital of the area, and the administrative centre for the Forest of Wensleydale. In each of the squares is a market cross; the one in the Swinemarket is called the Board Cross. This stands on a platform and consists of two stone blocks, one holding the badly eroded figure of a beast; the Warwick bear or the boar of Richard III.

The town has an interesting variety of dwellings; with a number of cottages ranging down the hill, and a row standing in front of the castle, where the outer baileys would have been. Next to the church is the Rectory, built in 1752 with three widely spaced bays.

The odd-shaped market square in the centre of Middleham contains a fine Georgian house with five bays, early eighteenth-century. There are also an interesting number of early and later nineteenth-century buildings with a range of bow windows and wide bays. Near the castle, there is another five-bay residence with a Tuscan porch.

The church of St Mary and St Alkelda is mainly of the fourteenth century, its tower housing a fireplace made from old tombstones. A memorial window to Richard III was placed in the south aisle in 1934 by the 'White Boar Society', and depicts Richard, his Queen and their son.

There has been a fortress at Middleham since the Norman Conquest. The early motte and bailey earthworks can be seen just south of the present **Middleham Castle** site. A Norman keep was built in the 1170s, and in the twelfth and thirteenth centuries a curtain wall was constructed with angle towers. Later additions included a chapel in the keep and living quarters round a courtyard. Close to the north-east tower is

Harsh journey

For hundred's of years the road from Coverham to Kettlewell was the main coach route from London to Richmond. The mind boggles at the thought of a coach and horses struggling up the one-in-five gradient of Park Rash. It was more than likely that passengers had to get out and push the coach up the earthen road. The surrounding desolate country was no place for either coach or travellers to meet with any kind of mishap.

the fourteenth-century gatehouse, and the tall keep was approached by an outer stone stairway, no longer in situ, but the doorway is still observable on the first floor. The south part of the castle contained a brew-house, a horse-mill and an oven, all these date from the fourteenth century.

In 1985, an exquisite piece of medieval jewellery a fifteenth-century gold pendant, was discovered in the vicinity of the castle. The Middleham jewel, as it became known, is now housed in the Yorkshire Museum in York. It is interesting to speculate whether it belonged to Richard III or one of his family. A replica of the pendant is now on display in the visitor centre at the castle.

Coverdale

To the west of Middleham lies Middleham Low Moor, which has become a training centre for racehorses. The open grassy moorland and pasture is eminently suitable for this and one will see strings of horses and their attendant jockeys, stable lads and apprentices at the gallops. The byroad leading to the gallops continues past Pinker's Pond, and bears left to Coverham Bridge over the River Cover. The bridge has an unusual pointed arch and parapets, and is of pre-Reformation age. Here, a narrow lane leads down beneath the inner gateway to the remains of **Coverham Abbey**. The Premonstratensian Canons moved here in 1212-13 from Swainby. It was never a large establishment, and only a little of it exists with some parts now combined with other buildings.

The most conspicuous piece is two arches of the arcade between the nave and south aisle. A nearby nineteenth-century house contains a low nine-light window from the abbey guesthouse, and a Georgian house, now called Coverham Abbey has effigies of knights and many other fragments of thirteenth and early fourteenth-century work.

Just north of Coverham Bridge stands the thirteenth-century church of Holy Trinity; it is quite alone, with no settlement nearby. The chancel is Early English and the south aisle is early fourteenth century. The church was heavily restored in 1854. Note the Anglo-Saxon stone with a carving of two figures cut into the lintel of the south doorway.

From Coverham two parallel roads run on each side of the river. The southern-most road passes close by to Caldbergh and East Scrafton to the village of West Scrafton. It then turns down to the river at Nathwaite Bridge and climbs to meet the other road. From Coverham the northern-most road reaches Carlton, with linking lanes to Melmerby and Agglethorpe. The solitary route follows the river through the small settlements of Gammersgill, Horsehouse, Braidley and Woodale. From then on it is a climb to the Hunters Stone, and across the moors down to Kettlewell in Wharfedale.

Coverdale is remarkable because of its austere beauty and the River Cover, the longest of the Ure's tributaries, has its beginnings at the head of the Dale. Although easily accessible, it is reasonable to say that this delightful area surrounding Coverdale is largely unspoilt. The Dale was a great favourite of James Herriot, and his stories brought it to the notice of discerning visitors who also admire its solitary splendours.

Horsehouse is a small Coverdale village of pleasant aspect with a terrace of stone houses looking across at the Thwaite Arms. In the days of the pack-horses, which gave the settlement its name, the horses and men rested and fed here. The church of St Botolph, 1869, built of dark stone, has a thin tower and a nave and chancel in one.

Carlton is the largest village in the dale and lines the road for nearly a mile. It is a place of peace and tranquillity, with a number of attractive and inter-esting houses, all on the north side of the road. A three-bay house, which was the home of Henry Constantine, the Coverdale bard, displays a stone tablet commemorating him, dated 1861. On the south side of the village street near to the inn, is the site of a conical motte, an early defensive stronghold.

Just to the west of Carlton a byroad bears left and descends to the River Cover. From Nathwaite Bridge the lane climbs into **West Scrafton**. The village is a closely packed group of ancient houses around a tiny green. One of its houses was originally one of the granges of the canons of Coverham Abbey.

From West Scrafton, a right of way rises up Great Bank, passing the old mine workings and climbing up to the remains of the West Scrafton Colliery at a height of 1,617ft (493m). The long rocky crest of Roova Pike 1,549ft (472m) stretches northwards. From the ridge one footpath descends to Colsterdale, and the other heads across the moor to South Haw and down to Nidderdale.

The southernmost valley road passes the farmsteads of East Scrafton, and op-posite, a right of way descends to the overgrown ruins of St Simon's Chapel. This is a lonely, hidden place surrounded by trees, with a wooded scar adding to its seclusion. Beyond, a footbridge, St Simon's Bridge, crosses the River Cover en-route for Melmerby. The hamlet of Caldbergh, which means, 'a cold hill', was the birthplace of Dr Miles Coverd-ale, Bishop of Exeter, whose translation of the bible was first printed in English in 1535.

From here the road meets the river at Coverham Bridge and then swings away to pass Braithwaite Hall. This is a remote seventeenth-century stone farmhouse, with fine original features including fireplaces, panelling and an oak staircase. Now owned by the National Trust, it is open by arrangement with the tenant.

East Witton

From the road past Braithwaite Hall or the main A6108 at Middleham one can travel east to **East Witton**. The houses stand in neat lines facing each other across a long narrow green decorated by trees. It is obvious that it was part of an ordered planning scheme, but the original nucleus of the settlement was some distance away, around the former church of St Martin.

Nearby Jervaulx Abbey was probably responsible for re-planning the old settle-ment, quite possibly after gaining a market and cattle fair charter in 1307. In 1809, the Earl of Ailesbury rebuilt the village, including the church of St John, with some types of standard cottages along the lines of the present layout. The church of St John is a substantial structure, with a broad tower, nave and aisles. It was remod-elled in 1872 to include a Perpendicular east window.

Jervaulx Abbey

Jervaulx Abbey is 2 miles (3.2km) to the east on the road to Masham. The Cistercian monks came here from Fors, higher up the valley, in 1156 in search of less inclement weather. The site is a beautiful one compared with the first foundation and the abbey prospered from the beginning. The church was one of the earlier buildings, but very little is left now. The bases of some of the piers remain with grave slabs in the nave. The church was late twelfth to early thirteenth century, and was 264ft (80m) long.

The lay brothers quarters, their dorter, west of the cloister, was probably built first. According to Cistercian custom, their accommodation was situated above the west range. The east range contained the monks' dormitory, again on the upper floor. The southern half of the dormitory wall with its range of nine lancet windows still survives.

At the approaching dissolution of the monasteries the opposing faction, the Pilgrimage of Grace, hoped that the Abbot, Adam Sedbergh, would join their cause. The rebels intimidated him by threatening to burn down the abbey, and he was hanged in 1537 at Tyburn Hill, for supposedly being involved in the rebellion. During the following year the abbey was destroyed, and like Middleham Castle, its fine stonework was taken and put to many other uses.

Today the Abbey is a fine place to visit at any time of the year with an atmosphere all its own. It is one of the few privately-owned Cistercian Abbeys, albeit in ruins, open to the public.

Masham was mentioned in Domesday as Massan, the name derived from 'Maessa's ham'. The heart of this busy market town is its wide square lined by attractive houses. There is the market cross, and at the south-east corner of the square is a grand church.

The church of St Mary has a very broad tower, the lower part of Norman age. Then in the late fourteenth or fifteenth century, a new bell stage lantern was placed on and a new spire added. the nave in its Norman form is very wide, and the arcades are probably Perpendicular. Outside the church is an important Anglo-Saxon, ninth century cross shaft.

The King's Head Inn stands guard over the market square. It was built in the middle of the eighteenth century, and was a coaching and posting house. Until the year 1850, the excise office was to be found there.

Masham in noted for its brewing industry, with the famous Theakston Brewery the home of the strong beer, Old Peculier. The Black Sheep Brewery is situated on the old former Lightfoot Brewery site. Each brewery has a visitor centre offering conducted tours.

Beyond Masham the Dale ends, although there is no sudden change; it is now gently rolling countryside criss-crossed by lanes and byroads. This marks the end of Wensleydale although the River Ure continues its journey to join the Swale and becomes the Ouse before entering York.

Selected Walks

1. Upper River Ure circular

Distance: 7 miles (11.2km)

Map: OS Outdoor Leisure 19 Howgill Fells and Upper Eden Valley, 1:25,000

From the road at Aisgill Moor cottages, (SD 779 962), note the footpath sign to Grisedale. Continue on a faint trod across a rough grassy fellside, pass through a number of gates and alongside a wall to reach the derelict farm of High Shaw Paddock. Slant to the right and ascend the slope across a meadow to a small gate. Continue across Rowan Tree Side through rushes and moor grass and aim for a small nick in the hill ridge. There's a wall also coming up to meet an angled wall on the left. Aim for a metal gate.

Walk ahead over moor, descend towards a distant plantation and head for the wall in immediate foreground. Bear right alongside the wall and follow a small road left towards East House. Keep on the road to Moor Rigg, and bear left just after farm – footpath sign to Garsdale Head. Ahead the route is waymarked via the tumbled homestead of Rowantree.

The stiles are clearly visible, especially at one gap stile where there is a notice board with the words 'BEWARE OF THE FARMER' – a lovely touch of humour. Pass the building of Blake Mire. The path crosses the moor ahead with a view of Garsdale Station in the middle distance. The steep slopes immediately on the right tumble down to Grisedale Beck. Follow the clear path in grassy surroundings and descend alongside a stone wall to a gap stile and gate.

Turn left along the main road for a short distance to a line of cottages. Opposite is a footpath signposted to South Lunds. Cross Garsdale Low Moor with a view of Dandry Mire viaduct. Continue to a ladder stile over a wall and head for the right-hand side of the house South Lunds. Cross an area of poor pasture to a stile. After crossing the footbridge over the railway proceed down the field to meet the B6259. Cross the road, footpath sign to Blades Bridge.

Keep on the left-hand side of the barn ahead and descend to poor pasture. Cross a small watercourse and up to stile in wall to the left of a barn. Slant across rushy pasture on the same heading to the footbridge across the River Ure. Keep straight on to gate and then alongside the fence to a stile in wall corner. Bear left alongside a wall, cross a watercourse to a stile. Ascend slope ahead and proceed across Cowshaw Hill to reach Lunds Chapel and burial ground.

Continue to stile, over a footbridge across a beck, to a gate leading into a track. Keep straight on to another gate and enter a walled track. The right of way heads across a mixture of rough pasture and improved meadow, passing a couple of barns en-route. Aim for an attractive barn ahead and the farm of Low West End. Proceed through a gap stile and down to farm and track. Pass the house and stone building after turning left. Go through a gate on the right, cross the beck and bear left. Keep left down through rushes to a stile in the far corner. Walk down the track to a gate and cross How Beck Bridge – actually the River Ure.

Turn right immediately over the bridge to corner of wall and go through a gate with an old railway notice – FASTEN GATE. Follow alongside the wall up the slope, bearing slightly right to a wall and step stile. Step down to cross the railway – STOP, LOOK, LISTEN BEWARE OF TRAINS. From step stile in far wall walk diagonally towards a barn, house and the B6259. Turn right for a short walk back to the starting point at Aisgill.

2. Snaizeholme

Distance 4 miles (6.4km)

Map: OS Outdoor Leisure 2 Yorkshire Dales – Southern and Western areas 1:25,000

For walkers, there is a right of way trailing into the Snaizeholme Valley from Snaizeholme Bridge (SD 833 884) on the B6255. The route follows Snaizeholme Beck to Low Houses, and continues over the beck half a mile beyond the farm. Carry on up the meadow and walk along the edge of the woodland, with a slight deviation towards the beck. Proceed through the Mirk Pot Nature Reserve, keeping to the path, and on towards Tow Hill and West Field to Stone Gill Foot. Turn right and head towards the Snaizeholme Road and turn right again. Follow the woodland boundary for a mile (1.6km) and proceed to Widdale Bridge. Bear right for a short walk along the B6255 to the starting point.

3. Bainbridge to Semer Water

Distance: 8¹/₂ miles (13.6km)

Map: OS Outdoor Leisure 30 Yorkshire Dales – Northern and Central areas 1:25,000

A few paces uphill from Bain Bridge brings one to a stile on the right just before the lane to Stalling Busk. Head across the pasture and keep to the left of a walled enclosure called Out Brough. The route climbs over Bracken Hill to a wall where two paths meet. Take the right-hand stile and follow the route markers. To the right, the green slopes drop steeply away to the gorge of the River Bain. On the far bank is Gilledge Wood and ahead lies Semer Water.

Selected Walks

Pass through several stiles in a gradual descent to the riverside pastures. A ladder stile points to a path along the river bank to reach the road bridge, and a few more steps lead to the gravelly shore of the lake. Semer Water is a relic of the Ice Age. As the ice melted, detritus blocked the foot of the valley and a large lake was formed.

Bear left for a short distance along the road and take the footpath on the right. The way proceeds through pastures bordering the eastern side of the lake. At this point, a steep cobbled track climbs up to the village of Stalling Busk. Keep straight on to reach a crossroad of paths and bear right down to the valley bottom. Cross the footbridges over Cragdale Water and then Raydale Beck and proceed along the track that follows Bardale Beck into ancient hamlet of Marsett.

Cross the stone bridge over the beck and take the second footpath on the left, a track leading to the fells. After a short distance, branch off to the right and ascend the pastures to meet a bridleway by Carlows. Continue straight ahead and descend by the side of Green Scar to meet the Roman road. Turn right, and follow this ancient route crossing the byroad from Burtersett and continue straight on to meet the lane from Countersett. Walk ahead on the road down into Bainbridge.

4. Waterfall stroll at Askrigg

Distance: 3 miles (4.8km) there and back

Map: OS Outdoor Leisure 30 Yorkshire Dales – Northern and Central areas 1:25,000

A stroll westwards from the church at Askrigg leads to the waterfall called Mill Gill Force. Set in a wooded ravine, a cascade of water pours through a notch in

Opposite: View of Askrigg from West End
Below: Looking towards Haylands Bridge
spanning the River Ure, Hawes

a limestone scar and tumbles on to a boulder-littered floor. Whitfield Gill Force lies further beyond along the same footpath through the woods.

5. Leyburn Shawl

Distance: 6$^1/_2$ miles (10.4km)

Map: OS Outdoor Leisure 30 Yorkshire Dales – Northern and Central areas 1:25,000

From the western end of Leyburn a footpath leads to Leyburn Shawl. This is a splendid limestone terrace that offers superb views across the dale. A location on Leyburn Shawl is called the Queen's Gap, where Mary Queen of Scots was supposed to have been captured as she tried to escape from Bolton Castle. However, the name Shawl is likely to be a corruption of the Norse word, 'skali', a hut, a temporary shelter used by shepherds or herdsmen. There's a fine view looking southwards from the Shawl but the opposite direction, hidden by trees, consists of a moon-like landscape of limestone quarry workings.

Extensive blocks of woodland clothe the terrace's southern slopes as the footpaths continue towards Preston-under-Scar. Upon reaching the village look for a footpath on the left just after two roads join and follow this down through the grounds of Bolton Hall. At a crossroads of paths shortly after, take the left fork to Wensley and from there the field paths back to Leyburn.

Places to Visit

Hawes

Wensleydale Creamery*

Gayle Lane, Hawes
Museum, shop and restaurant.
☎ (01969) 667664. Open: 9.30am–
5.30pm. All year – 7 days.
www.wensleydale.co.uk

Dales Countryside Museum*

Tourist Information and
National Park Centre, Hawes
Tells the story of the Yorkshire
Dales landscape. Displays,
events & demonstrations.
☎ (01969) 667210. Open: 10am–
5pm, daily except Christmas.
www.yorkshiredales.org.uk

The Hawes Ropemakers

Station Yard, Hawes
☎ (01969) 667487
Open: Mon–Fri, all year and Sat in
Jul–Oct. Closed on Sun. Wheelchair
walkway (Mon–Fri).
www.ropemakers.co.uk.

Aysgarth

Yore Mill Craft Shop

Aysgarth Falls ☎ (01969) 663496
Pictures, craft and pottery.

Raydale Preserves

Raydale, School House farm, Stalling
Busk
Preserves being made, tasting room.
☎ (01969) 650233. Open: daily,
May–Oct 10am–4pm.

The Forbidden Corner

Tupgill Park Estate, Coverham,
Middleham

Delightful four acre walled garden,
grotto with underground labyrinth
of chambers and passages. Pre-
booked tickets only please. ☎ (01969)
640638. Open: daily 12noon–6pm
Apr–Oct. Sun 10am–dusk. Nov–
Christmas.

Wensley

White Rose Candle Workshop

Wensley Mill
☎ (01969) 623544
Open: Please call for April opening
times. 10am-5pm, Jun–Oct; Thu, Fri,
Sat & Sun. 10am–dusk, Nov; Fri, Sat
& Sun. 10am–dusk, Dec, Fri, Sat &
Sun.

Castle Bolton

Bolton Castle, near Leyburn
☎ (01969) 623981
Open: 10am–5pm or dusk if earlier,
Mar–Nov. www.boltoncastle.co.uk

Leyburn & around

The Teapottery

Leyburn
☎ (01937) 588235
Open: Nov-Mar 10am–4pm, 7 days.
Apr-Oct 9am–5pm, 7 days. Closed
25-26th Dec and 1st Jan.
www.teapottery.co.uk.

The Wensleydale
Longwool Sheepshop*

Cross Lanes Farm, Garriston,
Leyburn.
Fleeces, hand and machine knitted
garments. ☎ (01969) 623840
Open: Tue–Sat, 10am–5pm
and Bank Holidays. From Nov

1st–31st Mar, open Tues. www.
wensleydalelongwoolsheepshop.
co.uk

Middleham Castle

The boyhood home of Richard III
☎ (01969) 623899. Open: daily, Apr–
Sep 10am-6pm. Oct-Mar 10am–4pm,
Thu–Mon (Closed 24-26 Dec & 1st
Jan). www.english-heritage.org.
uk/yorkshire

Jervaulx Abbey

A6108 between Middleham
and Masham
☎ (01677) 460391
Open: during daylight hours every
day, all year. Tearoom 10am–5pm
daily, Easter to Nov.

Constable Burton Gardens

A684 between Bedale and Leyburn
Large romantic terrace garden
surrounded by 18th century parkland.
Garden, trails & borders.
☎ (01677) 450428
Open: Mar–Oct 9am–6pm. www.
constableburton gardens.co.uk

Brymor Ice Cream Parlour*

A6108 between Middleham and
Masham
Thirty flavours of real dairy ice cream
plus tea, coffee and light snacks.
☎ (01677) 460377
Open: 10am–6pm daily, all year.

Theakston Brewery
& Visitor Centre

Masham
Bookings ☎ (01765) 680000
Open: Daytime and private evening
tours available.www.theakstons.co.uk

Black Sheep Brewery & Visitor Centre*

Wellgarth, Masham
☎ (01765) 689227/680100/
680101. Open: daily and evening
shepherded brewery tours. Group
tours and private parties. www.
blacksheepbrewery.co.uk

Thorp Perrow Arboretum & Falconry Centre

Thorp Perrow, Bedale
85 acres of woodland to explore. Bird
of Prey Centre.
☎ (01677) 425323. Open: 11am–3pm
weekends only, 19 Nov–18 Feb.
10am–5pm everyday 18 Feb–18 Nov.
www.thorpperrow.com

Wensleydale Railway

Passenger services information
☎ (08454) 505474
www.wensleydalerailway.com

Artbar Gallery

Nether Bar East, Appersett, Hawes
Oils, pastels and watercolour on
silk.
☎ (01969) 667782
www.artbargallery.co.uk

Uredale Glass

Market Place, Masham, HG4 4EF
☎ (01765) 689780
www.uredale.co.uk
An individual style of glass making
with a wide use of colour and
design.
Open: 7 days from Easter until 31st
Oct, 10am–5pm. Winter: 7 days,
10am–4.30pm, January – please
check opening hours.

6. Swaledale

The B6270 is an adventurous road that leaves the quiet charms of the Eden Valley to tackle the high land at the head of Swaledale. From the village of Nateby, just south of Kirkby Stephen, it climbs steeply below Tailbridge Hill to reach Lamps Moss at a height of 1,699ft (518m). At the dale head, the hill summits of Hugh Seat, High Seat, High Pike Hill and Nine Standards Rigg are the gathering ground of very many gills and watercourses that unite to form the Swale. The river becomes the dominant force, carving its passage deep into the landscape and creating its steep sided valley and numerous waterfalls. It is easy to see why Swaledale is regarded as a favourite dale and one of the grandest pieces of country in England.

Upper Swaledale

Having started on vast tracts of moorland amid peat hags, moor grass, rush and cotton grass, it is only slowly that scanty pastures and isolated barns begin to appear. From the barren peaty wastes east of Nine Standards Rigg, it is a pleasure to walk through walled pastures with gates and barns. Above the limestone scar of Cotterby, the swift-flowing Swale pours over **Wain Wath** falls in a frothy torrent. The falls can easily be seen from the roadside and from the bridge on the little road to Stonesdale.

Stonesdale Lane heads northwards to the farmstead and outbuildings that comprise West Stonesdale. Beyond Startindale Gill the road climbs gently amongst expanding and wide-ranging dun-coloured moorland. There are reminders of former industries now, partly softened by moss, rush and moor grass. Here on Stonesdale Moor coal of rather poor quality was mined, the highest and most important pit was the **Tan Hill** mine. There were numerous pits that dotted the surrounding moorland, and records point back to the time of the thirteenth century.

At one period, the coal was carried away on packhorses and donkeys and later as roads and tracks improved, lines of carts would be waiting for their loads. In many cases, farmers took two days on their journey from the lower valleys. Because of the coal pits, a turnpike road was made to Tan Hill through Arkengarthdale.

This is border country in a way up here, as the Tan Hill Inn lies on the

Tan Hill Inn

The Tan Hill Inn on lonely Stonesdale Moor is the highest in England at 1,732ft (528m). Tan Hill was not only a busy place for the nearby coal pits, for the inn was at a meeting place of four trails. Cattle drovers avoided towns and cultivated areas by taking to the hills and moorland. An experienced drover would be in charge of a herd of forty to fifty beasts, with a lad and a couple of dogs to help him. One route came from the Border hills, across Teesdale to Sleightholme and down into Arkengarthdale. They made their way through Wensleydale and Wharfedale to a great cattle fair on Malham Moor.

Tan Hill Inn would have been a lively place in those days; miners, drovers, farmers, pedlars and horse dealers would have frequented this famous hostelry. When the coal pits ceased operating and drovers no longer came, Tan Hill Inn lost a considerable amount of trade. However, with better roads and more visitors using motor vehicles, this lonely inn is no longer as isolated as it used to be. In more recent times, the creation of the Pennine Way, which passes the door, enables the inn to provide refreshment and accommodation. There is an important sheep fair held at Tan Hill each May.

boundary between North Yorkshire and County Durham, with the Cumbrian border just along the road. The boundary is also the northern limit of the Yorkshire Dales National Park and gazing out across a wilderness of moorland, it is also the watershed dividing the Swale and the Tees.

Keld and Muker

The village of **Keld** stands on a meadowy shelf above the Swale. In fact, the appearance of the countryside between Keld and Muker is almost alpine in character, with farms and barns perched on the edge of the fells. After landing in Ireland, the Norsemen moved across to the Lake District, then eventually crossed the Pennines and established their kingdom at York. These early colonists, whose former homes lay on steep valley sides, chose a familiar landscape to continue their pastoral farming traditions.

Keld is the first village in Swaledale, but visitors passing along the valley road may fail to notice the little cluster of stone buildings lower down the slope. The former shooting lodge lies on the top road together with a farm, a house or two and some barns. The houses and cottages of Keld are tidily arranged at the end of the little lane off the main road. Lintels are proudly carved with dates and initials, the various dwellings of cottage, larger house and chapel form a perfect picture of this community. There are public conveniences close by but parking is severely restricted in the small square.

Keld is a crossroads of the two long-distance paths, the Pennine Way and the

Coast to Coast path. A short descent from the village brings one to this junction of paths, and to the sound of the river. Here, the Swale is swift-flowing, sheltered by white limestone cliffs and enclosed by trees. The Pennine Way heads northwards, with nearby, the pretty stepped cascades of **East Gill Force**. **Catrake Force** lies on the west side of the village. Southwards, the Pennine Way follows a delectable route with a detour to **Kisdon Force**, and gradually climbs high over the deep gorge cut by the river.

The road from Keld to **Thwaite** gently descends, bobbing and weaving down the dale, beneath the impressive bulk of Kisdon Hill. This pleasant little place clustered round a bend in the road is compact and unassuming. Amongst its buildings there is a guesthouse and a shop. Just to the south, a byroad climbs the fellside overlooking Cliff Beck towards the Butter Tubs Pass.

From Thwaite, the road follows Straw Beck into **Muker**, where the village sits above the beck near to its confluence with the Swale. The view of Muker from just above the bridge is instantly recognised as the Dales – stone houses roofed with warm-coloured stone flags, standing together in perfect positions, as if they were actually posing. Overlooking all the houses built up against the green hillside is the tower of the village church pointing to Kisdon Hill.

The church was consecrated in 1580, when the building had a thatched roof. The church records date back to 1638, except for a gap from 1670 to 1699. The present church of St Mary has a fairly tall tower with bell opening, which is probably late seventeenth-century or early eighteenth-century. The church has no aisles, and the rest of the building is 1890.

The east window is a picture of Swaledale in stained glass; a splendid representation of the dale with Christ the Good Shepherd carrying a lamb as he leads his flock of Swaledale sheep. Other features include Kisdon Hill, Straw Beck and the Swale.

There is a small building in Muker called the Literary Institute, which has an attractive gable end. It was built about 1868, and is put to a variety of

The Kearton brothers

The little hamlet of Thwaite is remembered as the birth-place of the brothers, Richard and Cherry Kearton. As little boys, they astonished the local residents with their interest in, and knowledge of, birds and wildlife. Many a time they stood on the bridge over Thwaite Beck intently studying some object or small creature in the water.

Richard was to fall out of a tree and dislocate a hip, which was unsuccessfully set by a local vet, leaving him with one leg six inches shorter than the other. However, he eventually won fame as a writer and lecturer on wildlife, whilst Cherry became a pioneer of wildlife photography. His pictures were used to illustrate Richard's books. On one of the houses in Thwaite, a stone lintel with inscriptions of birds and animals marks their home, now the site of the Kearton Guest House.

community uses. The village is popular with visitors especially when it is Muker Show Day on the first Wednesday in September.

Back in the 1970s when the local economy was in a slump, a suggestion was made that local people might like to revive the hand knitting trade. At one time during the eighteenth century some 18,000 pairs of knitted stockings each year were made in the area. Machine methods and changes in fashion led to the trade dying out but it was decided to try to revive it. The result is **Swaledale Woollens** based in Muker. Some forty local people knit quality sweaters, gloves, hats and stockings in their homes. These are sold in the shop in Muker.

During early summer it is a great pleasure to follow footpaths through the local meadows. Here in this part of Swaledale the meadows are left to grow hay and are not heavily fertilised and cut for silage. The result is that they produce an abundance of wild flowers, such as, buttercups, pignut, daisies, clover, cranesbill, campion, pansies and speedwell. These flower meadow walks start from Muker towards Ramps Holme Bridge by the Swale, from Muker to Gunnerside and around Thwaite and Angram.

From Muker, the road and river are hemmed in the narrow valley between the encroaching high land of High Kisdon and Oxnop Side. At **Oxnop Bridge** a lane bears left for the hamlet of Ivelet and crosses over a beautiful single-arched bridge. This perfect example of a packhorse bridge rises high above the Swale and is one of the gems of Swaledale. The road that crosses the bridge may have been part of the Corpse Way, as there is a large stone towards one end on which the coffin was rested.

The stream flowing beneath Oxnop Bridge is Oxnop Beck. Higher up this little wooded valley, on its eastern side, was the site of the Spout Gill mines. They had been worked for lead in the seventeenth century by hushing, with water collected at first on Satron Moor. Spout Gill mines proved rich and were worked until about 1870.

Gunnerside and Healaugh

The valley road bends and crosses the Swale at Gunnerside New Bridge into the village of **Gunnerside**. At one time, the village was a centre of lead mining in the Dale and its closely-grouped dwellings housed the mining community. The miners also had small plots to cultivate vegetables and to grow grass for hay. These small fields are surviving examples of early enclosures. Amongst the buildings are a fine Methodist chapel, an inn, and a number of establishments catering for the accommodation needs of visitors.

On the eastern side of the village, a path leads up **Gunnerside Gill** to an extensive area of the former lead-mining industry. Taking a higher path on the eastern edge of the gill at Winter-ings, there are traces of early smelting places and in the valley bottom are the ruins of two crushing mills. Two miles from Gunnerside was the largest group of mines, with the Lownathwaite to the west and the Old Gang to the east. In Gunnerside Gill rich veins had been worked from an early date by hushing (see overleaf) – the Friarfold Hush and the Bunton Hush.

At the mouth of Blind Gill, on the western side of Gunnerside Gill, stand the ruins of Blakethwaite Smelt mill, built to smelt the ore from the mines at the very head of Gunnerside Gill. The beck is crossed by a huge stone slab close by the cloister-like ruins of the smelt mill that has a fine arched entrance. The flue comes down from the edge of Gunnerside Moor from a notch in the skyline. Note the well-preserved kiln to the right.

Many rights of way traverse and cross over the moorland on both flanks of Gunnerside Gill. Longer walks may be accomplished with a fine variety of moorland and beckside scenery. There is also the splendid option of returning

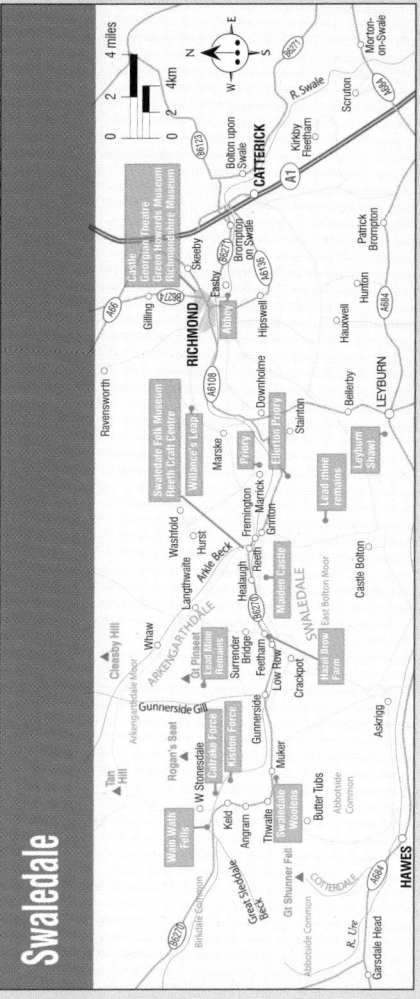

Hushing

In mining terms, a hush is a ravine engineered by prospectors on a steep hill slope. Water was dammed above the side of the ravine and suddenly released, causing a force of water to scour the surface and reveal any signs of minerals or veins. These hushes are very conspicuous and remain as permanent scars on the surface of the ground.

along the banks of the Swale.

On the south side of Gunnerside New Bridge, a lane bears left above Hag Wood to Spring End. The lane continues to Crackpot, which gets its name from a cave higher up Summer Lodge Beck, then branches left to descend alongside Haverdale Beck, with its waterfalls, and crosses Haverdale Beck Bridge. Just beyond, there's a left fork over Isles Bridge to reach the main road.

From Gunnerside, eastwards, there is a right of way that follows along the banks of the Swale, except for a short length of road opposite Rowleth Wood. At Strands there is a clearing bounded by the slopes of Rowleth Wood, an idyllic place for spring flowers. Here, the river is broad and shallow, in parts running over a gravelly bed; in others, its smooth flow interrupted by small cascades – a beautiful riverside scene at all seasons of the year.

The path quickly returns to the riverside and continues beneath Isles Bridge closely following the river to Feetham Wood. Another short stretch of road leads to a path on the left that heads across the lower pastures to

Barney Beck. A minor road takes one into the village of **Healaugh**. The surrounding land was at one time part of a large manor belonging to the Wharton family. The estate covered a large area of moorland that was heavily exploited by lead mining.

From Healaugh, High Lane runs along the east bank of Barney Beck, passing interesting farmsteads, such as Dagger Stones and Nova Scotia. Beyond Bleaberry Gill are the ruins of the **Surrender Smelt Mills** and on the hillside behind the mill the covered flue which carried smoke and fumes from the furnaces up to a chimney perched at a higher level. This smelt mill smelted ore from a large group of scattered mines.

A mile (1.6km) above **Surrender Bridge** are the most impressive ruins of the **Old Gang Smelt Mills**. Here, now roofless, stand many of the buildings: the furnace house, blacksmith's shops, stores, the Peat House and the mill chimney. Great quantities of peat were used, together with coal from Tan Hill. Lead ore was even carried through from the extensive workings above Gunnerside Gill to the Old Gang Smelt Mills.

Back in Healaugh, looking across the Swale in a south-south-east direction,

Well-known view

A little byroad crosses the Barney Beck at Surrender Bridge from Feetham and continues over to Arkengarthdale, just north of Langthwaite. The ford across Bleaberry Gill was the watersplash negotiated by Herriot's little car in the TV series *All Creatures Great and Small*.

one may perceive an earthwork on Harkerside. Close examination of the site is possible by travelling westwards along the B6270 from Healaugh for a short way, crossing the Swale at Scabba Wath Bridge. Turn left towards Grinton and proceed for 1 mile (1.6km); a footpath strikes uphill to **Maiden Castle**.

Commanding a good view of the valley, the fort is a circular banked enclosure 295ft (90m) across with an external ditch. From an entrance on the eastern side is an avenue of tumbled drystone walling stretching for about 361ft (110m). Just north of the end of the avenue is a large tumulus that is probably contemporary. The monument is thought to date back to the late Bronze Age or early Iron Age.

Between Gunnerside and Healaugh lie the settlements of **Low Row** and **Feetham**. A sword buckle unearthed locally in 1847, led to the discovery of several bodies slain in battle. They were probably killed during a clash with raiding Jacobites during the 1745 episode. They are buried in the churchyard at Low Row.

The church of Holy Trinity is the parish church of Feetham. It was built in 1810, and has a bellcote and short chancel. Gunnerside, Low Row and Feetham belong to the parish of Melbecks, but there is actually no such village, just a designation of the parish marked on the map.

In Low Row look out for the signs for **Hazel Brow Farm**, a typical working Swaledale farm. Visit in April and the Swaledale sheep will be giving birth. During the summer watch the cows being milked and bottle a 'pinta' to take home. Farm tours, a riverside walk,

young animals to see and cuddle, all add to the pleasure of a day here. The whole family can enjoy this taste of farm life and learn about the farming year.

The seventeenth-century Punch Bowl Inn is a high stone building, dating at least from 1636, standing above the main road. In front of the Punch Bowl, a byroad climbs steeply out of the Dale, and heads across the moor to Surrender Bridge and on to Arkengarthdale – two extensive and important lead-mining areas. This road was also an important drove road used by thousands of cattle en-route for a market or cattle fair. The Punch Bowl lay on the Corpse Route and burial parties bound for Grinton refreshed themselves while the dead rested in their wicker baskets in a building known as the 'dead house'.

After Feetham, the B6270 road travels delightfully alongside the Swale before the river turns away. It is about $1\frac{1}{2}$ miles (2.4km) from Healaugh to Reeth, and about the same distance by taking the footpath just beyond the village down to the Swale, and following the river bank. The last stretch is through the fields into Reeth.

Reeth

The village of **Reeth** is centred around a large irregular green, with wide views of the surrounding hills. Reeth's market charter dates from 1695, when Lord Wharton obtained permission for market each week and for four annual fairs. Reeth was formerly a centre for the lead mining industry but its importance dwindled when lead mining ceased and its present population is only a quarter of its former size. It is still a centre for the hill-farming community,

Selected Car Drive

Around Swaledale from Richmond

Distance: 54 miles (86.4km)

From the Market Place in Richmond join the A6136 and then turn left on to the A6108. The road bends round Friars' Close and passes a solitary tower. Take the next right turn by the cricket ground and follow this road to Marske. Cross Marske Bridge, and keep straight on following an undulating route, before descending to the B6270 at Low Fremington. Turn right and proceed into the centre of Reeth. Take the road leaving the north end of the green into Arkengarthdale. Follow the road up the dale eventually passing through the wild upper reaches of the dale and across Sleightholme Moor to England's highest pub, Tan Hill Inn.

Turn left, descend West Stones Dale, cross the Swale and turn left towards Keld. Continue down the dale through the attractive settlements of Thwaite, Muker and Gunnerside.

One mile (1.6km) beyond Feetham, turn right across Scabba Wath Bridge, then left, and proceed along the byroad, beneath Harkerside to Grinton. Turn left and then right to join the B6270. Travel for 3 miles (4.8km) passing Ellerton Abbey, and then branch off to the right on a byroad. After a little way, bear right again, and continue on to meet the A6108 at Walburn Hall. Go straight on.

Follow on for a short distance to a sharp bend, turn left and then second right. This road runs on a fairly straight course for 4½ miles (7.2km) before a right and left manoeuvre. Proceed through Tunstall cross over the A1 into Catterick to meet the A6136, turn left.

Head on past the Racecourse and cross the Swale at Catterick Bridge. Turn left on to the B6271, passing the road on the left to Easby Abbey and returning to Richmond.

The River Swale at Richmond

and events of special interest are the sheep sales and Reeth Show, which is held in late August; also the market has been revived.

Reeth is a pleasant place that attracts many visitors. As well as catering for the valley communities, it supplies the needs of the tourists: there are shops, inns and a number of bed and breakfast establishments. The village is an excellent base for spending a few days in Upper Swaledale.

For the motorist, there are touring excursions westwards to the Eden Valley and eastwards to Richmond and Ripon. Other byways connect Swaledale with Wensleydale and Teesdale. They climb steep slopes, bend round becks and gills, and pursue their lonely ways past scars and peat hags. Reeth offers a fine choice of walks, with a network of footpaths leading in all directions and suitable for a variety of grades and distances.

Visitors to Reeth should make a point of calling in at the **Swaledale Museum**. The former Methodist Sunday School near the green, houses a fine and interesting collection of memorabilia, which will help to explain about the old lead-mining days. Visitors will be able to understand the workings of the hushes, levels and the extraction processes and see the various tools used by the miners.

Another fascinating insight into their way of life is documentary evidence in the form of letters that include sad statements about leaving the Dale to seek for work in other areas and in other countries. There is information about farming life, how stone houses were built and what conditions were like for girls who worked in domestic

service. The implements used by the men and women of Swaledale will clearly illustrate what everyday life was like in years gone by.

In contrast the artistic skills of present-day inhabitants of the Dale are on show at the **Reeth Dales Centre** in Silver Street. Furniture, hand made rugs, clocks, sculptures and models can all be found here. Visitors can observe them being created and in some cases even join a class to learn for themselves.

Arkengarthdale

Arkengarthdale joins Swaledale at Reeth and extends in a north-westerly direction for 10 miles (16km) to the county boundary. This area is marked on the map as The Disputes, and the name arose from disputed ownership of land concerning mining rights. The Arkle Beck has its beginnings here and quickly becomes a busy, lively stream. The dale is noted for its many small communities like Arkle Town, High Eskeleth, Whaw and Langthwaite – the largest village in Arkengarthdale. This is a lonely dale, and in its upper parts, a wide, rolling area of moorland, is bleak and inhospitable. It is appreciated by those who prefer peace and tranquillity.

The small village of **Langthwaite** is a closely-formed huddle of grey stone houses. The church of St Mary, 1818-19 was built to serve Arkengarthdale. The church is a Commissioners' type, that is, tall for its width. The Methodist chapel is a large, Italianate style building, 1882, with windows in two floors. A short distance up the valley is the CB (Charles Bathurst) Inn, with two symmetrical bow-windows. All these buildings, church, chapel and inn, were built on a generous scale, due to the prosperity of the lead-mining industry at that time in the nineteenth century.

Eskeleth is an interesting name meaning 'a slope with ash trees and a spring'. Here, the early colonists found an ideal place to establish a home. The road down the valley form Dale Head was one of the great drove roads for thousands of cattle from Scotland. Further on up the Dale, the settlement of **Whaw** indicated that although the valley was reserved for hunting, here a small cattle farm was allowed.

On the hillside just east of Langthwaite is the huddle of houses called **Booze**. This is another early settlement that was originally called Bowehouse. The settlement lies above a bend in the river and during the height of lead-mining operations supported a considerable number of miners' houses. Despite its name, it does not possess an inn.

About a quarter of a mile north of the CB Hotel, between the road and the river, lie the interesting remains of the Old Octagon Mill. This was for some considerable time the main smelt mill for the Bathurst mines. The building is octagonal in shape, built about 1700, and a main flue runs half a mile up the hillside. A smaller building close by was a blasting mill, a powder house, built about 1804. However, another mill was eventually built higher up the fell.

Returning down the valley from Arkle Town, there is a very fine view across the river to the long escarpment line of Fremington Edge. Beyond to the north-east lie the moorland scars of the Hurst mining area. The quarries

on the steep slopes of Fremington Edge were worked for chert. This mineral is a hard flint-like stone that is ground into a whitish powder and used in the making of fine china.

Lower Swaledale

From Reeth, take the Richmond road and cross over Arkle Beck. Past Low Fremington the B6270 crosses the Swale into the village of **Grinton**. As the main road makes a sharp left turn, two other byroads enter, one from Harkerside and the other ready to make an ascent of Grinton Moor to the south. A variety of attractive cottages snugly line all the routes, making a very compact, sheltered community.

The church of St Andrew dominates the village and its size indicates its importance as a church in one of Yorkshire's largest parishes. This land stretched all along the upper dale to the old Westmorland border and its graveyard was the only one to serve this extensive area. A route linking the settlements in the upper dale was called the Corpse Way. The grey stone, low spreading church is Perpendicular in style with a Norman nave and a tower arch of the late twelfth century. The interior contains a Norman font that is drum-shaped, a Jacobean pulpit and some original stained glass fragments in the east window of the south aisle.

Grinton Youth Hostel is a nineteenth-century former shooting lodge on the edge of the moor $^3/_4$ mile (1.2km) south of the village. It has superb views overlooking Swaledale and Arkengarthdale. The byroad running south from Grinton divides just before the Youth Hostel; the right arm going to

Marrick Priory

Marrick Priory was founded in 1154-81 by Roger de Aske for Benedictine nuns. When it surrendered to the King's commissioners in 1539, it had a prioress and twelve nuns. The church was also the parish church of Marrick, a mile away on the hill behind. A stone causey with 375 steps, still a public footpath, runs from the priory through the wood to Marrick village.

In 1811, the nave of the church of St Andrew was pulled down and rebuilt out of the materials of the priory. The parts used were one arch and two half arches and two round piers. They form a shared division of three parts between the nave and chancel. The tall tower has a re-used, late thirteenth-century window of three lancet lights.

The remains of the priory are now partly concealed by new buildings occupied and used by an educational and training centre associated with the diocese of Ripon. A chapel of ease has been built in Marrick to serve the needs of the village.

Redmire and the left fork to Leyburn, both in Wensleydale. Grinton was once an important lead-mining centre and there are many signs of this industry across Grinton Moor. The old smelt mill up Cogden Gill is one of the best preserved in the area.

From Grinton return to Low Fremington and turn right along the Marske byroad. A little further on there is a well-trodden farm road in pleasant surroundings to **Marrick Priory**. The tower rises protectively above the old farmhouse, fine trees stand beside it and the site is sheltered beneath a well-wooded hillside. Here the River Swale has changed in character from its open hillside surroundings to a deep wooded valley, almost another land in comparison to its upper reaches.

From the old Reeth to Richmond road, a long and fairly straight switch-back lane to the north, the Stelling Road, reaches Washfold and Hurst. This was once a busy and thriving lead-mining area. It was believed that lead was mined here by the Romans and to confirm this supposition, a pig of lead was discovered in the eighteenth century bearing the inscription 'Hadrian'.

Today, the Hurst mining field is a lunar landscape but despite the bleak nature of the surroundings, there is much of interest to see. It will appeal to those who wish to explore quiet ways and little known dales and complete a moorland tramp beyond the border into County Durham.

Continuing along the old road to Richmond, the way descends to cross over the fifteenth-century stone bridge. Here, full of charm and natural beauty, is the small village of Marske. It lies snugly sheltered amongst fine trees in the narrow valley of Marske Beck. This glacial groove in the hills is edged by limestone cliffs and the beck has its beginnings on the distant heather moors.

The church of St Edmund with some Norman features has an ancient double bellcote. The restoration of 1683 has interesting features, including two south windows, the chancel arch with its strange corbels and the north arcade's octagonal piers. Marske Hall was for centuries the home of the Hutton family, who provided two Archbishops of York, one of whom, Matthew, became Archbishop of Canterbury in 1757.

The Hall was one of the earliest houses built by John Carr in the Palladian style in the mid-eighteenth century. It has a classical pillared doorway and symmetrical frontage. The building has now been altered into flats after the sale of the estate. In the grounds of the Hall stands a 60ft (18m) obelisk, erected in memory of Captain Matthew Hutton.

Beyond Marske, the road climbs Clapgate Bank and at a point $2^3/_4$ miles (4.4km) from the village a footpath on the right leads to Whitcliffe Scar. The inscribed stones on the edge of Whitcliffe Scar commemorate the remarkable escape from death of Robert Willance in 1606. While out hunting a fog descended, and not realising where he was, he galloped his horse over the edge of the cliff. The horse was killed but Willance escaped with a broken leg.

The south bank of the Swale Valley from Grinton is approached by the main road, the B6270. Across the river from the village of Marrick, and a short distance by river ford to Marrick Priory, is the site of **Ellerton Priory** situated on private land. A solitary tower is the remaining part of the Cistercian nunnery, one of the smallest in England.

Close by to the west, stands Ellerton Abbey, formerly Ellerton Lodge. In 1827, the owner of the shooting lodge extended his home by taking stone from the priory buildings. The house was featured in the television series *All Creatures Great and Small* as the home of Mrs Pumphrey and Tricki-Woo.

A short distance towards Richmond, a minor road bears right and soon joins the A6108 by **Walburn Hall**. This is an impressive fortified house, with an embattled wall along the road. The wall is of moderate height with a wall-walk. The Elizabethan east wing has mullioned windows and a superb five-light oriel window. To the north-west is an earlier sixteenth-century range which has a flat oriel window facing a courtyard. The road descends into the valley of the Swale beneath the wooded slopes of Hag Wood, crosses Lownethwaite Bridge and enters the town of Richmond.

Richmond

Richmond is a visually impressive small town, a unique place and rich in relics of the past. It has its distinctive market-place of Georgian appearance. Its massive castle keep and fortress walls stand high above the Swale and its steep streets lead down to the river. The name of Richmond was given to it by the Normans after one of the Richemonts in France.

The large and powerful **Richmond Castle** was part of the early castle building programme in England, and was constructed soon after the Conquest by Alan the Red in 1071. The earliest masonry is the curtain wall of

A barn in Swaledale near Thwaite

shale blocks on the east and west sides. The southern part of the west wall has a roundheaded archway flanked by shallow buttresses. The eastern curtain wall formerly had four projecting towers (one has almost collapsed). The original gateway was converted into a tower keep, and a new gateway, defended by a portcullis, was made through the curtain wall beside it. The keep, attributed to Earl Conan (1146-71), was constructed of worked stone.

Situated in the south-east corner of the bailey is Scolland's Hall, an eleventh-century building, the main floor of which was entered by a wooden stair on a rubble base. The ground floor was used for storage purposes and the

Georgian theatre

The **Theatre Royal** in Victoria Road, is a beautifully preserved little Georgian theatre, one of the two oldest in England. It was built in 1788 by an actor/manager, Samuel Butler and it formed part of a theatre circuit which included places as far away as Kendal and Whitby. In 1848, the long association with the Butler family ended, and the building was used for many purposes.

Restoration work began in 1960 and the theatre was reopened in 1963 with many of the original features on view. Regular performances take place often starring well-known actors. The **Georgian Royal Museum** houses a unique collection of playbills related to the theatre. There is also the oldest and complete set of Georgian scenery in Britain.

Lead Mining in Arkengarthdale

The Dale was once a bustling mining centre, dating back to the seventeenth century, when it was bought by Dr John Bathhurst, who was physician to Oliver Cromwell. He purchased Arkengarthdale in 1656 and began mining there. For centuries the mines were owned by the Bathurst family; this connection is remembered in the name of the CB Hotel, which stood for Charles Bathurst, the grandson of Dr John Bathurst.

Remains of the lead-mining industry – tips, hushes, levels, flues and ruined buildings – comprehensively cover many parts of Swaledale and Arkengarthdale. One of the earliest methods was to dig a shaft down to a vein and work along it until the ore gave out or was difficult to work. Then a new shaft was dug nearby, until eventually, there was a row of shafts across the moor. Later, with improved technology, adits or horizontal levels were driven into a hillside. These levels provided access, drainage (water was the miners' greatest enemy) and transport. For the latter, ponies were used to pull the tubs containing the ore.

Many of the mines were situated high on the moors in remote and dreary places. One is tempted to think of the employees, particularly women, and boys as young as seven, working on the dressing and washing floors with no protection against the harsh Pennine weather. The miners fared little better,

building was extended westwards in the twelfth century. At this time, the curtain wall was extended round the cliff edge above the River Swale.

The castle formed part of the Honour of Richmond, that was all the country south of the river Tees, including the area drained by the rivers Swale and Ure to the watershed of the rivers Nidd and Wharfe. The castle seemed to have a peaceful existence, being a little off the beaten track as far as any serious action was concerned. Its one claim to fame was that it served as a royal prison for a while, holding William the Lion, King of Scotland.

The castle is an excellent starting point for a tour of Richmond. The splendid view from the top of the keep not only encompasses the town, but also covers a wide area of the surrounding countryside. Beyond the spacious market place with its obelisk, is a pattern of stone roofs, flags and pantiles that give the town its distinct appearance. The town hall dates from the Georgian period and the central church of the Holy Trinity now fulfils another role. The building contains the **Regimental Museum of the Green Howards** and everything has been beautifully displayed. There is a documented history and a collection of uniforms, medals and relics.

working by candlelight in damp and dangerous conditions.

In the nineteenth century, water-power was used to drive water wheels, which operated crushing machinery and large bellows for the furnaces. This led to the construction of long flues up the hillsides to increase draught and to carry away fumes. One of the disagreeable tasks that boys had to do was to crawl inside the flues and scrape down the residue.

Many of the farmers in the Dale took on a dual role as farmer and miner. According to the price of lead, men could not always rely on income from mining. So, small plots of land, often intakes on the edge of the moor, were acquired to grow a few crops, or keep a cow and a few sheep, to supplement their income. To make the money go round, the families used to knit stockings, which were sold to dealers who called to collect them. These stockings then found their way into the towns and cities.

By the middle of the nineteenth century, due to cheaper foreign imports, the price of lead fell. Towards the end of that century, many mines in Swaledale were worked out although the Arkengarthdale mines carried on until 1912. Care should always be taken in old mine areas and no attempt should be made to explore old workings. Information on conducted walks to look at lead-mining sites can be obtained at the nearest National Park Visitor Centres at Aysgarth and Hawes. Excellent information on lead mining in Yorkshire may be found on the website: www.ayresnet.swinternet. co.uk/archbold.htm. In addition there is the Museum of Yorkshire Dales Lead Mining at Earby on the A56, 6 miles (9.6km) south-west of Skipton. ☎ (01282) 815686 for further details.

Just off the Market Place Richmond boasts another fascinating museum, the **Richmondshire Museum**. A collection of artefacts and displays tells the story of Richmond's history, traditions and culture from the Stone Age to the present day. There are more reminders here of James Herriot with the surgery set from the film *All Creatures Great and Small*.

From the Market Place, New Road leads down to the town bridge; this thoroughfare was an eighteenth-century addition. The Bar, a narrow street, contains an old gateway, a tiny fragment of the old town walls. The steep streets, including cobbled Bridge Street, display a fine diversity of Georgian houses. Just above the Swale, the Green presents a neat and architecturally attractive appearance. From here, one can look up to the ornate Georgian folly the **Culloden Tower**, built to commemorate the English victory at Culloden in 1745.

Turning up Cravengate, brings one to Newbiggin, an ancient road going back to medieval days. Just above here is Victoria Road that faces Friars' Close. There was a Franciscan Friary established here in 1258, but the remains of their church are of the fifteenth century.

The church of St Mary lies outside

Selected Walks

1. Keld to Thwaite and Kisdon Force

Distance: 5 miles (8km)

Map: OS Outdoor Leisure 30 Yorkshire Dales – Northern and Central areas 1:25,000

From the centre of the little community of Keld, walk up to the top road (B6270) and bear left. Continue along the road for about a quarter of a mile, ignoring the first right of way on the left. Then take the next path on the left. This pleasant way enters and crosses a succession of walled pastures, with a variety of stiles, as the path bypasses the hamlet of Angram. There follows another short distance along the road before taking the next path on the left, a grassy route beneath the slopes of Kisdon Hill. Note the typical squeeze-through stiles and the magnificent Swaledale stone barns. Follow the Skeb Skeugh Brook almost into Thwaite. Bear left and then left again and follow the Pennine Way signs. The exit from Thwaite is through small walled enclosures and then head in a north-easterly direction across a field. The path climbs up to Kisdon Cottage with helpful waymarkers.

From now on the way runs along a limestone terrace with capital views across the Swale Gorge where on the western side of Swinner Gill is Crackpot Hall. The ruins of this house stand out against the background slopes of Hall Side. Many years ago, probably due to mine workings underneath, the walls began to bulge and tilt and windows slipped at crazy angles.

A short way on, a small detour to the river bank will reveal the splendour of Kisdon Force waterfall. The variety of scenery present on this walk, the Swale along its wooded ravine, limestone outcrops and wild flowers, makes it a very special walk. The path begins to descend along the edge of woodland to meet a barn and a gate. Follow the track, Keld Lane, back into the village; or bear right towards the river for a possible picnic.

2. Industrial heritage in Gunnerside Gill

Distance: 6¹/₂ miles (10.4km)

Map: OS Outdoor Leisure 30 Yorkshire Dales – Northern and Central areas 1:25,000

From Gunnerside village take the Ivelet byroad to the west for just over a half a mile and bear right up the slanting track (SD 941 983). This bends and terraces along the western slopes of Gunnerside Gill. It curves round Botcher Gill and continues northwards past the foot of the North Hush to Blakethwaite Smelt Mill. Proceed a little further to where the route joins a path on the opposite side of the stream, and return down the eastern side of the gill. The route crosses the barren, disturbed ground left by the hushes and proceeds down the valley past Middle Bank. At this point, the path descends to Gunnerside Beck and pursues a delightful course alongside the stream back to the village.

3. Reeth and Fremington Edge

Distance 6$^1/_2$ miles (10.4km)

Map: OS Outdoor Leisure 30 Yorkshire Dales – Northern and Central areas 1:25,000

Leave Reeth by the Richmond road, and after crossing the bridge, take the stile on the left and proceed eastwards across the fields to High Fremington. On entering a narrow lane, turn almost immediately up the walled track to the left to meet another lane. Proceed left, ignoring a bridleway branching off, and head towards Fremington Edge.

Keep on this lane, when it becomes a track, passing White House away to the left. Continue climbing to reach the top. From the gate in the wall bear left and walk along Fremington Edge Top for a distance of 1$^1/_4$ miles (2km) with rewarding views across Arkengarthdale to Calver Hill and Great Pinseat.

On approaching the end of the escarpment walk, a bridleway appears from the right in an area of mine tips. This bridleway now descends from the edge, (GR NZ 031 021) through a gateway towards the mine workings ahead. Keep to the lower side of them and follow a level course with North Rake Hush lying directly ahead across Slei Gill. Head round to the left and descend the slope to a gate. Proceed down by a wall to reach a farm lane. Turn left at Storthwaite Hall, then go along the lane to the next farm. From here walk across two fields to a gate in front. Continue alongside Arkle Beck and then follow blobs of yellow paint on a number of trees. The way crosses more fields, using stiles, to reach farm buildings.

Ahead, the route passes a derelict farmhouse to meet the beck once again. As the path forks, take the left-hand track, go through a gateway and continue alongside a wall. Pass through two stiles and then take one on the right descending past a barn. There are two more stiles and a wall to another stile. Proceed through two more fields to reach Reeth Bridge.

Down shafts and adits with plug and feather,
With light from candles in nobs of clay..

From 'The Dales' by Ron Scholes

Places to Visit

Muker

Swaledale Woollens*

Strawbeck, Muker in Swaledale
☎ (01748) 886251.
Open: Every day from Mar–Oct,
10am–5pm, Nov–Feb; 10am–4pm
Apr–Dec. www.swaledalewoollens.
co.uk

Reeth

Hazel Brow Farm*

Low Row, nr Reeth
Award-winning attraction, guided
tours, demonstrations, farm shop &
café. ☎ (01748) 886224
Open: 31st Mar – 30 Sep, 11am–
4.00pm; Mon & Fri school and group
bookings only except bank holidays.
www.hazelbrow.co.uk

Swaledale Museum*

Off the village green, Reeth
☎ (01748) 884118
Open: Easter to end of Oct. Wed–Fri,
Sun & Bank Holiday Mon, 10.30am–
5.30pm. museum@swaledale.org,
www.museum@swaledale.org

Cabinet Maker

The workshop & Gallery
Reeth Dales Centre, Silver Street,
Reeth. DL11 6SP
☎ (01748) 884555
Open: Mon–Sat, 9am–5pm
Occasional Sun and evening
openings through the year.

Clock Works

Reeth Dales Centre, Silver Street,
Reeth. DL11 6SP
☎ (01748) 884088
Open: Tue–Fri, 10am–4.30pm, Sat
10am–12.30pm, Sun closed. Other
times by appointment.
www.clockmakers.co.uk

the town walls with a tower not as imposing as Greyfriars. The interior has some twelfth-century work in the west bays of the arcades. Look for the misericords, they include two pigs dancing to a bagpipe played by a third. There is a wall painting in the south chapel, the Angel of the Annunciation, fifteenth century.

At the eastern part of the town is the particularly fine old railway station. When the line closed it was well converted into a garden centre.

The interesting ruins of **Easby Abbey** lie on the east bank of the Swale, about 1 mile (1.6km) east of Richmond. A pleasant walk wanders between the river and high wooded banks. This religious house was a Premonstratensian abbey of the White Canons and is now in the care of English Heritage. The gatehouse is well preserved and extremely fine and has hardly been altered since the fourteenth century. Another impressive feature is the refectory, with walls rising to their full height, and containing beautiful window tracery.

Below: Richmond
Castle, built soon
after the Conquest

Richmond

Richmond Castle

☎ (01748) 822493
Open: Apr–Sep 10am–6pm daliy.
Oct–Mar 10am–4pm Thu–Mon.
Closed 24–26 Dec & 1 Jan. www.
english-heritage.org.uk/yorkshire

Georgian Theatre Royal and Museum*

Victoria Road
Britain's oldest working Georgian theatre in its original form.
Tours: Mon–Sat; on the hour 10am–4pm. To pre-book a group tour of 10 or more – ☎ (01748) 823710. Box Office (01748) 825252. www. georgiantheatreroyal.co.uk

Green Howards Museum*

Trinity Church Square
☎ (01748) 822133
Open: Apr to Christmas, Tue–Sat, 10am–4.30pm and Sun 1–4pm.

Richmondshire Museum*

Ryders Wynd
☎ (01748) 825611
Open: Daily 1 Apr to late Oct, 10.30am–4.30pm.

Easby Abbey

1 mile (1.6km) south-east of Richmond off B6271
Open: 10am–6pm daily, Apr–Sep, 10am–5pm daily in Oct.

Swaledale Festival

A celebration of music and the arts taking place at venues in Swaledale, Wensleydale and Arkengarthdale. End of May to beginning of June. ☎ (01748) 880019, www.swaldale-festival.org.uk

The church of St Agatha, the parish church lies close to the gatehouse of the abbey and within its outer court. It is a long, low building with a small bellcote. Much of it is Early English, although the chancel arch is Victorian by Sir Giles Gilbert Scott, 1869.

The magnificent Easby Cross, the finest piece of Anglo-Saxon sculpture in the country, now resides in the Victoria and Albert Museum. Dating from about 800 AD, it is carved with scrolls, interlace, birds and beasts. At the top is seated Christ with two figures, then tiers with apostles under arches. A cast of the Easby Cross is to be found inside the church. Mid thirteenth-century wall paintings in the chancel include: *Creation of Eden, Temptation, Adam and Eve Ashamed, Expulsion, Annunciation to the Shepherds, Adoration of Magi* and *The Passing of the Seasons.*

Easby is an admirable place to stop at the beginning or end of a tour of Swaledale. It is pleasant to stroll round the ancient buildings or to walk along the attractive riverside at Richmond.

7. Nidderdale & Ripon

Nidderdale is a winding valley, some 25 miles (40km) long, which has been carved mainly out of rocks of the Millstone Grit series. During the last ice age, a glacier was formed in the upper part of the Dale on the slopes of Great and Little Whernside. Its gouging action produced the U-shaped section of the valley below the village of Lofthouse.

As the glacier retreated, it left successive moraines across the valley floor. This proved particularly useful in the choice of a site for the Gouthwaite Dam. The soils produced from the Millstone Grit strata are sandy, porous and infertile, while the shales erode into heavy clays. A combination of the two can form a depth of loam, which is acid in nature.

However, when this land is drained and limed it makes rich pasture.

The natural vegetation on the summit slopes and ridges is still coarse grass, cotton grass and peat; but due to the impact of man, the hillsides and valley bottoms have been cleared and transformed.

History of the dale

In the middle of the twelfth century, most of the surrounding area, and the Dale itself, was depopulated after the Norman campaign of murder, destruction and devastation – the Harrying of the North. In the twelfth and early thirteenth centuries, the abbeys of Fountains and Byland secured control of the whole of Nidderdale Chase. To develop their farming interests, the abbeys established a series of granges. Many of these were much bigger than peasant farms, and the abbeys' flocks and herds ranged far and wide.

It is easy to admire the determination and efficiency with which the monks set about reclaiming the waste, and bringing field and dale back to production after the destruction by the Normans. However, there were many cases of monastic clearances, when peasants were removed from their homes. There were occasions when the monks condoned callousness, avarice and even theft to gain more land and property. It is recorded how the monks of Byland Abbey attempted to evict a troublesome Ramsgill farmer in Nidderdale, by using a brand on two of his neighbour's sheep, and hoping that he would be convicted as a thief.

In the middle of the eighteenth century most of the dwellings were thatched, and the roads were rough, narrow tracks, with surfaces and gradients more suitable for packhorses than for wheeled carts. The time between the 1750's and the 1870's saw a dramatic change in the appearance of the countryside. In this period, miles of stone walls were built and hedges were laid, during the enclosure of the common pastures.

Before the arrival of the reservoirs of Angram, Scar House and Thruscross, water in the Dale played a different role. The middle of the nineteenth century saw a growth of small industrial hamlets using water-power. There was an abundance of fast-flowing streams, and in 1835, some sixty water wheels were at work powering corn, flax and smelt mills, and lead-mining machinery.

Upper Nidderdale

At the head of the Dale, Bradford Corporation was embarking on the construction of two large reservoirs, **Scar House** and **Angram** and in order to transport men and materials to the construction site, they built the **Nidd Valley Light Railway** from Pateley Bridge to Angram. Passengers services were run on the first six miles of the line, with stations at Pateley, Wath, Ramsgill and Lofthouse. The Nidd Bridge to Pateley line opened on 1st May 1862. These railways enabled people from Leeds or Bradford to enjoy a day out in the countryside.

The dam wall of Scar House is a massive structure that towers 170ft (52m) high; it is the largest stone-built dam in Europe. However, to be technically correct, the dam is stone-faced with a core consisting of large blocks of stone set in concrete. The stonework is of the highest quality, from beautifully dressed facing stone on the dam to the stone-lined culverts.

It was a tremendous achievement to undertake a project of this nature at the beginning of the twentieth century. At the height of operations, there was a workforce of well over 1,000 men. To house this number, a completely new village was built with over sixty bungalows for the staff, and hostels for the navvies. The workforce was looked after by housekeepers, cooks and cleaners. Each section of accommodation had electric light and running water, with inside toilets and bathrooms.

Missed opportunity

The workers living in the temporary settlement near the dam sites provided the main passenger traffic on the Nidd Valley Light Railway. There must have been many a boisterous journey along this stretch of the line, with navvies returning after a night out visiting the pubs in Pateley Bridge.

As the construction work on the dams neared completion, the running of the trains became uneconomic, and what had been England's first municipally-owned railway passenger service was closed in 1926. When Scar House Reservoir was finished in 1936, the line was taken up. With hindsight what wonderful tourist attractions these little railways would be today running through such superb scenery.

There was a well-staffed little hospital as well as a school and a cinema. Scar House Reservoir was begun in 1924 and completed in 1936.

The fish-tailed shape of Angram Reservoir with its 130ft (40m) dam above the watercourse contains half the capacity of its Scar House. The catchment area beyond, contains the beginnings of the River Nidd, and many other sources lying on the flanks of Little and Great Whernside. Angram was begun in 1904 and finished in 1919.

For hill walkers in Upper Nidderdale, as well as the ridge from Dead Man's Hill, there are paths from Lodge to Long Hill Sike Head, and one from Middlesmoor, above the How Stean Beck Valley to Sandy Gate. All these routes lead towards Wharfedale. Returning down the valley towards Lofthouse, the present road follows the old track-bed of the railway.

There is an interesting feature of the local geology in the upper part of Nidderdale, where carboniferous limestone outcrops on the west side of Greenhow Hill. There are two inliers in the Millstone Grit to the east between Newhouses and Lofthouse. In the upper dale, the River Nidd has cut through the grits into the underlying limestone for a length of two miles. The river disappears through a great hole in the river-bed, when in spate, at **Goyden Pot**, a short distance from Limley Farm. About 400yds (366m) further upstream, the river disappears into its bed at Manchester Hole and emerges near Lofthouse. In dry weather, it is safe to examine the mouth of Goyden Pot; it must be remembered that any further exploration should be left strictly to the experts.

Lofthouse to Pateley Bridge

The stone-built village of **Lofthouse** sits in the valley bottom, at the foot of the byroad that climbs steeply up Trapping Hill. The settlement was established around a grange belonging to the monks of Fountains Abbey. At Lofthouse one can see the old station building with its cast-iron pillars and station platforms and a drinking trough with the following rhyme on its side:

If you want to be healthy, wealthy and stout,

Use plenty of cold water inside and out.

Turn right at the southern end of the village, cross over the River Nidd and take a right turn up to the hillside village of **Middlesmoor**. The settlement's very stones speak of years long past, and the quaint corners and cobbled ways add to its engaging character. Standing at 950ft (290m) above sea level, the view from the churchyard affords panoramic views down Nidderdale. The church of St Chad dates from 1866 although the first church was consecrated here in 1484.

Descend the spiralling road from Middlesmoor, and turn right along the How Stean Beck for a short distance to reach the **How Stean Gorge**, known as Yorkshire's Little Switzerland. The limestone gorge in places is 80ft (24m) deep with an abundance of lichens, ferns and mosses growing beside the water and woodland trees, including ash, hazel and oak line the ravine.

There is a walk through its confines, assisted by footbridges and an opportunity to explore Tom Taylor's Cave; it is entered from the gorge down narrow

Nature Reserve

Gouthwaite Reservoir was built in 1899, as a compensation reservoir, on the site of a glacial lake. The Water Authority decided that the 2-mile (3.2km) long lake should be declared a nature reserve. The road runs alongside the reservoir, and the immediate area is a favourite spot for birdwatching with a special viewing facility. Very many species of birds have been recorded, including, duck, birds of prey, grebes, divers and waders.

steps. The site includes a restaurant which offers home cooking.

Take the road past Lofthouse and accompany the Nidd to the village of **Ramsgill**. It lies at the head of Gouthwaite Reservoir and is considered to be Nidderdale's prettiest settlement. The village is centred round the Yorke Arms Inn, formerly a lodge belonging to the Yorke family. The cries of peacocks can often be heard as they strut round the village green, and the whole scene affords much pleasure. The monks from Byland Abbey established a grange here, together with a small chapel. A fragment of this early building can be seen in the east wall of the nineteenth-century church.

The valley road to **Pateley Bridge** crosses Foster Beck. Here the Foster Beck Mill, with its huge 35ft (10.6m) water-wheel was a hemp mill but is now the Watermill Inn. Although the wheel is no longer working, its existence is a reminder of the importance

Cottages in Lofthouse, Nidderdale

of water-power for Pennine industries – lead mines, smelt mills and textile mills.

A little further on, the valley road meets the B6265, and crosses the Nidd by the Pateley Bridge to enter the town. The town is centred round the main street that climbs steeply from the river bridge. The buildings are of dark millstone grit but in summer, are brightly decorated with flowers in window boxes and containers. In between the houses and shops are secluded courtyards and little alleyways.

In the past, it was an important industrial centre for lead mining. The main workings, which lay principally on nearby Greenhow Hill, declined over the years as the richer seams became exhausted. By the nineteenth century, stone-quarrying had succeeded lead mining. The main quarries were at Scotgate Ash high above the town. Also, at the same time that the demand for lead disappeared, textiles such as flax and cotton became more important.

The award winning **Nidderdale Museum** is housed in the Victorian workhouse, and visitors will find out how local life was lived in the past.

Annual events

Pateley Bridge is the home of the Nidderdale Show and the Nidderdale Festival. Over 100 years old, the show is held on a Monday in the middle of September and is considered to be the premier agricultural show in the Dales. Farmers display their finest stock. There is a splendid Grand Parade and a dog show claimed to be second only to Crufts. The Festival is earlier in the summer, usually late June and early July, and offers music of all kinds in many different settings. Crafts are on show and parades and drama in the open air take place in a celebration of Dales' culture.

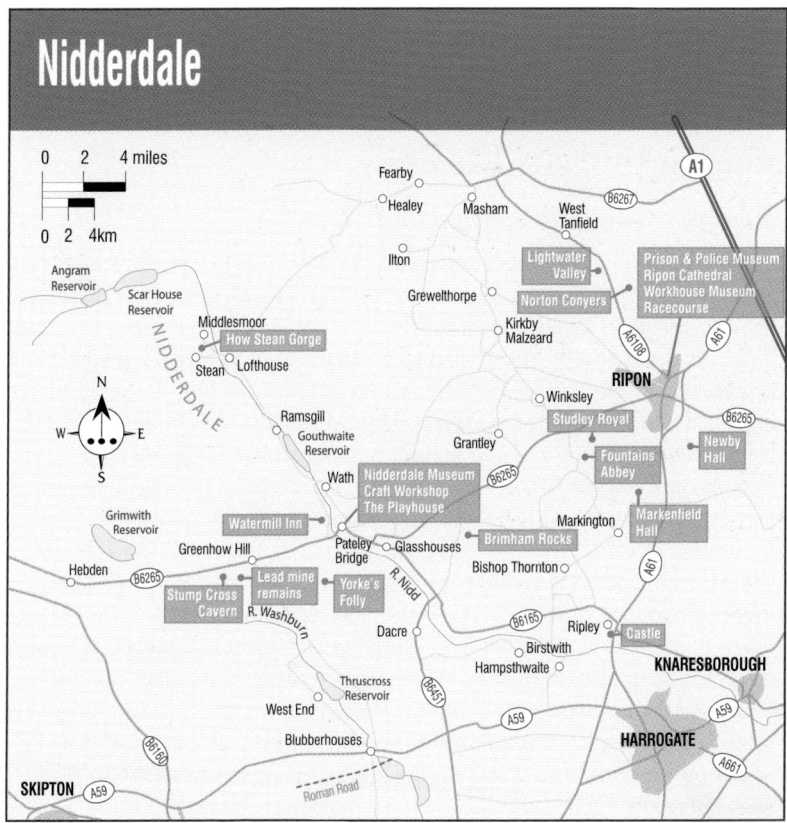

Nidderdale

0 2 4 miles

0 2 4km

Fearby
Healey Masham West Tanfield
A1
B6267

Ilton

Angram Reservoir
Scar House Reservoir
Lightwater Valley
Prison & Police Museum
Ripon Cathedral
Workhouse Museum
Racecourse

Grewelthorpe
Norton Conyers

Middlesmoor
How Stean Gorge
Stean Lofthouse

Kirkby Malzeard
RIPON
A6108
A61

NIDDERDALE

Ramsgill
Gouthwaite Reservoir
Wath
Winksley
Studley Royal
B6265
Newby Hall

Grantley
Fountains Abbey

Nidderdale Museum
Craft Workshop
The Playhouse
B6265

Grimwith Reservoir
Watermill Inn
Greenhow Hill
Pateley Bridge
Glasshouses
Brimham Rocks
Markington
Markenfield Hall

Hebden
B6265
Bishop Thornton
A61

Lead mine remains
Stump Cross Cavern
Yorke's Folly
R. Washburn
R. Nidd

Dacre
B6165
Ripley
Castle

Thruscross Reservoir
Birstwith
Hampsthwaite
KNARESBOROUGH
B6451

West End
A59
A59

Blubberhouses
HARROGATE
A661

SKIPTON A59
B6160
Roman Road

Among the displays are a cobbler's shop, a village shop and a solicitor's office. Here too is a history of the reservoirs and displays of minerals and fossils.

The town has a wide selection of small interesting shops that cater for all the needs of the visitor: gifts, foodstuffs, cafes, outdoor wear, maps, craft goods and paintings. Behind the museum, are the **King Street Craft Workshops** where local craftsmen make and sell their goods. It also has one of the smallest theatres in the country, **The Playhouse**, where performances of all sorts are held throughout the year.

The church of Old St Mary, lies in ruins at the top of a steep hill. It has a tower of 1691, a nave and aisles. The nearby church of St Cuthbert, dates from1827.

Around Pateley Bridge

Bewerley is situated just across the river and looks out across the Nidd towards Pateley Bridge. In the village there is a small roadside dwelling. The house was first built as a chapel and priest's cell by Marmaduke Huby the last abbot of Fountains Abbey (1495-1526). From Bewerley, a road leads to Middle Tongue, once a cluster of houses occupied by quarry workers.

Selected Walk

Pateley Bridge to Wath

Distance: 5$\frac{1}{4}$ miles (8.4km)

Map: OS Explorer 26 Nidderdale 1:25,000

From the north end of the bridge at Pateley Bridge take the footpath signposted to Wath. The route follows the line of the old Nidderdale Railway through fields close to the river. At Wath cross over the old packhorse bridge and the road, and climb across the hillside, as the path runs between a block of woodland and a large lonely tree. Looking back, there are wide views eastwards to the moors above Pateley Bridge. To the north-west, there is a fine aspect of Gouthwaite Reservoir.

Walk through a gate in the wall at the top of the slope to pass a farmyard and emerge on to the road. Bear right to pass the corrugated iron chapel at Heathfield Just past the chapel a bridleway heads to the left along a farm track which curves up to the brow of the hill. Proceed straight ahead through a gate and follow the wall down towards Spring House Farm. Just before the farm, the route runs diagonally across the field and through a farmyard, leaving the yard by the right-hand metal gate. Follow the hedgeside and descend to join the metalled road alongside Ashfold Side Beck. Turn left and walk past some caravans as far as the new metal gate and into the caravan site. From the gate, keep on the track between the caravans and over the beck. Follow the track up the bank and descend the walled green lane to Mosscarr Bottom and the footbridge over Brandstone Beck.

Climb steadily up the valley side above the beck. This is an opportunity to admire the wilder landscape of this part of Nidderdale. Where the path meets the road, turn left and walk past Ladies Riggs to a point where the large area of woodland meets the road. Take a path opposite on the left, and follow the field boundaries descending to Bridgehouse Gate. Cross the Wath Bridge road by the chapel and cut through to the Greenhow Hill road. Bear left and return to the starting point.

Before reaching Middle Tongue, there is a gate signposted 'Moorhouses via White Wood'. This is a beautiful path through beechwoods, leading to a lake surrounded by rhododendrons. The path continues towards a lane leading back to Bewerley.

Also from Bewerley, a road crosses Turner Bridge and ascends the hillside via Nought Bank Road, as it swings round some quarry workings to reach **York's Folly**, otherwise known as Two Stoops. The folly consists of two stone pillars said to have been built by one of the prosperous Yorke family for the purpose of providing employment.

From this point there are splendid views across the valley of the Nidd.

Returning to Turner Bridge, turn left and climb through Middle Tongue to reach the B6265 road. The village of **Greenhow Hill**, is the highest in Yorkshire at 1,280ft (390m). Appropriately, the village pub is named the Miners arms, with the surrounding moorland a scene of desolation, scarred and pock-marked by generations of lead mining. Greenhow Hill has been described like a piece of cheese in which men have burrowed like mice.

The Greenhow lead-mining field dates back to the Romans, a fact a confirmed by the finding of two pigs of lead at Dacre in Nidderdale. These pigs bear the inscription IMP. CAES. DOMITIANO.AUG. COS.VII and are therefore dated to around 81 AD.

Fountains and Byland Abbeys were granted the Chase of Nidderdale in the twelfth century, and Fountains erected a smelt mill at Smelthouses in about 1445. The eighteenth and nineteenth centuries saw greatly increased activity but eventually poor financial practice, lack of capital, and the drop in the price of lead resulted in closure of the mines in 1896.

A short distance west of Greenhow Hill are the **Stump Cross Caverns**. In 1860, lead miners stumbled into caves long sealed off in the last ice age. The miners had been sinking a

The flax industry

The flax spinning mill at **Glasshouses** on the Pateley Bridge to Harrogate road. Glasshouses was originally a corn mill, and was rented to spin flax in 1812. It is interesting to note the scale of wages paid in 1833:

Under 10 years of age	1s 6d per week
10-12 years of age	2s per week
14-16 years of age	4s per week
Over 21 years of age	12s per week

During the nineteenth century there were alternate booms and slumps in trade, not helped by production problems due to the water level in the river. At Glasshouses a 120hp waterwheel was installed in 1851, eventually superseded by a steam engine in 1862.

These fluctuations in fortune were a general state of affairs in the Nidd Valley. Generally by the 1870s there was a decline in the flax-spinning industry due to the competition from cotton and mills were converted into cotton spinning, weaving, hemp spinning, etc. Some mills continued to make linen cloth, tea-towels and shirtings.

Then foreign competition and the arrival of artificial fibres threatened to drive hemp products out of this field altogether. Some mills were demolished and others put to different uses. At Glasshouses, the old mill dam is now used for water sports in summer and skating in winter.

Fountains Abbey

History of Fountains Abbey

In 1132 the Benedictine Abbey of St Mary at York had been established for fifty years. A group of thirteen dissident monks, wishing to pursue a life of greater austerity, were led by Thurstan the archbishop to a wild wasteland in the narrow valley of the River Skell.

The story of Fountains starts as one of great hardship and near starvation. Their first winter was spent sheltering under the rocks while they built a hut and a chapel. Fortunately Hugh, Dean of York, retired to Fountains bringing considerable wealth. The great northern families of Mowbray, Percy and others began to grant extensive gifts of land to the abbey. Their holdings were soon impressive with granges in Nidderdale, Wensleydale, Colsterdale, Wharfedale, Littondale, Malham, Ribblesdale and even in Cumberland.

Fountains was now one of the most powerful religious houses in the north of England. Farming was an important source of wealth, particularly wool from sheep rearing. Many of the granges developed specialised activities, such as mining, smelting, forging, quarrying and fishing. Financial maladministration brought the abbey into debt, followed by Scottish attacks after Bannockburn and a complex legal struggle as who was to be the next abbot.

Stability was restored in the second part of the fifteenth century and Fountains prospered under the leadership of Marmaduke Huby. He is remembered as the builder of the great tower, and as a tireless worker in the repair of the abbey's granges and chapels. The last abbot, Marmaduke Bradley, surrendered the abbey and all its possessions on 25 November 1539 to the king.

Today, the great church is still quite magnificent, with its imposing Perpendicular tower overlooking the roofless nave and transept. The strength of the massive pillars is much in contrast with the fine tracery of the sightless windows. The cloister court with its dominant Norman arches and the chapel of the nine altars are still awe-inspiring after seven centuries. This is a very special place, well deserving of its World Heritage Site status.

Above: The fantastic shapes of Brimham Rocks

Left: Ripon Cathedral

Selected Car Drive

Explore Nidderdale from Masham

Distance: 58 miles (92.8km)

Leave the Market Square in Masham, and join the A6108 towards Leyburn. At the western edge of the town, turn off left on the byroad to Fearby and Healey. After crossing the River Burn, the road passes Leighton Reservoir, and climbs over the moorland to Jordan Moss, then descends steeply to Lofthouse. Bear right and then right again, for the short climb to the interesting hill village of Middlesmoor. Return to the foot of the hill, where a right turn leads to How Stean Gorge. Otherwise, bear left to Lofthouse and continue down Nidderdale, passing Gouthwaite Reservoir to Bridgehouse Gate. Bear left into Pateley Bridge.

Return and cross the Nidd on the B6265, and climb up to the former lead mining area of Greenhow Hill. A short distance along the road lies the location of Stump Cross Caverns. Return to Greenhow Hill and turn right to Thruscross Reservoir. From the cross roads, a road descends to the reservoir, where there is a parking area. Return to the crossroads, turn right and continue south for 1 mile (1.6km), then turn left for Birstwith. In the village, turn right by the church, and then left to cross over the Nidd and on to Clint. The road travels on to meet the B6165, turn left.

After a short way to Burnt Yates, branch off to the right on a byroad, and proceed for 3 miles (4.8km), then turn right for Brimham Rocks, parking area. Return to the road, turn left, and continue on to meet the B6265, turn right. After 4 miles (6.4km) signposts announce the turn for Fountains Abbey and Studley Royal. Return to the B6265 for the journey into Ripon. Note that having crossed the River Laver approaching Ripon, keep an eye out for a turning left prior to the city centre. Take this byroad to Kirkby Malzeard and Grewelthorpe, and from the north-east corner of the latter village, a lane leads back to Masham.

shaft near the Stubbe or Stump Cross, when they accidentally came upon the caves at a depth of 49ft (15m). These water-worn caverns were used as ancient shelters, and on exploration yielded many different animal remains dating back some 90,000 years. Also discovered was a wealth of stalagmites and stalactites which can still be seen as the caverns are open to the public. The B6265 descends from Greenhow Hill into Pateley Bridge, and continues along the valley road before branching left towards Ripon.

The B6265 climbs out of Nidderdale for 3 miles (4.8km) to reach Crossgates, and a road on the right signposted to **Brimham Rocks**. There is no other place in the country quite like Brimham Rocks. On the edge of high heathland, centuries of wind, rain and frost have sculptured these outcrops of exposed gritstone. Some rise up as tall pillars and stand precariously balanced on others, while yet more are of massive girth. The rocks are spread over about 60 acres (24 hectares) of Brimham Moor.

Some appear to represent animal shapes or other recognisable forms – a dancing bear, an oyster, elephant rock, a frog, a tortoise, a tiger and many other creatures, with an Idol Rock, a Druid's Circle and a Cannon Rock for good measure. The area of Brimham Rocks is now under the guardianship of the National Trust. There are ample car parking facilities and information points.

Fountains Abbey

Return to the B6265 and follow the signs to **Fountains Abbey**. This is a World Heritage Site and the preservation of its historic buildings is the responsibility of English Heritage. The site, comprising the spectacular ruin of a twelfth-century Cistercian abbey, an Elizabethan mansion, and one of the best surviving examples of a Georgian water garden is managed by the National Trust. There is a National Trust Visitor Centre, good footpaths through the estate and excellent parking arrangements.

After some time in the attractive Visitor Centre, visitors may wander along the pathway to the abbey ruins. Tracks then continue to the series of formal lakes of the **Studley Royal Water Garden**. This makes a delight-

---

Wakeman's ceremony

On the south side of Ripon market place is the Georgian town hall, 1801, with the inscription: 'Except Ye Lord keep Ye Cittie, Ye Wakeman Waketh in Vain'. The old custom of 'setting the watch', a thousand year old ceremony, takes place at nine o'clock every evening. This is carried out by the Wakeman, in full regalia, who blows the Wakeman's Horn. The Wakeman's House is a two-floored timber-framed building.

---

ful setting for the classical statues and temples, and the surrounding gardens.

Another attractive approach is from the B6265 and the small village of Studley Roger. A path continues through the deer park where stands the church of St Mary, built by the Marchioness of Ripon in 1871-8; the architect was William Burges. It has a tower with spire and pinnacles, and bell openings with gables. The interior of the church is pure Victorian, Early English in style, with excellent stained glass and a fine mosaic floor. There is a monument to the First Marchioness of Ripon, 1908, consisting of a large white marble effigy.

Ripon

It is only a short journey by road along the B6265 from Fountains Abbey into the large market town of Ripon, with its cathedral to give it the status of a city. The settlement developed at the confluence of the Rivers Skell and

Ripon Cathedral

The Cathedral Church of Saint Peter and Saint Wilfrid was originally a minster. Following the creation of the new Diocese of Ripon it became the Cathedral in 1836.The first church existed for only five years, when it belonged to a monastery founded by Scottish monks in the seventh century. Wilfrid, an Anglo-Saxon noble, made a journey to Rome to meet the Pope. He took holy orders and eventually became an abbot, rebuilding the church on the present site. The crypt belongs to that early building. Wilfrid's church was destroyed by the Northumberland king, Eadred, in 950 and the whole church was rebuilt from about 1180, but the west front was not probably reached until 1220.

Towards the end of the Middle Ages, a number of important additions and alterations were made. The fine west front of the cathedral is Early English. The two towers originally had spires, removed in 1664. Above the portals are five tall lancets, with dog-tooth decoration.

The nave is entirely Perpendicular of the early sixteenth century. What appears certain is that the twelfth-century nave had no aisles. It must have appeared very tall and narrow. The chancel is a fine, architectural part of the church, with the work being carried out in about 1175, similar to Canterbury. It has a wooden vaulted ceiling with fine fourteenth-century bosses, including the Creation of Adam, God speaking to Eve, the Annunciation, Christ in Glory, the Expulsion from Paradise and two Bishops.

The stalls contain an outstanding series of misericords, the work of the famous school of Ripon carvers. The stalls are dated 1489, and a bench-end 1494. The latter carries a representation of the Elephant and Castle, others have poppy-heads.

In Wilfrid's time the Cathedral would have been magnificently furnished with the finest available workmanship. Today the only artefact of that period that remains is the Ripon Jewel found near the Cathedral in 1976. The small gold roundel, just over 1 inch (2.5cm) in diameter is set with amber and garnets but the central inlay is now missing. The exact purpose is not known but it provides a fascinating link with the past.

A more recent link that may not be appreciated is that the father of Lewis Carroll, creator of Alice in Wonderland, was a Canon at Ripon from 1852 to 1868. Sharp-eyed visitors will be able to spot carvings in the choir that inspired characters in Alice. The Cheshire Cat, the Queen of Hearts and even the white rabbit disappearing down his hole, are there somewhere.

Laver and near to the navigable River Ure, which was an important factor in Ripon's trade and commerce. Recently, the final stretch of the Ripon Canal and the local basin has been reopened after problems with roads and bridges. This rejuvenated waterway now allows access for leisure craft into the heart of the city. Ripon is the most northerly point of the canal system of England and Wales.

The attractive market square comes to life on market days when, each Thursday at 11am, a bell is rung for the official start of trading. Standing on the square, is the tall obelisk erected in 1781 to commemorate the sixty years that William Aislabie of Studley Royal had been MP for Ripon.

The narrow medieval streets, such as Kirkgate and Low Skellgate, cause problems to modern traffic, but the combination of seventeenth, eighteenth and nineteenth century buildings add to the city's charm. Along the north side of the Cathedral in Minster Road, remains one thirteenth century archway with dog-tooth decoration. Behind the arch is the Court House of late Georgian date. Then there is the former Deanery with a seventeenth-century façade.

Going south from the front of the cathedral, at Bedern Bank, there is a fine brick, early Georgian house called The Hall. Turning left into High St Agnesgate one arrives at the Thorpe Prebend

The Market Square in Ripon

171

House, seventeenth century; then the former chapel of St Anne's Hospital. Following on, is St Agnes Lodge that dates back to 1630.

Walking north into St Mary Gate, there is a late seventeenth-century house, now converted into flats. On the north side of St Mary Gate are strangely built eighteenth-century prison cells. These have been converted to **The Prison and Police Museum**, which houses documents, prints and artefacts depicting the history of law and order over 1,100 years. Early punishments and conditions in Victorian Prisons are shown in the cells on the first floor.

St Mary Gate continues to Stonebridge Gate, where stands a chapel of a former leper hospital; it has a medieval south doorway, with a re-used Norman arch and a Perpendicular east window.

Just outside the town centre is the **Ripon Workhouse Museum** housed in the Men's Casual Wards of Ripon's Victorian workhouse. The galleries give an insight into the conditions suffered by the poor and destitute in the nineteenth century.

Markenfield Hall lies some $3^1/_2$ miles (5.6km) south-west of Ripon via the A61. This building is a fortified house with a forecourt surrounded by a moat. Markenfield is a remarkable house having survived a web of political and religious intrigue. The Markenfields lost all after attempts to re-establish a Catholic monarch on the throne. Sir Thomas Markenfield fled to the continent after the failed Rising of the North in 1569. The Hall was presented to the Lord Chancellor, and he and other owners kept the structure in excellent condition.

Beyond Markenfield the A61 heads south towards Harrogate. After $4^1/_2$ miles (7.2km) the road reaches, and bypasses, the village of **Ripley.** This attractive village is very much centred on the castle, which has been in the possession of the Ingilby family since the fourteenth century. Now free of busy traffic the village centre is a pleasant spot to stroll and admire the houses. The settlement is an eighteenth-century estate village modelled to the ideas of Sir William Ingilby who based it on a village in Alsace Lorraine. It consists of one straight street with houses in a variety of Gothic to Tudor styles; these can probably be dated from between 1780 and 1860. It has a village hall in the style of a French Hotel de Ville.

Ripley Castle has lost its fortress-like appearance and is, in fact, a family home which is open to the public. There is a short tower block, which was part of the original house, although the adjoining hall was removed in 1780. The tower boasts a secret priest's hole and one large upper room has an early Jacobean plaster ceiling. The grounds, with lakes and a magnificent kitchen garden, were laid out by Capability Brown. Visitors can enjoy walks through the extensive gardens or see the lovely displays in the hot houses.

The church of All Saints was rebuilt in 1395 and contains several monuments to the Ingilby family. In the churchyard is an unusual medieval 'weeping cross'; a base with eight niches to kneel into. There are marks in the church wall made by bullets fired at Royalist prisoners who were lined up and shot.

Places to Visit

Lofthouse

HowStean Gorge

Lofthouse. ☎ (01423) 755666
Restaurant & tea room, cycle hire.
Open: All year, 10am–6pm. Evening
bookings by arrangement. Closed
Mon & Tue Oct–Easter. Open
weekends only in Jan.
www.howstean.co.uk

Pateley Bridge

Nidderdale Museum*

King Street. ☎ (01423) 711225
Open: Nov–Easter 1.30–4.30pm (Sat
& Sun). Easter–Nov 1.30–4.30pm
daily. (10.30am–4.30pm Aug only).
www.nidderdalemuseum.com

King Street Studio Workshops*

Pateley Bridge. ☎ (01423) 712570
Range of craftspeople demonstrate
their skills, finished articles on sale.
Open: 9.30am–5.30pm Mon–Fri,
weekends by appointment. www.
kingstreetworkshops.co.uk

The Playhouse*

Pateley Bridge
The Little Theatre in the Dales.
☎ (01423) 712196

Yorkshire Country Wines*

Glasshouses Mill, Pateley Bridge
☎ (01423) 711947

Stump Cross Caverns*

Greenhow Hill, 5 miles (8km) west of
Pateley Bridge on B6265

☎ (01756) 752780. Tearoom & gift
shop. Open: Daily 10am onwards,
1st Mar – end of Nov. Winter
openings: weekends and school
holidays. Schools, evening groups
and coach parties always welcome.
www.stumpcrosscaverns.co.uk

Brimham Rocks (NT)

Summerbridge. ☎ (01423) 780688
Strange and fascinating rock
formations. Spectacular views. Open:
site open daily, 8am–dusk. Facilities:
Please phone, times may vary. www.
nationaltrust.org.uk

Fountains Abbey and Studley Royal Water Garden

Nr Ripon. ☎ (01765) 608888
Abbey and Garden, Shop and Mill:
1 Mar – 31 Oct; 10am–5pm
1 Nov – 28 Feb; 10am–4pm
Restaurant:
1 Apr – 30 Sep; 10am–4.30pm
1 Oct – 31 Mar; 10am–4pm.
www.nationaltrust.org.uk

Ripon

Prison and Police Museum*

St Marygate
☎ (01765) 690799
Open: daily from 31 Mar to 28 Sep,
Oct from 1–4pm (11am–4pm during
chool holidays).

Ripon Cathedral*

☎ (01765) 602072
Open: from 8am to after 5.30pm.
Evensong daily, and the crypt and
treasury close at 4.45pm.

Places to Visit

Below: Nidderdale Museum
Right: Lightwater Valley Country Theme Park

www.riponcathedral.org.uk
Admission free although a donation of £3 per person is suggested.

Workhouse Museum*

☎ (01765) 690799
Open: times as for Prison & Police Museum.
www.riponmuseums.co.uk

Ripon Racecourse

On B6265 just outside Ripon
Some 14 flat racing meetings per year. ☎ (01765) 602156
www.ripon-races.co.uk

Newby Hall & Gardens*

East of Ripon, about 3 miles (4.8km)
Renowned Adam house with superb contents including the Gobelins Tapestry Room and Chippendale furniture. 25 acres of gardens and an adventure garden for children. Shop and restaurant. Open: 31 Mar to 30 Sep, Tue–Sun, 11am–5.30pm. Open bank holidays and Mon throughout Jul and Aug. ☎ 0845 4504068.
www.newbyhall.co.uk

Norton Conyers*

Near Wath, about 3 miles (5km) north of Ripon
16th–17th century house.
Please call for house and garden opening times ☎ (01765) 640333.
Please call for house and garden opening times.

Lightwater Valley Country Theme Park and Country Shopping Village*

3 miles (4.8km) north of Ripon on A6108

Rides and attractions for all the family with Lightwater Village and Factory Shopping next door.

☎ (0870) 4580040. Open: April 10th–23rd; May week ends. Daily May 29th–Aug 31st. September week ends.

Ripley

Ripley Castle & Gardens*

Ripley, Nr. Harrogate, A61 7 miles (11.2km) south of Ripon

☎ (01423) 770152

Romance and drama, all feature in the fascinating, 700-year history of Ripley Castle. Tours are very entertaining and informative.

Guided tours: gates open 9am, 1st tour 11am, last tour 3pm.

Castle: Open: Apr–Oct daily; Nov & Mar: Tue, Thu, Sat, Sun; Dec, Jan, Feb: weekends only. The castle is open daily for pre-arranged group tours.

Gardens: Open daily throughout the year (except christmas day) 9am–5pm (4.30pm winter months). No dogs allowed except for Guide Dogs.

www.ripleycastle.co.uk

Ripley Castle

Getting there

Airports

There are four airports close to the Yorkshire Dales:
Leeds/Bradford ☎ (0113) 2509 696
Manchester ☎ (0161) 489 3000
Newcastle ☎ (0870) 122 1488
Teeside ☎ (01325) 332811

Bus/coach

Regular coach services from around the country to the larger towns around the Dales.
Enquiries: National Express ☎ 0870 580 8080 or www.eurolines.co.uk

Car

A network of major roads surrounds the Dales, the M1/A1 on the eastern side and the M6 on the western side, both run north-south. In an east-west direction the A66 crosses to the north and the A65, A59, A629, M62 and M65 cross to the south.

Ferry

The Yorkshire Dales are readily accessible from the ferry ports of Hull and Newcastle.

Colorline
Bergen & Stavanger to Newcastle
☎ (0191) 2624444

P&O North Sea Ferries
Rotterdam & Zeebrugge to Hull
☎ (0870) 5202020

Rail
There are regular services to all major cities around the Dales while the Lancaster to Skipton line and the Settle to Carlisle line cross the area.
National Rail Enquiries ☎ (0845) 7484950
Internet enquiries www.nationalrail.co.uk

Accommodation

There is a wide range of types of accommodation in the Yorkshire Dales. The most up-to-date details will always be obtained from the local Tourist Information Centres that are listed in this fact file. However a selection of addresses are given here for immediate reference.

Hotels, Inns and Bed and Breakfast

Milton House
Askrigg
☎ (01969) 650217

Stow House Hotel
Aysgarth Falls
☎ (01969) 663635

West Winds
Buckden, Wharfedale
☎ (01756) 760883

Redmire Farm
Buckden, Wharfedale
☎ (01756) 760253

The Red Lion Hotel
Burnsall
☎ (01756) 720204

The Wheatsheaf
Carperby
☎ (01969) 663216

St. Mark's
Cautley, Sedbergh
☎ (01539) 620287

New Inn Hotel
Clapham
18th-century coaching inn.
☎ (015242) 51203

Stone Close
Dent
☎ (01539) 625231

Sportsman's Inn
Cowgill, Dent
☎ (01539) 625282

The Austwick Traddock
Austwick
☎ (015242) 51224

The Moorcock Inn
Garsdale Head, nr Sedbergh
☎ (01969) 667488

Harts Head Hotel
Belle Hill, Giggleswick
☎ (01729) 822086

Springroyd House
Grassington
☎ (01756) 752473

Ashfield House
Summers Fold, Grassington
☎ (01756) 752584

Laburnum House
The Holme, Hawes
B & B and tearoom
☎ (01969) 667717

Crown Hotel
Horton-in-Ribblesdale
☎ (01729) 860209

Low Raisgill
Hubberholme
☎ (01756) 760351

Rombalds Hotel and Restaurant
Wells Road, Ilkley
AA Rosette Restaurant.
☎ (01943) 603201

Ingleborough View
Ingleton
☎ (01524) 241523

Springfield Hotel
26 Main Street, Ingleton
☎ (01524) 241280

Dalegarth House
Gunnerside
☎ (0748) 886275

Tan Hill Inn
Nr Keld, above Swaledale
☎ (01833) 628246

The Buck Inn
Malham
Traditional country inn, home cooked food.
☎ (01729) 830317

River House Hotel
Malham
Interesting menu and wine list.
☎ (01729) 830315

Fletcher House
Kirkby Stephen
☎ (017683) 71013

Street Head Inn
Newbiggin-in-Bishopdale
☎ (01969) 683282

Roslyn Hotel
9 King Street, Pateley Bridge
B & B and evening meal.
☎ (01423) 711374

Charles Bathurst Inn
Arkengarthdale, Reeth
☎ (01748) 884567

Unicorn Hotel
Market Place, Ripon
☎ (01765) 602202

Lime Tree Farm
Grewelthorpe, Nr Ripon
☎ (01765) 658450

The Marton Arms Hotel
Thornton-in-Lonsdale
Good food, bar meals and en-suite accommodation.
☎ (015242) 41281

Kearton Guest House
Thwaite, Swaledale
☎ (01748) 886277

Self-catering agencies

Robin Hill and Brewhouse Cottages
Settle
☎ (01729)

Yorkshire dale Country Cottages
Shaw Ghyll, High Shaw, Simonstone, Hawes
☎ (01969) 667359

Helm Pasture Lodges
Hartwith Bank, Summerbridge, Harrogate
☎ (01423) 780279

Cawder Hall Cottages
Skipton
☎ (01756) 791579

Dales View Hoilday Homes
Jenkins Garth, Leyburn
☎ (01969) 622808

Holiday Cottage

Elm Hill Holiday Cottage
Askrigg
☎ (01969) 624252

Caravan and camp sites

Dalesbridge Centre
Austwick
B & B, bunkhouse, electric hook ups.
☎ (015242) 51021
e-mail: info@dalesbridge.co.uk

Bainbridge Ings Caravan and Camping Park
Hawes
☎ (01969) 667354

Harden & Bingley Hoilday Park
Goit Stock Estate, Harden
☎ (01535) 273810

Lower Wensleydale Caravan Site
Harmby, Leyburn
☎ (01969) 623366

Woodclose Caravan Park
Kirkby Lonsdale
☎ (015242) 71597

Langcliffe Park
Settle
☎ (01729) 822387

Lindale Holiday Park
Bedale
☎ (01677) 450842

Sleningford Watermill Caravan & Camping Park
North Stainley
☎ (01765) 635201

Knight Stainforth
Little Stainforth, Settle
☎ (01729) 822200

Howgill Lodge
Barden, Skipton
☎ (01756) 720655

The Camping & Caravaning Club Site
Bar Lane, Roecliffe, Boroughbridge
☎ (01423) 322683

Youth Hostels

Youth Hostels at Baldersdale, Dentdale, Earby, Grinton Lodge, Hawes, Haworth, Ingleton, Kettlewell, Kirkby Stephen, Malham, Mankinholes and York. To book a Youth Hostel visit: www.yha.org.uk or call your chosen Youth Hostel ☎ (0870) 770 8868.

Camping barns

Camping barns and bunk barns are available throughout the Dales: Brompton, Chipping, Downham, Leyburn, Lovesome Hill, Low Row, Richmond & Trawden. ☎ (0870) 770 8868.

Also at: Husband's Bunk Barn, Stainforth ☎ (01729) 822240
Old School Bunkhouse, Bishopdale ☎ (01969) 663856
Dalesbridge, Austwick ☎ (015242) 51021

Caving in the Yorkshire Dales

www.josslane.freeserve.co.uk

Guided Minibus Tours

Throstlenest Dales Tours, Walk Mill Lane, Leyburn. DL8 5HF
☎ (01969) 624755. www.throstlenesttours.co.uk

Cycling

For information on road cycling visit: www.cyclethedales.org.uk
For information on mountain bike routes visit: www.mtbthe dales.org.uk
National Cycle Network: ☎ (0845) 1130065.

Eating Out

Throughout the Dales there are tearooms, restaurants, pubs and hotels where excellent refreshment is offered, usually including local specialities and fresh local produce. Those listed are just a selection of the many available. Details were correct at the time of going to press.

The King's Arms Hotel
Askrigg
☎ (01969) 650258

Town End Farm End Shop & Tearoom
Airton
☎ (01729) 830902

The White Rose Hotel
Askrigg
☎ (01969) 650515

New Inn Hotel
Clapham
☎ (01524) 251203

The Cart House Tearoom
Hardrow
☎ (01969) 667691

The Coverbridge Inn
East Witton
☎ (01969) 622115

The Dales Kitchen
51 Main Street, Grassington
☎ (01756) 753208

Lury Fold Tearooms
Garrs Lane, Grassington
Light lunches, afternoon teas, high

tea, cakes, scones, morning coffee.
☎ (01756) 752414

Foresters Arms
Main Street, Grassington
Meals served lunch-times and evenings. ☎ (01756) 752349

The Bridge Inn
Grinton nr Richmond
☎ (01748) 884224)

Cockett's Hotel and Restaurant
Market Place, Hawes
☎ (01969) 667312

Herriot's Hotel
Main Street, Hawes
☎ (01969) 667536

Stone House Hotel & Restaurant
Nr. Hawes
☎ (01969) 667571

The Thwaite Inn
Horsehouse-in-Coverdale
(01969) 640206

Bettys Café Tea Rooms
The Grove, Ilkley
Open: 9am-6pm including Sunday.
☎ (01943) 608029

Cow and Calf Hotel
Cowpasture Road, Ilkley
Panorama Restaurant: lunches,
dinners, snacks.
☎ (01943) 607335

Red Lion Inn
Langthwaite
☎ (01748) 884218

Box Tree Restaurant
Church Street, Ilkley
Lunches and dinners; licensed.
☎ (01943) 608484

Muffins
Corner of Brook Street and Railway
Road, Ilkley
Coffee, lunches, teas, snacks.
☎ (01943) 817505

Whoop Hall Inn
Burrow with Burrow, Kirkby
Lonsdale
☎ (015242) 71284

Golden Lion Hotel
Leyburn
☎ (01969) 622161

Barbon Inn
Barbon, Nr Kirkby Lonsdale
☎ (015242) 76233

The Royal Hotel
Market Place, Kirkby Lonsdale
☎ (015242) 71217

**Copper Kettle Licensed
Restaurant**
Market Street, Kirkby Lonsdale
☎ (015242) 71714

Mad Hatters Tearooms
Market Place, Masham
☎ (01765) 689129

The Richard III Hotel
Market Place, Middleham
☎ (01969) 623240

Barbara's Tea Rooms
Bridgehousegate, Pateley Bridge
☎ (01423) 711013

The Buck Hotel
Reeth
☎ (01748) 884210

The King's Arms
Reeth ☎ (01748) 884259

The King's Head Hotel
Market Place, Richmond
☎ (01748) 850220

**The Shambles Fish Restaurant
and Take Away**
Settle
☎ (01729) 822652

Kearton Guest House
Thwaite
☎ (01748) 886277

The Three Horseshoes Inn
Wensley
☎ (01969) 622327

The Wensleydale Heifer
West Witton
☎ 01969 622322

Early Closing Days

Shops in these places may be closed for the afternoon on the following days, especially in the winter.

Tuesday	Keighley
Wednesday	Aysgarth, Gargrave, Hellifield, Hawes, Ilkley, Kirkby Lonsdale, Settle, Reeth, Leyburn, Middleham, Richmond
Thursday	Bedale, Bentham, Grassington, Ingleton, Kettlewell, Masham, Pateley Bridge, Sedbergh

Events – annual

March–April
- **North Country Theatre**, Richmond. The Zetland Centre. ☎ (01748) 825288
- **Wensleydale Tournament of Song**, Leyburn Methodist Hall. ☎ (01969) 625641
- **Jazz on the Swale**, Reeth, The Buck Hotel. ☎ (01748) 884821
- **Book Fair**, Gargrave, Village Hall. ☎ (01617974786)
- **Harrogate Spring Flower Show**, Harrogate, Great Yorkshire Showground. ☎ (01423) 561049
- **The Three Peaks Race**, Horton-in-Ribblesdale. ☎ (01423) 870326

May
- **Yoredale Art Club Annual Art Exhibition**, Leyburn, Methodist Hall. ☎ (01748) 824514
- **Otley Show Bridge End**, Otley, the Showground. ☎ (07961) 966952
- **Sedbergh Gala**, Back Lane, Sedbergh. ☎ (015396) 20764/ ☎ (015396) 21267
- **Gaping Gill Winch Meet**, Bradford Pot Hole Club. Gaping Gill ☎ (01484) 683260
- **Swaledale Festival**, various locations throughout Swaledale. Office: ☎ (01748) 880018 Bookings: ☎ (01748) 880019

June
- **Swaledale Marathon**, Reeth. ☎ (01748) 822446
- **Grassington Festival of Music & Arts**, Grassington. ☎ (01756) 752691
- **Skipton Horse Trials**, Skipton. ☎ (01756) 792809
- **Broughton Game Show**, Broughton Hall, Skipton. ☎ (01756) 720262
- **Hawes & District Gala**, Dairy Field, Hawes. ☎ (01969) 667192

July
- **Nidderdale Festival**, various locations throughout Pately Bridge. www.nidderdalefestival.org.uk

August

- **Clogfest**, Skipton canal basin. ☎ (01282) 868040
- **Great Yorkshire Show**, Harrogate. ☎ (01423) 541000
- **Masham Steam Engine Rally and Fair Organ Rally**, Masham. ☎ (01765) 689569
- **Skipton Horse Trials**, Carleton, Skipton.
  ☎ (01756) 792809
- **Ripley Show**, Ripley Castle Park, ☎ (01943) 466654
- **Kettlewell Scarecrow Festival**, Kettlewell.
  ☎ (01756) 760887
- **Aldbrough Village Feast**, Aldbrough St. John, Nr. Richmond. ☎ (01325) 374112
- **Lunesdale Agricultural Show**, Kirkby Lonsdale.
  ☎ (015242) 61047
- **Brough Agricultural Show**, Brough.
  ☎ (017683) 42610
- **Gaping Gill Winch Meet**, Graven Pothole Club, Gaping Gill. www.cravenpotholclub.org
- **Watercolour Exhibition by Patricia Jones**, Linton.
  ☎ (01282) 816130
- **Festival of Books & Drama**, Sedbergh, England's Book Town, Various venues. Sedbergh.
  ☎ (015396) 20125
- **Settle Festival**, Settle and Giggleswick.
  ☎ 0870 777 5929

September

- **Muker Show**, Muker. ☎ (01748) 886564
- **Ripon International Festival**, Ripon Cathedral & other venues. ☎ (01765) 605508
- **Harrogate Autumn Flower Show**, Harrogate.
  ☎ (01423) 561049
- **Nidderdale Show**, Pateley Bridge. ☎ (01969) 650129
- **Masham Sheep Fair**, Masham Market Place.
  ☎ (01765) 689300

October

- **Masham Arts Festival**, various venues in Masham.
  ☎ (01760) 680200
- **Ingleton Folk Weekend**, Ingleton. ☎ (015242) 41049

November

- **Wensleydale Flower Club Open Flower Demonstration**, Harmby, Village Hall.
  ☎ (01969) 663381

December

- **Masham Victorian Fair**, Market Place and Town Hall.
  ☎ (01760) 680200
- **Skipton Medieval Festival and Market**, Skipton.
  www.skiptononline.co.uk
- **Grassington Dickensian Festival**, Grassington.
  ☎ 0845 0942 894

Facilities for the disabled

Most attractions are able to accommodate visitors with disabilities. Full access for people with certain disabilities is not always possible due to constraints of old buildings or natural features. It is advisable to telephone individual attractions before visiting to avoid disappointment.

The Yorkshire Dales National Park Authority offers a wide selection of events and guided walks. Advice on suitability for disabled participants may be obtained from the Interpretation Officer ☎ (01756) 751690.
Email: grassington@yorkshiredales.org.uk

Fishing

Fishing is allowed on many stretches of river in the Dales. Enquire at the nearest local tackle shop or Tourist Information Centre for details.

Hawes and HA Angling Association has 15 miles (24km) of river for trout and grayling. ☎ (01969) 650304

Kilnsey Park, Wharfedale, two trout fishing lakes. ☎ (01756) 752861
Fishing for brown trout in Malham Tarn is allowed from boats.
Day tickets available from Tarn House, Malham Tarn. ☎ (01729) 830331.

Blackburn Farm Gayle. ☎ (01969) 667524

Guided walks

The Yorkshire Dales National Park Authority organises a full programme of guided walks throughout the year. Full details may be found in the current edition of The Visitor, the free newspaper published annually by the Park Authority. Walks vary from easy to strenuous and enable participants to see many facets of Dales life.

The Friends of Settle/Carlisle Railway offer an extensive programme of free guided walks based on the stations on the line. ☎ (01729) 825454. Friends of DalesRail also have a programme of guided walks. Contact Tourist Information Centres or National Park Centres for details.

Rambler's Association, quote YHAG ☎ (020) 733 8500
www.ramblers.org.uk

Horse Riding

Booking is advisable at all centres.

Arklemoor Riding Centre
Arkengarthdale ☎ (01748) 884731
www.arklemoor.com

Swaledale Ponies
Angram ☎ (01748) 886682

Kilnsey Trekking and Riding Centre
Homestead Farm, Conistone
☎ (01756) 752861
www.kilnseyriding.com

Coverdale Equestrian Enterprises
West Scrafton, Leyburn
☎ (01969) 640663

Trail Riding Holidays
D&P Equestrian, Low Haygarth Farm, Cautley, Sedbergh
☎ (015396) 20349

Maps

The following Ordnance Survey maps cover the area:

OS Outdoor Leisure 2 *Yorkshire Dales – Southern and Western areas* 1:25,000

OS Outdoor Leisure 19 *Howgill Fells and Upper Eden Valley* 1:25,000

OS Outdoor Leisure 30 *Yorkshire Dales– Northern and Central areas* 1:25,000

OS Explorer 298 *Nidderdale* 1:25,000

OS Explorer 297 *Lower Wharfedale and Washburn Valley* 1:25,000

OS Explorer 302 *Northallerton & Thirsk* 1:25,000

OS Explorer 287 *West Pennine Moors* 1:25,000

OS Explorer 288 *Bradford & Huddersfield* 1:25,000

Market Days

Monday	Keighley, Kirkby Stephen, Skipton, Thirsk
Tuesday	Bedale, Hawes, Settle
Wednesday	Keighley, Masham, Sedbergh, Skipton
Thursday	Keighley, Kirkby Lonsdale, Richmond
Friday	Ingleton, Keighley, Leyburn, Skipton
Saturday	Keighley, Masham, Richmond, Skipton

National Park Information Centres

These centres have a wealth of information on all aspects of the Park. They are often the starting points for guided walks. Information on the various activities that are organised in the Park such as cycling, caving, pathfinder days, farm walks, painting workshops, craft events and many more, will be available here.

Aysgarth Falls	☎ (01969) 662910
Grassington	☎ (01756) 751690
Hawes	☎ (01969) 666210 (Dales Countryside Museum)
Malham	☎ (01969) 652380
Reeth	☎ (01748) 884059
Sedbergh	☎ (01539) 620125

The centres are open 10am-5pm daily from April to October and for more limited times during the winter.

Public Transport

There is a good network of public transport within the Yorkshire Dales. A free publication Getting Around is available from National Park Information Centres and Tourist Information Centres. This gives details of all bus and train services in the area. Further bus information may be obtained from Yorkshire Dales Traveline: ☎ (0870) 6082608. www.traveldales.org.uk

Railway

Wensleydale Railway Association

For details of current passenger services between Leeming Bar – Bedale – F inghall – Leyburn and Redmire, please see: www.wensleydalerailway.com or phone ☎ 08454 505474.

Settle – Carlisle Railway

Settle. Open all year. Website: www.settle-carlisle.co.uk
Discounts for groups of 10+, please call ☎ (0800) 9800766.National Rail Enquiries: ☎ (08457) 484950.

Rock Climbing

There are excellent areas for rock climbing in the Yorkshire Dales. Limestone climbing is particularly good at Malham, Gordale and Kilnsey. Brimham Rocks, Almscliff and Ilkley are the main gritstone areas. Further information can be obtained from the **Leeds Mountaineering Club**.
Leeds has a climbing wall at 100a Gelderd Road, Leeds, LS12 6BY. Further information about local climbing may be obtained here, ☎ (0113) 234 1554.

Swimming pools

Keighley Leisure Centre
Victoria Park, Hard Ings Road
☎ (01535) 681763

Craven Swimming Pool
Aireville Park, Gargrave Road, Skipton.
☎ (01756) 792805
Heated indoor pool, Squash Courts, Sauna, Jacuzzi, Steam Room, Solarium.

Long Ashes Leisure Centre
Threshfield, near Grassington
☎ (01756) 753520
Indoor pool, outdoor pool and outdoor sports.

There are also swimming pools at Harrogate, Ilkley, Knaresborough, Richmond and Ripon.

Tourist Information Centres

(see also National Park Information Centres)

* open all year

Bradford, City Hall*	☎ (01274) 433678
Harrogate, Royal Bath Assembly Rooms*	☎ (01423) 537300
Haworth, 2-4 West Lane*	☎ (01535) 642329
Horton-in-Ribbleside, Penyghent Café*	☎ (01729) 860333
Ilkley, Station Road*	☎ (01943) 602319
Ingleton, Community Centre Car Park	☎ (015242) 41049
Kirkby Lonsdale, 24 Main Street	☎ (015242) 71437
Kirkby Stephen, 22 Market Street	☎ (017683) 71199
Knaresborough, 35 Market Place	☎ (01423) 866886
Leeds, Leeds City Station*	☎ (0113) 2425242
Leyburn, Railway Street*	☎ (01969) 623069
Pateley Bridge, 18 High Street	☎ (01423) 711147
Richmond, Friary Gardens*	☎ (01748) 850252
Ripon, Wakemans House	☎ (01765) 604625
Saltaire, 2 Victoria Road*	☎ (01274) 774993
Sedbergh & Dent, Main Street*	☎ (01539) 620125
Settle, Town Hall*	☎ (01729) 825192
Skipton, Old Town Hall*	☎ (01756) 792809
York, Railway Station*	☎ (01904) 621756

Long distance Walks

Long distance walking routes: The Pennine Way, The Dales Way, Wainwright's Coast to Coast Walk, Herriot Way, Swale Way, Brontë Way, Calderdale Way and *Coast to Coast on the Ravenber Way.
* For information, please contact the author: ron.scholes@btinternet.com

Weather

Before undertaking outdoor activities such as walking, climbing, caving etc, a daily forecast for the Dales area may be obtained by telephoning any of the National Park Information Centres.

Against the sunset's bright repose,
The moorland rim is black and steep,
The swelling lines of ancient fields fade as the dale now falls asleep.

From 'The Dales' by Ron Scholes

Index

Published by
Landmark Publishing Ltd,
Ashbourne Hall, Cokayne Ave, Ashbourne, Derbyshire DE6 1EJ England
Tel: (01335) 347349 Fax: (01335) 347303 e-mail: landmark@clara.net
Website www.landmarkpublishing.co.uk

Published in the USA by
Hunter Publishing Inc,
222 Clematis Street, West Palm Beach, FL 33401
Website www.hunterpublishing.com

3rd edition
ISBN 13: 978 184306 388 9

British Library Cataloguing in Publication Data: a catalogue record for this
book is available from the British Library.

Print: Cromwell Press, Trowbridge
Design: Sarah Labuhn
Cartography: Mark Titterton

Front cover: Meadows near Langcliffe
Back cover top: Malham National Park
Back cover Bottom: Pately Bridge

Picture Credits
All photography supplied by the author except:
International Photobank: 106, 123T
John Robey: 81, 93L, 101
Wensleydale Creamery: 118, 119B
Harrogate International Conference Centre: 159, 167T,
171, 174 both, 175
Images below are from Shutterstock with copyright to:
Front cover and page 69: **Kevin Eaves**
Back cover top and page 79: **W H Chow**
Page 42: **Tom Curtis**
Page 51T: **Andrew Barker**
Pages 86, 99T, 122 & 138: **Steve Smith**